Stories of Lancastrians

TAKEN FROM LANCASHIRE STORIES

BY FRANK HIRD

Selected and Edited by

PRINTWISE PUBLICATIONS LIMITED
1991

This compilation and edition published 1991 by PRINTWISE PUBLICATIONS LTD.
47 Bradshaw Road, Tottington, BURY, LANCS, BL8 3PW.

Warehouse and Orders —
40-42 Willan Industrial Estate, Vere Street,
(off Eccles New Road), SALFORD,
M5 2GR.
061-745 9168

'Stories of Great Lancastrians' have been selected from
'Lancashire Stories'
2 vols. Published about 1911, written by Frank Hird.

Prints and text chosen, researched and edited by

©

Cliff Hayes

ISBN No. 1 872226 23 X

Printed & bound by Manchester Free Press,
Paragon Mill, Jersey Street, Manchester M4 6FP.
Tel: 061-236 8822.

DEDICATED

To my wife Sylvia, who put up with the hours spent
on this series of books and my daughter Alison.

Foreword

It's a curious irony when you think about it, that as the world gets progressively smaller, with travel to exotic and historic places increasingly easier, there seems to be a most welcome upsurge of interest in things close around us, and particularly in our own local history.

It's easy to become blasé about Bermuda, matter-of-fact about Miami, and tiresome about Thailand as jets get bigger and air-fares — against all the odds — become cheaper. Perhaps it is not so surprising after all that as more and more of us see and learn this and that about touches of other places' history and traditions, we should become keenly interested in discovering or re-discovering more knowledge about our own.

It's also a curious irony that a Cheshire lad should be invited to write a word or three about Famous Lancashire Men, men whose names at first glance would have you believing they were dredged from some fictional radio-drama series... John Bradford, Tim Bobbin, John Dee. No messing-about names, those, Stark and simple, Just like their stories in this book.

But then, my birth-place was so close to the Red Rose county border that I have always considered myself to be at least half-Lancashire. I was born in Sale, about 600 yards from its boundary with Stretford.

I commend the tales in this book, and I heartily commend the editor and writers of this and all its sister-publications for putting down for posterity stories and history which otherwise would be in danger of being ignored and forgotten.

When this Cheshire lad becomes literary dictator of Britain, his one dictum will be that the law of the land will offer safe protection to the lore of the land.

Each and every one of us has access to potential material for safe-keeping through our elders and friends. How I wish, for instance, that I had kept a copy of the old monologue that my dear late Mum used to regale us with each Christmas, sometimes so often that it was received with initial horror, but always ended with renewed delight. It was called "The Newsboy's Debt" and was a real, old-fashioned tear-jerker. If you know of it, please let me know so that I can at least replace one small brick in the home of my own history.

Bob Greaves

Original Foreword

FROM whatever point of view it may be approached—topographical, archæological, commercial or romantic — no county possesses so varied a history as Lancashire.

Lancashire has had many historians, such as Whitaker, Baines, Harland and Whatton. There is a literature, dealing with the county from every aspect, which fills many pages in the British Museum catalogue. But, although the greatest pains in research have been taken to ensure historical accuracy, *Lancashire Stories* does not claim to be a history. It may be described as the result of a consideration of the history of the county entirely from the human point of view ; and, that there should be variety and constant change of interest, no order of dates has been followed. Human nature is the same to-day as it was in the days of the Normans ; the story has been the one object of the writer, not the period.

It has been suggested that a bibliography should be printed with this work, but in a publication destined for the general reader, rather than for the historian and archæologist, such a list would be out of place. The authorities are given in the text wherever it has been deemed essential to the interest and value of the story.

Ready and most courteous help has been extended to me by the Lancashire libraries in the search for material and for illustrations to these stories. All the books, old prints, etc., in their possession were freely placed at my disposal, permission at the same time being given for photographs to be taken of anything germane to my purpose. My warm thanks are therefore due for this valuable assistance to Mr. A. E. Sutton, of the Manchester Reference Library ; Mr. George T. Shaw, of the Liverpool Reference Library ; Mr. R. J. Gordon, of the Rochdale Public Library ; Mr. Charles Madeley, of the Warrington Public Library ; Mr. Charles Leigh, of Owens College Library, Manchester ; Mr. J. N. Dowbiggin, of the Public Library, Storey Institute, Lancaster, and to the Harris Free Library, Preston and Mr. James Brockbank, of the *Manchester Courier*, and Mr. J. L. Edmondson, of the Manchester *Daily Mail*, for their valuable suggestions.

My acknowledgments are specially due to the London Library and its assistants.

FRANK HIRD.

Introduction

I have, for a long time, tried to find a book of stories, tales or myths of Lancashire. A book that was not a long history or just the bare facts, but one of the unusual, and of the characters of what is the most fascinating county in England. After much searching and help from the second-hand trade I came across a large bulky two volume "Lancashire Stories" by Frank Hird, written about 1910 and very popular at the time. It was just right, it had just the story-tellers feel that I was looking for. It was informative, and factually correct but not over long. Tony Gibb first showed me the book and it was on his suggestion I first read it.

Printwise has now published three books from those massive books and they have been well received. The light gossipy style made easy reading stories, and by splitting up the areas we hope that we have re-introduced many local stories to today's readers and given those readers an introduction to each area and its history.

Also in that original book was a section on "Famous Lancashire Men" and is is that section, added to, edited and enlarged that is presented here. May I introduce some of the people who made Lancashire the great county it is today (Government boundary moves forgotten). The families whose history is so closely interwoven with the story of the land itself. The style remains easy to read and the names come to life and introduce themselves like old friends.

Very little is known about Frank Hird, and even enquiries to the usually helpful Lancashire Library didn't bring up any personal details. But I am very grateful that he wrote the original book, and I hope that you agree that, between us we have produced an interesting and informative book.

Cliff Hayes

P.S. Please remember that they were written in approximately 1910 so if it refers to 40 years ago, it refers to 1870. If the story states 100 years ago then it means 1810 etc...

Contents

Harrison Ainsworth..7

Richard Arkwright..18

"Tim Bobbin", John Collier – The Burns
   of Lancashire...29

John Bradshaw – The Regicide.....................37

John Bradford – The Martyr........................47

John Byrom...55

Humphrey Chetham..62

Samuel Crompton and His
   Spinning Mule...71

John Dalton – Father of Chemistry.............81

James, Earl of Derby.......................................87

Francis Egerton The Last
   Duke of Bridgewater....................................100

George Fox, The Quaker...............................113

John-o Gaunt – the Great
   Duke of Lancaster.......................................121

The Romance of The Peel Family...............128

George Romney...138

William Roscoe...149

The Townleys of Townley Hall....................158

Ulverston's Famous Son –
   Sir John Barrow..167

HARRISON AINSWORTH

"THE Lancashire Novelist," as he has been called, gave the world some forty romances, but none of them are more romantic than the story of his own life. Born in 1805, the elder son of a well-to-do lawyer, Thomas Harrison, he became one of the most striking figures in the literary world of the nineteenth century, and at the outset of his career even rivalled Dickens in popularity.

Harrison Ainsworth was born in Manchester, at 21 King Street, at that time a street of fine old Georgian houses, and the residence of the leading and most prosperous men of the town. King Street was then the Park Lane of Manchester. On his father's side the novelist traced his descent back through five hundred years to the Ainsworths of Tottington, and on his mother's side through seven hundred years to the Touchets, of whom there is a clear record back to the days of William the Conqueror. Orme Touchet, from whom Harrison Ainsworth was descended, was harper to that sovereign. His mother also was descended from the Mosleys of Ancoats, the Bayleys, one of the oldest and most influential merchant families in Manchester, and from the Harrisons, another old Lancashire family. Early in the eighteenth century an Ainsworth had married an heiress, Jane Berry, who brought with her a house and property called Spotland Gate, near Rochdale. This house and land were ultimately inherited by the novelist, who is entered in Burke's *Landed Gentry* as "William Harrison Ainsworth of Spotland, Co. Lancaster." His father and mother, however, never occupied the old sixteenth-century house, which was pulled down in 1902, to make way for the development of the estate for building.

From his earliest childhood Ainsworth had a passion for romantic stories, especially concerning highwaymen. The elder Ainsworth took a keen interest in this subject, and long before he could read or write the boy would sit spellbound upon his father's knee listening eagerly to the tales of the wild doings of other days. Stories, too, in which mysteries and supernatural happenings played a part, appealed strongly to his vivid imagination; thus, the foundation of those romances which have delighted and engrossed many thousands of readers was laid by his father in the old house in King Street. Manchester at that time, with its quaint black-and-white houses with their gables and lattice windows, and the many ancient halls which still stood in its outskirts, was the very spot to foster the boy's natural love of romance and history, and that it left indelible marks upon his mind is shown by the frequency with which he placed the scenes of his books in the old town.

One of the elder Ainsworth's stories, which was a particular favourite of the future novelist, concerned a robbery at Hough, near Rostherne, in Cheshire, where the family spent a certain portion of each year, by Dick Turpin, the highwayman. "Turpin was the hero of my boyhood," says Ainsworth. "When a boy I have often lingered by the side of the deep old road where the robbery was committed, to cast wistful glances into its mysterious windings, and when night deepened the shadows of the trees, have urged my horse on its journey, from a vague apprehension of a visit from the ghostly highwayman."

When he was twelve, Ainsworth was sent to the Manchester Free Grammar School, whose head-master was Dr. Smith, a noted classical scholar. In *Mervyn Clitheroe*, which was published in 1851, and which was mainly autobiographical, Ainsworth described the Grammar School of his day. It had been rebuilt some thirty-six years previously.

"I cannot say much of the architectural beauty of the school; for if truth must be spoken it was exceedingly ugly. The building was comparatively modern, and did not date back from the period of which I write more than twenty or thirty years. It was raised on a high sandstone bank, overlooking the little river Irk, not far from its confluence with the Irwell; and viewed on this side, in connection with the old and embrowned walls adjoining, its appearance was not unpicturesque —certainly more pleasing than when viewed from the noisy and crowded thoroughfare by which it was approached. It was a large, dingy, and smoke-begrimed building, with copings of stone, and had so many windows that it looked like a lantern. In front, between the angles and the pointed roof, was placed a stone effigy of the bird of wisdom,[1] which seemed to gaze down at us with its great goggle eyes as we passed by, as if muttering, 'Enter this academic abode over which I preside, and welcome, but you'll never come out as clever as I . . .' The school was divided into two rooms, each occupying a whole floor, and the lower school—in those days a very confined, dirty-looking place, utterly unworthy of such an establishment—was reached by a flight of steps descending from the little court I have described." This court was made by a wall of the Chetham College, which faced the school entrance. "But, happily, I knew nothing from personal experience of the dark and dismal hole, being at once introduced to the upper school, which, if it had no other merit, was airy and spacious enough. There were four fireplaces and four tables, those at either extremity being assigned to the head master and the second master, and the others to the two ushers. Each master had two classes, so that there were eight in all. The walls were whitewashed, and like the flat roof, without any decoration whatever, unless the oak wainscoting at the back of the boys' benches which surrounded the whole schoolroom can be so considered. These benches, the desks in front of them, and the panels behind, were of the hardest oak; and it was well they were so, for they had to resist the ravages of a thousand claspknives. In some places they were further secured with clamps of iron. Everybody cut his name on the desks or wainscot, like the captives in State prisons in the olden time; and amongst these mementoes I suppose I have somewhere left mine. I know that while once carving on the

[1] An owl was part of the armorial bearings of Bishop Oldham, the founder of the school.

leads of the Collegiate Church I nearly carved off my fingers. The place was not so bright as might be conceived from the multitude of windows, for they were never cleaned, and the panes of glass were degrees of thickness, tied with tatching-end to prevent them from splitting; and for all these he found employment. While calling us round for punishment he got as red in the gills as a turkey-cock, and

HARRISON AINSWORTH AS A YOUTH

(After the miniature by Stump. Reproduced by the kind permission of Mr. S. M. Ellis from his "Harrison Ainsworth and his Friends," and the publisher, Mr. John Lane)

yellow and almost tawny from the reeky atmosphere. . . . The Rev. Robinson Elsdale, under whose care I was first placed, was a sound classical scholar, but a severe disciplinarian. He was one of those who believe that a knowledge of Latin and Greek can be driven into a boy, and that his capacity may be sharpened by frequent punishment. Under this impression he was constantly thrashing us. In his drawer he had several canes of various lengths, and of various occasionally rose up to give greater effect to the blows. Some boys were so frightened that they couldn't learn their tasks at all, and others so reckless of the punishment which they knew must ensue, whether or not, that they intentionally neglected them. I have seen boys with 'blood blisters,' as they called them, on their hands, and others with weals on their backs, but I do not recollect that the castigation did them any good, but the very reverse. But our preceptor had

9

other ingenious modes of torture. He would make us stand in the middle of the school for a whole day, and even longer—sometimes on one leg; and the effect of balancing in this posture with a heavy dictionary in hand, and a Virgil under the arm, was ludicrous enough, though rather perplexing. It must not be imagined that I escaped the cane. I had enough of it and to spare, both on shoulders and hands."

A year before Harrison Ainsworth went to the Grammar School his father had bought what was then a country house, called Beech Hill, in Smedley Lane, as a summer residence, the house in King Street being used for the winter. The saying, " The child is father of the man," is certainly exemplified in Ainsworth's case. At Beech Hill his great delight was to play games representing highwaymen, and as his most recent biographer, Mr. S. M. Ellis, says, " It would almost seem as if Ainsworth utilised his subsequent literary powers to consummate and preserve the fancies which had originated in his boyhood. A great deal of the boy in other respects remained in the man throughout his life. He always retained the impetuousness, the open-hearted generosity of youth; and the careless, sunny temperament which characterised the lad was never lost in the after years despite many troubles."

The Fates were indeed kind to Harrison Ainsworth, for, in addition to the encouragement of his taste for romance which he received from his father, when he was at a most impressionable age, he made the friendship, destined to last throughout his life, of a boy of similar mental outlook. This was James Crossley, who came from Halifax, a youth of seventeen, to be articled clerk in the firm of solicitors of which the elder Ainsworth was a partner. Crossley was then seven-

teen, Harrison Ainsworth was twelve, but a very precocious twelve. Crossley was a great reader, and already had made quite a good-sized collection of books. It was the meeting of two kindred spirits, a meeting that had lasting effect upon the career of the younger. When he was fifteen Ainsworth wrote two plays. They were acted before his admiring relatives in the cellar of the King Street house, which he had converted into a theatre. For this performance Crossley wrote the Prologue, and it was of sufficient literary merit to find a place in *Blackwood's Magazine* shortly afterwards.

In every moment of leisure afforded by his schooldays Ainsworth was busily employed in writing verses, romances and articles, work of such power and merit that it was gladly accepted by several magazines, and amongst them the *Edinburgh Magazine* and *Arliss's Magazine*.

He left school when he was seventeen, and being destined to follow his father in the prosperous and old-established firm of Halstead and Ainsworth in Essex Street, he was articled to another leading solicitor of the town, called Kay, to be trained for the law, but more especially in conveyancing, which was the branch his father wished him to follow. The arrangement, however, did not work well. Kay was an austere man, and had no sympathy with his clever young pupil's dabbling in literature. When Ainsworth should have been at the office studying ponderous legal tomes, or learning the technicalities of his profession, he was spending hours of delight with old-world historians, dramatists and romancers in the Chetham Library. His favourite seat was the recess in the oriel window with the finely-groined roof, and the sixteenth-century table at which Sir Walter Raleigh is supposed to have sat. At this table Ainsworth wrote the majority of his stories and articles as a youth, but the tradition that asserts he likewise penned *Rookwood* and *The Lancashire Witches* in this same secluded and delightful spot has no foundation. As will be seen, these two famous books were written far away from Manchester, and in scenes widely differing from the monastic calm of the Chetham Library. His father's library and the Old Exchange Library (now the Reference Library) likewise afforded material for the boy's all-absorbing passion for books dealing with history and romance. Manchester, therefore, laid the foundations upon which Harrison Ainsworth built his fame.

So able and complete a lawyer as Kay could not see his pupil's neglect of his legal education with anything but disfavour : and he did not hesitate to express his opinion freely, both to the young man himself and to his father. " Mr. Alexander Kay was anything but an idle man," Harrison Ainsworth said, " and became disgusted with his idle clerk " ; whilst his father remarked, and not without bitterness, " He's an idle dog—he never will work."

The young man hated the law, all he cared for was literature. His father, notwithstanding his own literary tastes, could not understand him. There were angry scenes, remonstrances, which brought a perfunctory attendance at Mr. Kay's office. Then the young scribbler was off once more to his favourite nook in the Chetham Library.

A year after he left school Harrison Ainsworth published a collection of his stories and articles collected from the *Edinburgh, London, European* and *Arliss's* Magazines, under the title of *December Stories*. The gloominess of thought, the " blighted hopes," at that time made fashionable by Lord Byron, are the dominant themes of these youthful stories,

yet for a boy of seventeen they show a remarkable command of language and expression.

Although Harrison Ainsworth devoted many hours a day to the study of his beloved authors, he had nothing of the recluse in his nature. On the contrary, he was a most sociable being. He was singularly handsome, he had a fine figure, he sang well, and had a most charming manner—in short he possessed all the attributes which make a young man an acquisition in any society. It is said he was " petted and spoiled . . . by a bevy of fair ones of the *élite* of Manchester Society." But from this pleasant dabbling with literature and social gaieties he was rudely awakened. In June 1824 his father died suddenly, and Harrison Ainsworth found himself called upon to take his place as head of the firm of Ainsworth, Crossley and Sudlow. He was in no way fitted for such responsibility, but the unexpected call was met bravely, and in order to finish his legal studies, and so fit himself to take his father's place, he went to London in the winter of that year. When he left Manchester with the firm resolution of becoming an efficient lawyer, the future novelist little thought that he would never live in his native town again.

Immediately after his arrival in London, Ainsworth attended at the chambers of Mr. John Phillips, in the Temple, a barrister and a noted conveyancer. At first he studied with the most laudable zeal, but gradually the pleasures - of London and the claims of literary society weakened his purpose. His companions in John Phillips's chambers were not attractive, " dull, dreary, plodding unintellectuals — black-whiskered, grossest-eyed, odiously muddy-cheek'd fellows, blessed with talents of the happiest mediocrity," was his description of them. Ainsworth must have appeared as a rose amongst nettles in that dingy Temple office. Edward Harrison, his cousin, described him at this time as being "as beautiful as a woman," and Ainsworth himself, in a letter to his friend Crossley, speaks of still keeping "my complexion, which you know is proof against clime, and it commands unusual respect in a place where such things are rare." At the end of the same letter he adds, "I am not vain, but I cannot but wonder

Majesty's solicitors in the Court of King's Bench, and after divers perils in the shape of Judges, clerks, affidavits, etc., I feel myself comfortable and happy with my admission in my pocket." Six months later his first book—an early work arranged in collaboration with a Manchester friend. J. P. Aston, but actually written by Ainsworth, was published, and in October he was married. A month later he had given up the law and started

BEECH HALL, SMEDLEY LANE, MANCHESTER
(*Reproduced by kind permission of Mr. S. M. Ellis and Mr. John Lane*)

what there is in one which attracts the notice of the fair sex."

Throughout his whole life Harrison Ainsworth was most popular with women, and in turn no one was more susceptible to feminine influence. Yet both his marriages turned out unhappily.

In most lives one year marks the turning point—"the tide in the affairs of men." With Harrison Ainsworth this year was the year of his majority. On the 4th of February, 1826, he attained his twenty-first birthday, on the 8th of the same month he wrote to his old friend Crossley, "This morning has seen me installed in the office of one of His

in London as a publisher—a step which meant resignation of the senior partnership in his late father's firm and a large and certain income.

Having been admitted as an attorney, Ainsworth should have packed his trunks and taken the first coach back to Manchester, there to occupy his father's chair in the office of Messrs. Ainsworth, Crossley and Sudlow, but the Fates ordained otherwise. Early in that same year he had made the acquaintance of John Ebers, a publisher and librarian, and also the lessee of the Opera House in the Haymarket; this acquaintance altered the whole course of Ainsworth's life. Ebers was a Hanoverian by birth, his father having come over to England in the suite of Caroline of Brunswick, the unhappy wife of George IV. The Opera exercised a great fascination over Ainsworth, and from constantly attending the performances he became acquainted with Ebers, who invited the brilliant and handsome young man to his house. He was a widower with two daughters, and Ainsworth promptly fell in love, at first sight, with the younger girl, Fanny, who was said to be one of the most beautiful girls in London. She was the same age as himself. Why Ainsworth kept his engagement and marriage secret from his friends and family until two days before the ceremony is unknown, unless it was for the reason he gave to his friend Crossley: "Really, I had so much unhappiness on a former occasion, that I made a resolution, which I have kept, not to divulge it to a creature till the very moment of its celebration. This post only acquaints my mother with the circumstance." Only the bride's relatives were present at the ceremony in Marylebone Parish Church on October 11, 1826.

Shortly after the return from their honeymoon, acting upon the advice of Ebers, Ainsworth definitely abandoned the law and became a bookseller and a publisher, practically taking over his father-in-law's business. At first the undertaking was successful, but Ainsworth was not a business man, and the reasons that led him to embark upon the project were not such as make for monetary success. "His was not the speculation of an ordinary publisher; his aim was to promote the interests of literature, to advance his own reputation as a writer, and to surround himself with authors as it was alike honourable to serve and be associated with; he thought that he might bring forward sterling works, rejected,

perhaps, as not 'fashionable,' and assist writers of a better class than those who aspired to merely fleeting popularity." Such aims, especially in the publishing trade, could only lead to failure. But during the three years he played the part of intellectual publisher, Ainsworth made a very definite position for himself in the worlds of art and letters. One newspaper called him the "Adonis of booksellers," and we have this description of him from William Carter Hall :—

"When I knew him in 1826, not long after he married the daughter of Ebers . . . and 'condescended' for a brief time to be a publisher, he was a remarkably handsome young man—tall, graceful in deportment, and in all ways a pleasant person to look upon and talk to. He was, perhaps, as thorough a gentleman as his native city of Manchester ever sent forth."

The next four years of Ainsworth's life were not very profitable. His gay entertainments at his house in London, his travels abroad and his life of pleasure, caused his Manchester friends and kinsfolk to wag their heads. So far he had done nothing. It is true he started a "legal agency" in 1830, but this did not last long. But in 1833 he began to work seriously upon his first novel, *Rookwood*, which he had already commenced in 1831 and put on one side because of the ruin that befell his father-in-law, Ebers. With the publication of this book, in 1834, Harrison Ainsworth achieved immediate fame. It was a time of the flabby sentimental novel; this story of the highwayman, Dick Turpin, came at the moment when the reading public was weary of the silly love-stories of fashionable folk. In *Rookwood* they found real men and women, exquisite descriptions of scenery, and no stint of supernatural horrors. Turpin's ride to York, which

13

brings the book to its thrilling conclusion, is a striking instance of an author's imagination actually making history. This famous ride never took place; it was created by Ainsworth. Yet, to this day, there are thousands who believe that the notorious highwayman's dash from London to York upon his wonderful mare, Black Bess, actually took place. It has preserved the name of Dick Turpin. Ainsworth himself thus describes how the famous " ride " was written :—

" The ride to York was completed in one day and one night. This feat—for feat it was, being the composition of a hundred ordinary novel pages in less than twenty-four hours—was achieved at "The Elms"—a house I then occupied at Kilburn. From the moment I got Turpin on the high road till I landed him at York, I wrote on and on without the slightest sense of effort. I began in the morning, wrote all day, and as the night wore on, my subject had completely mastered me and I had no power to leave Turpin or the high road. Well do I remember the fever into which I was thrown during the time of composition. My pen literally galloped over the pages. So thoroughly did I identify myself with the flying highwayman, that once started, I found it impossible to halt. Animated by kindred enthusiasm, I cleared every obstacle in my path, with as much facility as Turpin disposed of the impediments that beset his flight. In his company I mounted the hill-side, dashed through the bustling village, swept over the desolate heath, threaded the silent street, plunged into the eddying stream, and kept an onward course, without pause, without hindrance, without fatigue. With him I shouted, sang, laughed, exulted, wept. Nor did I retire to rest till, in imagination, I heard the bell of York Minster toll forth the knell of poor Black Bess. The whole panorama of the country between London and York seemed to pass before me ; and being personally a good horseman, passionately fond of horses, and possessed moreover of accurate knowledge of a great part of the country, I was thoroughly at home with my work. I must, however, confess that when the work was in proof, I went over the ground between London and York to verify the distances and localities, and was not a little surprised at my accuracy. The pains of authorship are great; but its pleasures, when they occur, are greater. And among the latter I may instance the composition of this Ride to York."

Those were the days of the " bucks," as the dandies were called in the reign of William IV., and, upon the success of *Rookwood*, Ainsworth took his place amongst those young men of fashion who moulded themselves upon Count d'Orsay, then the supreme arbiter in male attire. Ainsworth and the Count were strikingly alike, and as he galloped or cantered in Hyde Park, the young author was frequently mistaken for " the glass of fashion and the mould of form—really a complete Adonis," as d'Orsay was described. The late George Augustus Sala said, " Count d'Orsay and William Harrison Ainsworth were two of the best-looking and the best-dressed men in London." Henry Vizetelly, writing of the summer of 1834, says that Ainsworth " was the literary lion of the day. He was somewhat of a fop in dress, but that was the way with good-looking men in those days, and made an unnecessary display of the many rings he wore, but his manners were singularly pleasant, and there was not a particle of conceit."

Amongst other houses which were opened to him by the success of *Rookwood* was that of the Countess of Blessington, where he met all the most famous men of the time. His good looks, his cleverness, speedily made him a noticeable figure even in that assembly of wit and talent, as they did also at Holland House, where Lady Holland held a *salon* no less remarkable than that of Lady Blessington. But, unfortunately, Mrs. Ainsworth had no share or place in her husband's success and the attention it brought him from society. After eight years of marriage, differences arose which ended in a separation, the wife going to her father, and the husband taking up his residence with his relations, Mrs. James Touchet and Miss Buckley her sister, at Kensal Lodge on the Harrow Road, then in the midst of the country. The view from this house —now covered thickly with houses for miles around— Ainsworth described in *Jack Sheppard*. It was at Kensal Lodge, and later, in the Manor

HARRISON AINSWORTH AT THE AGE OF
THIRTY-ONE
(*After the portrait by D. Maclise*)

House near by, that Ainsworth gathered round him at his famous dinner parties, men whose names are household words wherever the English language is spoken—Thackeray, Dickens, Maclise the painter, George Cruikshank the illustrator, Benjamin Disraeli, Bulwer Lytton, Samuel Lover, Richard Barham, the author of *The Ingoldsby Legends*, and many more. As Mr. Ellis says, Ainsworth's residence at Kensal Lodge and the Manor House "made the Harrow

Road the most noted and popular literary rendezvous of the early Victorian era."

Ainsworth was ever the most generous of men, not only with his purse but in helping others. In 1834 he made the acquaintance of a young man of twenty-two who was a reporter on *The Morning Chronicle*, and who, at the same time, was contributing tales and sketches to *The Old Monthly Magazine* and *The Evening Chronicle*. These tales and sketches impressed Ainsworth by their humour and originality ; he therefore urged the young reporter to publish them in book form, and introduced him to George Cruikshank and Macrone, his own publisher. Cruikshank illustrated the tales, Macrone published them. The young reporter was Charles Dickens, and the book was *Sketches by Boz*.

Dickens also owed two of his most lovable characters to Ainsworth—the Cheeryble Brothers in *Nicholas Nickleby*. Visiting Manchester with Ainsworth, the latter introduced William and Daniel Grant to his brother-novelist, with the result that their kindly memory has been for ever perpetuated.

Out of the forty historical romances which bear Ainsworth's name *The Lancashire Witches* appeals most directly to his native county. No one but Ainsworth could have written this book with its perfect descriptions of the wild scenery of Pendle Forest, and its thrilling account of the ghastly rites practised by the witches. For some time Ainsworth had had the intention of writing a book on witchcraft in Lancashire, but it was his friend Crossley who suggested that he should use the account of the witches' trial at Lancaster in 1612, written by the Clerk of the Court—Pott's Discoveries of Witches—as the basis for his story. Ainsworth at once adopted the idea, and although the book was written during the year 1848, he was taking infinite pains in the collection of material during the two previous years. Thus in May 1846 he wrote to Crossley, "I have some intention of running down into Lancashire to see the Witch Country once more"; and in August of the following year, "I shall soon be in Manchester, as I want to pay another visit to Whalley." Those were only two of many visits to Pendle and the neighbourhood. He completed the plan of the book in December 1847, and on the third of that month he was able to write to his friend:—

"It has been settled that I do *The Lancashire Witches*, so you may look out for the first chapters on New Year's Day." The story was taken by *The Sunday Times* for serial publication, the price paid being one thousand pounds, a large sum for that time.

"He's an idle dog—he never will work," the elder Ainsworth prophesied concerning his son. Yet no man ever worked harder. In addition to the steady stream of romances which flowed from his pen year after year, he owned and edited, at different times, three important magazines. From the date of the publication of *Rookwood* (1834), until 1853, Ainsworth was in the heyday of literary and social success. Every one who was distinguished in the world of art and letters met at his hospit-able table; no writer had ever before entertained so largely. But in the summer of 1853 all this was altered. He then gave up Kensal Manor House, to which he had removed from Kensal Lodge, and went to live at Brighton. "He ceased to be the leader of the brilliant band of literary and artistic people who had gathered around him for many years at Kensal," says Mr. Ellis, "and his former hospitality—once so prominent a feature in London life—became but a pleasant memory." From Brighton he went to Hurstpierpoint, and then finally to Reigate, where he died in 1882, after passing the last years of his life practically in seclusion.

The year before his death he was entertained at a public banquet by the Mayor of Manchester, "as an expression of the high esteem in which he is held by his fellow-townsmen and of his service to literature." This was the first public recognition of his fame made by his native town, but the popularity of his writings amongst his fellow-townsmen is shown by the statement, made by the Mayor at the banquet. "In our Manchester public free libraries there are two hundred and fifty volumes of Mr. Ainsworth's different works. During the last twelve months these volumes have been read seven thousand six hundred and sixty times, mostly by the artisan class of readers. And this means that twenty volumes of his works have been perused in Manchester by readers of the free libraries every day all the year through." His last novel, *Stanley Brereton*, was published in 1881. In the following list of his books, with their dates of publication, *The Lancashire Witches, Guy Fawkes, The League of Lathom, Beatrice Tyldesley, Preston Fight, The Manchester Rebels*, and *Mervyn Clitheroe* give a continuous history of Lancashire from the reign of Henry VIII. down to Ainsworth's own boyhood and youth.

LIST OF HARRISON AINSWORTH'S NOVELS

Rookwood	. . . .	1834	Myddleton Pomfret	. .	1865
Crichton	. . . .	1837	The Constable de Bourbon	.	1866
Jack Sheppard	. .	1839	Old Court	. . .	1867
The Tower of London	.	1840	The South Sea Bubble	.	1868
Guy Fawkes	. .	1841	Hilary St. Ives	. .	1869
Old St. Paul's	. .	1841	Talbot Harland	. .	1870
The Miser's Daughter	.	1842	Tower Hill	. . .	1871
Windsor Castle	.	1843	Boscobel	. . . .	1872

St. James's, or the Court of Queen Anne . . . 1844
The Lancashire Witches . 1848
The Star Chamber . . 1854
The Flitch of Bacon, or the Custom of Dunmow . 1854
The Spendthrift . . 1856
Mervyn Clitheroe . . 1857
Ovingdean Grange . . 1860
The Constable of the Tower 1861
The Lord Mayor of London 1862
Cardinal Pole . . . 1863
John Law, the Projector . 1864
The Spanish Match, or Charles Stuart in Madrid 1865

The Manchester Rebels, or the Fatal '45 . . . 1873
Merry England . . . 1874
The Goldsmith's Wife . . 1874
Preston Fight, or the Insurrection of 1715 . . 1875
Chetwynd Calverley . . 1876
The League of Lathom, a Tale of the Civil War in Lancashire . . . 1876
The Fall of Somerset . . 1877
Beatrice Tyldesley . . 1878
Beau Nash 1880
Auriol and other Tales . 1880
Stanley Brereton . . 1881

Strolling Players Performing in an Inn-yard

17

RICHARD ARKWRIGHT

DURING his lifetime no man was the subject of more controversy than Richard Arkwright. Some people roundly asserted he had stolen the inventions which he patented, and which revolutionized the cotton industry; others as roundly declared him to be their sole creator. At this distance of time it is easy to perceive, from the many accounts of Arkwright's career, that both his detractors and supporters were equally right and equally wrong. Arkwright was not a mechanic, but he had a marvellous insight into the capabilities of mechanism, and possessed the power of adapting by head-work the hand-work of others. There is no proof that he actually stole any invention, but on the other hand he certainly adapted what he saw, or what he heard described. And, unlike most inventors, he had the energy and resource to push his inventions and make a fortune out of them—a circumstance not easily forgiven by those who lacked his strong business instincts.

Richard Arkwright was a native of Preston, being born there in 1732. His parents were in humble circumstances and poor, and as he was the youngest of thirteen children his education was of the scantiest. So indifferent indeed was it, that at the age of fifty, in the full tide of his success, feeling his deficiencies in conducting his correspondence and the management of his business, he cut off two hours' sleep each night in order to learn English grammar and to improve his writing and spelling.

From his infancy Arkwright must have been familiar with spinning by distaff and spindle, for at that time Preston already had a considerable manufacture of linen. But whether he ever had practical experience of spinning is not known; the only fact that history records of him until his twenty-third year, being that he was apprenticed to a barber called Nicholson. In this year a son was born to him who survived him ·and inherited his great wealth. From the fact that his wife was the daughter of a schoolmaster called Holt, at Bolton, it is not improbable that on the termination of his apprenticeship at Preston, Arkwright set up in business for himself in Bolton. Five years after the birth of his son he was certainly settled there, for, his first wife dying, he married Margaret Biggins, the daughter of "a respectable inhabitant of Leigh who had lived many years in the town," and he was described in the register as "Richard Arkwright of the parish of Bolton, barber."

The second Mrs. Arkwright possessed

a small property of her own, " perhaps of the value of four hundred pounds," which, although settled upon herself, was doubtless of use in assisting her husband to develop his business. Either shortly before or shortly after his second marriage Arkwright removed his small barber's shop, in Churchgate, to a larger one at the end of the passage leading to what was then the White Bear public-house. He also engaged an assistant, a man from Leigh who was particularly skilled in making the strong country wigs then in use. Not content with his growing business Arkwright began to travel about the country for the purpose of buying human hair. He attended the hiring-fairs frequented by young girls seeking places as domestic servants, and was said to be most successful in persuading them to part with their locks. By some means he had become possessed of a valuable chemical secret for dyeing hair. When he had cleaned, prepared and dyed the hair he sold it to the wigmakers, speedily gaining the reputation, " Arkwright's hair was esteemed the best in the county."

It has been said that the gradual disuse of wigs and the consequent lessening of his income led Arkwright to turn his attention to mechanical inventions. But no man of Arkwright's keen intelligence, living in a place like Bolton, could have failed to be impressed by a subject which was a matter of general conversation and speculation—that the demand for yarn by the weavers was greater than the supply from the spinners, a circumstance brought about by the invention of the flying shuttle by Kay of Bury. Throughout the whole of the district spinning and weaving, sometimes separately, sometimes together, formed part of the occupation of most households. Arkwright, in his search for hair, visited the cottages as well as the fairs, and con-

sequently must have become familiar with the growing discrepancy between supply and demand, and the spectacle of the spinners working at high pressure whilst the weavers stood idle. To a keen, practical man like himself whose native ingenuity and " push " had already been demonstrated in his barber's business, it must have been obvious that a large profit was to be made from any improvement in the method of spinning by the old hand-wheel. Hargreaves had completed his spinning-jenny in 1767, but the thread spun by it was only suitable for weft, and the roving process had still to be carried out by hand. The only solution of the increasing difficulty was a method of spinning by machinery, and what is more natural and probable than that a man of Arkwright's turn of mind seeing the golden opportunity should set his keen wits to work ?

In this year of 1767 when Hargreaves had completed his experiments, Arkwright asked John Kay, a watchmaker at Warrington (who must not be confused with John Kay of Bury, the inventor of the fly-shuttle) " to bend him some wires, and turn him some pieces of brass." As it has been said, Arkwright was no mechanic, and all his models had to be made for him. And this was the reason given for his request to Kay. The watchmaker was a neighbour at Leigh of a man called Highs, who not only had invented a spinning-jenny (which was unsuccessful) but had conceived the possibility of spinning by rollers. He had taken Kay into his confidence, and had employed him in the construction of his models. Highs was represented as a poor, friendless man, and not at all pushing ; and in the hope of ultimately procuring capital with which to test and work his invention of rollers, he kept the models by him. Arkwright was a constant visitor to Leigh, where his father-in-law, Mr. Biggins, had secured him clients. The story affirms that hearing some word of Highs's invention, and of Kay's share in the work, he kept the latter under close observation. About the year 1767 Kay left Leigh for Warrington, where he was shortly afterwards visited by Arkwright, ostensibly to "bend him some wires and turn him some pieces of brass," but in reality to get from him the secret of Highs's invention. Eighteen years later, in his evidence during a suit brought against Colonel Mordaunt by Arkwright for infringing his patent rights, Kay stated on oath that he made two models of Highs's invention of spinning

ARKWRIGHT'S ADVERTISEMENT AS A WIG-MAKER

by rollers, and that Arkwright took them away.

"He asked me whether I could make a small model at a small expense.

"'Yes,' says I, 'I believe I can.'

"Says he, 'If you will, I will pay you.' I went and bought a few articles and made him a small wooden model, and he took it

20

with him to Manchester, and in a week or a fortnight's time, I cannot say which, he comes back again, and I make him another."

" Before you go further, who did you get the method of making these rollers from ? "

" From Mr. Hayes." [The name was so given throughout the trial.]

" From Mr. Hayes, the last witness. Did you tell Mr. Arkwright so ? "

" I told him I and another had tried that method at Warrington."

" You made him a model ? "

" I made him two models and he took one to Preston."

There were a good many discrepancies in Kay's evidence, not the least glaring of which was his statement that he and another man had tried the method of rollers at Warrington. Highs and Kay had worked at Leigh. Kay had been for some time in Arkwright's service, which he had left hurriedly under a charge of felony. On his own admission Kay was not over scrupulous, and he had clearly told Hargreaves that the spinning-rollers were his own invention, otherwise Hargreaves would not have advised him, as he did, to lodge a *caveat* when Arkwright took out his patent for them in 1769.

When the verdict at the trial just mentioned deprived Arkwright of his patent in the spinning-rollers, he drew up a *Case* in which his life-story was set out. It began : " Mr. Arkwright, after many years' intense and painful application, invented, about the year 1768, his present method of spinning cotton by rollers, but upon very different principles from any invention that had gone before it." Believers in Arkwright imputed Kay's story to the malicious invention of a servant " discharged on an ignominious accusation of felony." But the other side asked, and with reason, why, if Arkwright was the actual inventor of the rollers, did he not apply to a clock-maker at Bolton to make the model for him ? Why should he go eighteen miles off to Warrington in search of Kay ? It was also said that the journey to Warrington was made very suddenly. " One gentleman near Bolton had informed us that his grandfather, having ordered a wig of Arkwright, was required to pay a guinea in advance. Before the wig could be made, Arkwright had left the town in pursuit of his spinning-wheel project, on which the whole energies of his mind had become bent." In Aikin's *General Biography* we are told that after Arkwright's visit to Warrington, " Kay and Arkwright applied to Peter Atherton Esq." (apparently a watchmaker) " of Liverpool, to make such an engine ; but from the poverty of the appearance of the latter, Mr. Atherton refused to undertake it, though afterwards, on the evening of the same day, he agreed to lend Kay a smith and watch-tool maker to make the heavier part of the engine, and Kay undertook to make the clock-maker's part of it, and to instruct the workmen." If Kay's story in the witness box was true, it is clear that he made himself a willing party to Arkwright's alleged theft of Highs's invention. But the journey to Liverpool is believed to be an invention, since Mr. Atherton then lived in Warrington, and the model of the " engine " appears to have been made there, and not in Liverpool.

The next step was to procure capital to test the machine, and with this object Arkwright, accompanied by Kay, went to Preston, where he applied to an old friend, John Smalley, " a liquor merchant and painter," for help. Smalley was so much impressed by the possibilities of the invention " that he joined Arkwright with hand and purse."

Secrecy above all things being necessary,

a room in the house of the master of the Free Grammar School, which was hidden by a garden filled with gooseberry bushes, was chosen as the scene of trial. This room became the birthplace of modern cotton-spinning. But the very secrecy of Arkwright's and Kay's operations almost brought about their undoing. Two old women who lived near by declared they heard strange noises coming from the schoolmaster's parlour, as if the devil was tuning his bagpipes and Arkwright and Kay were dancing a reel. It was generally believed they were engaged in some kind of witchcraft or sorcery. Many were inclined to break into the place to see what was going on, but, happily for Arkwright, matters did not go so far. If the neighbours had made a forcible entry the invention would undoubtedly have been destroyed. As it was, Arkwright was spending all the money he could procure in perfecting the rollers, and was reduced to such straits that he declined to record his vote at the Preston election unless he were given a new suit of clothes, his own being in rags. "The wardrobe of the future knight was in so tattered a condition, that a number of persons subscribed to put him into decent plight to appear at the poll-room."

When Arkwright was satisfied with the trials of his invention, the great question to be decided was, where it should be set up. Only a year before Hargreaves had been driven out of Blackburn, because of his spinning-jenny, after the mob had destroyed his machines. Feeling all over Lancashire was so strong against the introduction of machinery, that to open a mill in any part of the county was only to court disaster. Arkwright, therefore, followed Hargreaves's example and went to Nottingham. Now Nottingham was one of the principal seats of the stocking manufacture, but the stockings were of silk or worsted, the lack of a suitable cotton-yarn making the production of cotton hosiery an impossibility. As Arkwright rightly argued, if his machine could spin good cotton-yarn, there was a big market for it at Nottingham, and no "vested interests," as in Lancashire, to be annoyed by its success.

Some bankers in Nottingham made advances on condition of sharing in the profits of the invention, but the machine not being perfected as soon as they had anticipated they advised Arkwright to seek other assistance, and recommended him to Samuel Need. This recommendation laid the foundation of Arkwright's fortunes. Samuel Need was the partner of Jedediah Strutt of Derby in the manufacture of ribbed stockings, of which they possessed the patent—an invention of Strutt. Both men were much impressed by Arkwright's invention, but more particularly Strutt, and it was with his help that the Bolton barber built a mill at Nottingham a year after his arrival there.

"The first cotton-mill erected in the world was built between Hockley and Woolpack Lane 1769, by Richard Arkwright, who removed hither from Lancashire."

In the same year (1769) Arkwright took out his patent for his spinning-rollers, and by a strange coincidence James Watt took out his first patent for his steam-engine. In later years the application of Watt's invention to Arkwright's rollers revolutionized the cotton-trade.

Arkwright used horses to drive his rollers in his Nottingham mill, but finding this method too expensive as well as impossible upon any large scale, he decided to use water, which had already been applied to a silk-mill on the Derwent; and entering into partnership with Need and Strutt, built a mill at Cromford in Derbyshire, in a deep, picturesque valley near the Derwent, where he had command of a never-failing supply of water power, from a spring of warm water which scarcely ever froze, even during the severest winter. This gave Arkwright's invention its name of "water-frame"; when steam took the place of water it was called the "throstle."

Whether the spinning-rollers were Arkwright's own invention, or an adaptation and improvement of the inventions of others, is a point which never can be made clear. "The spinning-frame of Arkwright was the result of an inventive power of a higher and rarer order than that necessary to originate the spinning-jenny. It was much more than a mere development of the old hand-wheel. It implied the application of a new principle, that of spinning by rollers; and in the delicate adjustment of its various parts, and the nice regulation of the different mechanical forces called into operation, so as to make them properly subordinate to the accomplishment of one purpose, we have the first adequate example of those beautiful and intricate mechanical contrivances which have transformed the whole character of the manufacturing industries. The spinning-frame consisted of four pairs of rollers, acting by tooth and pinion. The top roller was covered with leather to enable it to take hold of the cotton, the lower one fluted longitudinally to let the cotton pass through it. By one pair of rollers revolving quicker than another, the rove was drawn to the requisite fineness for twisting, which was accomplished by spindles or flyers placed in front of each set of rollers. The original invention of Arkwright has neither been superseded nor substantially modified, although it has of course undergone various minor improvements."

The yarn produced by Arkwright's machine being much harder and firmer in texture than that spun by the jenny, it was specially suited for the warp, but the Lancashire manufacturers resolutely declined to have anything to do with it. Consequently Arkwright and his partner were left with a large stock upon their hands. As an experiment some of the yarn was woven into hose, which was found to be greatly superior to those woven from hand-spun cotton. For some time, therefore, the spinning-rollers were used to supply the material for stockings. But in 1773 Arkwright began to use it as warp for the manufacture of calicoes instead of the linen warp, which, until then, had always been used with the cotton weft, and thus he had the distinction of producing a cloth made solely of cotton for the first time in England.

There was a great demand for the new material, but here again the jealousy of the Lancashire manufacturers threw a large stock of material upon the hands of Arkwright and his partners. In 1736 an Act of Parliament had been passed for the protection of the woollen manufacturers of England against Indian calicoes, which had to pay double duty, that is sixpence a yard. The Lancashire manufacturers contended that Arkwright's calico, being made entirely of cotton, came within the meaning of the Act, and it was by their insistence that the authorities demanded the double tax. "The orders for goods which they had received being considerable," says the *Case*, "were unexpectedly countermanded, the officers of Excise refusing to let them pass at the usual duty of threepence per yard as being 'Indian calicoes' though manufactured in England; besides, these calicoes when printed were prohibited. By this unforeseen obstruction a very considerable and very valuable stock of calicoes accumulated."

Neither Arkwright nor Strutt were men

to accept such a situation. They boldly faced the forces arrayed against them and appealed to Parliament for a new Act. In 1736 the rivalry of two great Lancashire interests—the cotton and the woollen—had brought about the Act which placed heavy duties on Indian calicoes, and made it penal to use or wear them if they were printed upon. But now, "a solitary firm was pitted against a combination, that of the Lancashire manufacturers seeking to strangle in its

lawful for any person or persons to use or wear, within the kingdom of Great Britain, either as apparel, household stuff, furniture or otherwise, any new manufactured stuffs wholly made of cotton spun in Great Britain, when printed, stained, painted or dyed with any colour or colours, anything in the said recited Act of the seventh year of his late Majesty King George the First, or any other Act or Acts of Parliament notwithstanding." Up to this time Arkwright

HARGREAVES' SPINNING JENNY

cradle the infant industry which, a hundred years after their opposition to it, was to clothe half the world, enrich their descendants, and to make their county what it is!"

After a heavy expense Arkwright and his partners triumphed over the opposition, and in 1774 Parliament passed an Act which specially exempted from extra taxation the "new manufacture of stuffs wholly made of raw cotton wool." A further provision of the same Act reads oddly to-day: "It shall and may be

and his partners had spent nearly twelve thousand pounds upon machinery, with little or no return, but with the new Act a golden tide of prosperity set in.

Arkwright took out a second patent, which included all the processes for preparing cotton to be spun, as well as the spinning-processes themselves, known as the "carding patent," in December 1775; and five years later he was able to say that there had been "sold to numbers of adventurers, residing in the different counties of Derby, Leicester, Nottingham,

Worcester, Stafford, York, Hertford and Lancashire, many of his patent machines. Upon a moderate computation, the money expended in consequence of such grants amounted to at least sixty thousand pounds; and Mr. Arkwright and his partners also expended in large buildings in Derbyshire and elsewhere, upwards of thirty thousand pounds; and Mr. Arkwright also erected a very large and extensive building in Manchester at the expense of upwards of four thousand pounds, and a business was formed which already employed upwards of five thousand persons, and a capital on the whole of not less than two hundred thousand pounds." Such was the early result of the invention of the spinning-rollers.

The Bolton barber had become a wealthy man, but in 1779, both his peace and his prosperity were seriously disturbed. Ten years before, the spinners of Blackburn had driven Hargreaves and his spinning-jenny out of the town. Now the spinners in other districts, believing that all these inventions of machinery would deprive them of their livelihood, rose up in fury. Arkwright had a mill at Chorley in which all his inventions were at work. This was the first object of attack. It was completely destroyed. In the *Annual Register* for 1779 we have an account which gives us a clear impression of the widespread terror caused by this revolt against machinery—

"*Manchester, October* 9.—During the course of the week several mobs have assembled in different parts of the neighbourhood, and have done much mischief by destroying the engines for carding and spinning cotton-wool (without which the trade of this county could never be possibly carried out to any great extent). In the neighbourhood of Chorley the mob destroyed and burned the engines and buildings erected by Mr. Arkwright at a very great expense. Two thousand, or upwards, attacked a large building near the same place on Sunday, from which they were repulsed, two rioters killed, and eight wounded taken prisoners. They returned, strongly reinforced, on Monday, and destroyed a great number of buildings, with a vast quantity of machines for spinning cotton, etc. Sir George Savile arrived (with three companies of the York Militia) while the buildings were in flames. The report of their intention to destroy the works in this town [Manchester] brought him here yesterday noon. At one o'clock this morning two expresses arrived—one from Wigan, another from Blackburn—entreating immediate assistance, both declaring the violence of the insurgents and the shocking depredations yesterday at Bolton. It is thought they will be at Blackburn this morning, and at Preston by this afternoon. Sir George ordered the drums to beat to arms at half after one, when he consulted with the military and magistrates in town, and set off at the head of three companies soon after two o'clock this morning for Chorley, that being centrical to this place, Blackburn, and Wigan. Captain Brown of the 25th Regiment, with seventy invalids [probably pensioners], and Captain Thorburn of Colonel White's Regiment, with about one hundred young recruits, remained at Preston; and for its further security, Sir George Savile offered the justices to arm three hundred of the respectable house-keepers if they would turn out to defend the town, which was immediately accepted. In consequence of these preparations the mob did not think it prudent to proceed to any further violence."

Arkwright's loss by this destruction must have been considerable, for, in addition to the mill he owned at Chorley, he had valuable patent-rights in machinery destroyed in other places. In the same year his wife separated from him, it was said because she would not agree to join him in selling some property which could only be sold with her consent. Probably it was her own inheritance. Then a rain of troubles descended on Arkwright. Scarcely two years after the destruction of his mill at Chorley he found that the infringements of his patents were so numerous that he was obliged to appeal to the law for protection as he was threatened with the loss of one of his most valuable sources of profit. The greatest care was taken by the infringers of his patent to prevent any knowledge of their action leaking out, none but persons sworn to secrecy being employed by them as workmen. But after exhaustive inquiries Arkwright obtained evidence against nine firms. His first case was against Colonel Mordaunt, who admitted his use of Arkwright's machine, but pleaded insufficiency of specifications in the patent. This was technically correct, and Arkwright lost the day. Whether it was brought about by the verdict is obscure, but the partnership between Need, Strutt and Arkwright was dissolved very shortly afterwards.

Four years later (1785) Arkwright made another effort to prove the validity of his second patent by bringing an action in the Court of Common Pleas against its infringement. The plea of insufficiency of specification was again set up, but the case was decided in Arkwright's favour.

When the verdict became known in Lancashire there were indeed " racings and chasings on Cannaby Lea." In the four years that had elapsed since the Mordaunt trial, the unauthorized use of the patent had become so great that over thirty thousand persons were employed in the mills in which it had been set up, the building of which had cost about thirty thousand pounds. The cotton spinners who, acting upon the first verdict, had annexed Arkwright's patent, saw themselves threatened with complete ruin by the second. They therefore combined together and obtained a writ for a new trial. The case was heard in the Court of the King's Bench on June 25, 1785, before Mr. Justice Buller and a special jury. All cotton-spinning Lancashire was agog with excitement, and when the news reached the county palatine that even Arkwright's claim to the invention was being disputed, excitement rose higher still. John Kay gave his evidence, a portion of which has been quoted; Highs gave evidence—they were the principal witnesses brought forward by Arkwright's opponents. But Kay's evidence was trebly tainted. To begin with he confessed himself guilty of fraud by stating that he revealed the secret of Highs's spinning-roller to Arkwright; then not only had he fled from Arkwright's service when threatened with a charge of felony, but he had also represented himself to be the inventor of the rollers. Highs could produce no machine on which he had ever spun cotton.

After hearing the evidence on both sides the judge told the jury there were three points upon which they had to decide—

1. Is the invention new?
2. Is it invented by the defendant?
3. Was it sufficiently described in the specification?

The summing up was dead against Arkwright, and the jury without a moment's hesitation gave their verdict against him.

Such an issue would have crushed an ordinary man, but in the following November we find Arkwright petitioning for another trial on the ground that he had new evidence which would refute that adduced against the originality of his invention. His application was refused, and so far as the law was concerned Arkwright was declared to be not the inventor of the machinery which revolutionized the cotton-trade, and brought millions of money to Lancashire.

So far as one point pleaded against him was concerned, the lack of proper specification in taking out his second patent, which actually covered the first, Arkwright had placed himself hopelessly in the wrong. It was proved beyond all manner of doubt he had given directions that the plans should " be as obscure as the nature of the case would admit," but besides this, it was also proved that he had introduced matter intended to render them unintelligible. Some of the articles, on the specification upon which the patent was granted, would have spoiled the cotton if they had been put into operation. All this Arkwright practically admitted in his *Case*, but he gives as his reason that, instead of wishing to perpetrate a fraud, he was " anxiously desirous of preserving to his native country the full benefit of his inventions." But he had more reason to fear infringements or copying of his patents in England than abroad, and this was doubtless his reason for the wilful obscurity of the specifications, an obscurity that lost him the verdict.

The cancelling of Arkwright's patents made no difference, however, to his prosperity. He had the start in manufacturing all cotton goods ; this, allied to his experience and remarkable business capacity, placed him at the head of the cotton manufacturers, and " for several years he fixed the price of cotton twist, all other spinners conforming to his prices." He built new mills both in Derbyshire and Lancashire, and had some share in the erection of those mills at New Lanark in Scotland, where, at a later date, the Co-operative movement had its birth under Robert Owen. Not only did he become a man of wealth ; he became a man of position. When George III. escaped assassination by the dagger of Margaret Nicholson, Arkwright was chosen by the wapentake of Wirksworth to present its congratulatory address to the sovereign, and in reward received a knighthood. This was in 1786 ; the next year he was chosen as High Sheriff of Derbyshire. Then he bought the Manor of Cromford, obtaining the grant of a market for the town ; and was busily engaged in building a home worthy of his fortune—Willersley Castle—when he died in 1792, at the age of sixty.

Few men have passed through thirty so strenuous years as Richard Arkwright, or years more fraught with opposition, failure and success. Few men have triumphed more completely. The secret, perhaps, lies in this description : " Arkwright possessed an energy which would scarcely allow him a moment's rest. He generally laboured in his multifarious concerns from five in the morning until nine at night, and utilized all his time to the best possible advantage. Bad or careless work roused his stern wrath. For the success of his schemes he was ready to endure any personal inconvenience and suffer the severest sacrifices. From the beginning he was so sanguine of the vast result that would follow his inventions ' that he would make light of discussion on taxation, and say that he would pay the National Debt.' "

Whether Arkwright stole his inventions or originated them himself, he created a system of labour which completely altered the domestic conditions of the Lancashire spinners and weavers. He introduced the factory system with its minute division of labour, and the highly organized co-operation of many workers in the different processes of machinery. "In overcoming the prejudices of workers, in accustoming them to unremitting diligence during the stated hours of labour, in training them for their particular tasks and inducing them to conform to the regular celerity of the machinery, Arkwright displayed an energy and perseverance perhaps of a higher kind, if less rare, than that which enabled him to originate his invention. His whole arrangements were framed with the utmost forethought and care, and from the beginning he enforced scrupulous cleanliness and the most systematic order." His plans of management are practically those which obtain to-day.

Arkwright was succeeded by his only son, who was already making twenty thousand a year out of a mill his father had given him at Bakewell. He left a fortune of nearly half a million sterling, part of which went to his daughter, part to his son. Arkwright only had these two children—the son by his first wife, the daughter by the second. Richard Arkwright the younger completed Willersley Castle and died in 1843, worth considerably more than a million of money. Millionaires were not so plentiful in those days as they are now, and Arkwright's son was described as being "except Prince Esterhazy the richest man in Europe." He had a pleasant habit of wrapping a ten-thousand-pound banknote in the table-napkins of each of his ten children for a Christmas Box.

RICHARD ARKWRIGHT

"TIM BOBBIN"

JOHN COLLIER

The Burns of Lancashire

"TIM BOBBIN," as John Collier is always known, was the Burns of Lancashire. He was the first author who wrote in the Lancashire dialect, and for nearly two hundred years his name has been a household word in the county. His *Tummus and Meary* stands unrivalled as a dialect story.

Tim Bobbin's father was a poor curate or deacon, combining the work of village school-master with his clerical duties, at Urmston, where Tim, his third son, was born in 1710. Telling his own story in the third person, Tim Bobbin thus speaks of his father and his own childhood—

"In the reign of Queen Anne he was a boy and one of the nine children of a poor curate in Lancashire, whose stipend never amounted to thirty pounds a year, and consequently the family must feel the iron teeth of penury with a witness. These indeed were sometimes blunted by the charitable disposition of the good rector (the Rev. Mr. Haddon, of Wigton). So this T. B. lived as some other boys did, content with water porridge, buttermilk and jannock, till he was between thirteen and fourteen years of age, when Providence began to smile on him on his advancement to a pair of Dutch looms,[1]

when he met with treacle to his pottage, and sometimes a little in his buttermilk, or spread on his jannock. However, the reflection of his father's circumstances (which now and then start up and still edge his teeth) make him believe that Pluralists are no good Christians." It was a period when many livings and benefices were held by one man who enjoyed the revenues, paying poor curates like Tim Bobbin's father to do the work. The remembrance of his father, blind and half-starved, with nine children and only thirty pounds a year upon which to bring them up, never left Tim Bobbin, and in after life he never ceased, both with tongue and pen, to pillory and satirize those parsons who grew rich by the holding of several livings. It was a scandalous state of affairs, but it was not confined to Lancashire; it was common all over England.

The poor curate had destined his third son for the Church, but his poverty made this impossible, and having given him what smattering of education he could, he apprenticed the boy to a weaver. "I went 'prentice in May 1722," says Tim,

[1] "The Dutch looms were brought to England by some Flemish artisans in the beginning of the eighteenth century, and their principal settlement was at Bolton-le-Moors. Those who adopted them had an advantage over the old English looms. The shuttle was thrown and caught by the hand of the weaver, and the Dutch loom continued to be popular until the invention of Kay's fly-shuttle, for which there was a patent in 1753."

" to one Johnson, a Dutch-born weaver, at Newton Moor, in the parish of Mottram, but hating slavery in all shapes, I by divine Providence, vailing my skull-cap to the mitres, in November 1727, commenced school-master at Milnrow." From this it seems probable that Tim persuaded his master to cancel his indentures half way through the term of his apprenticeship. To enter upon a career as a school-master at the age of seventeen with a stock of knowledge gained only from his father's tuition up to the age of twelve, and supplemented by his own studies in the scanty leisure afforded to apprentices, was a step not only of ambition, but of daring. This action of the youth was characteristic of the man, and it is to Tim Bobbin's determination to be a school-master, and not a weaver, that Lancashire owes its first dialect literature.

But Tim antedated the " vailing " of his " skull-cap to the mitres," that is, procuring a licence to teach from the Bishop of the diocese, by some fifteen years. When he forsook the loom he became a travelling school-master, going from place to place, and holding classes. Bury, Middleton, Oldham and Rochdale, with the neighbouring villages, was the district he selected, and wherever he made his head-quarters for the time being he held a night- as well as a day- school. His earnings, notwithstanding his teaching both by day and night, were most meagre, but the knowledge he gained laid the foundation for the work by which he became famous throughout Lancashire. As one of his biographers, Mr. Espinasse, says, "A thorough knowledge of the Lancashire dialect, nowhere so pure as in that district, Tim could not fail to acquire as he shifted his tent from village to village, and he began early to note down what was quaintest and raciest in its phraseology.

The oddities and peculiarities of Lancashire rusticity were forced on his attention, and the eye of the young humorist was not slow to apprehend and seize them." So unsatisfactory were the proceeds of his itinerant teaching, that after a while Tim was grateful to accept the post of assistant-master at a free school at Milnrow, near Rochdale, with the princely salary of £10 a year. The master, Mr. Pearson, was also the curate of Milnrow ; his salary was only £20 a year, which he divided with his assistant. This free school at Milnrow had been built by Mr. Townley, of Belfield Hall, who nominated its masters. His son, Colonel Townley, was much attracted by Tim Bobbin's (or rather John Collier, as he was then known) intelligence and ready wit ; throughout Tim's life the colonel remained his constant friend and patron, and at his death became his biographer.

Ten pounds a year represented independence to the young school-master. He considered it, Colonel Townley says, " as a material advance in the world, as he could still have a night-school, which answered very well in that very populous neighbourhood, and was considered by him, too, as a state of independency, a favourite idea ever afterwards with his high spirit. Mr. Pearson not very long afterwards falling a martyr to the gout, my honoured father gave Mr. Collier the school, which not only made him happy in the thought of being more independent, but made him consider himself a rich man." As a matter of fact Tim was assistant-master at Milnrow for twelve years before he succeeded Mr. Pearson in 1739, and it was three years later that " vailing my skull-cap to the mitres," he obtained his licence to teach from the Bishop. In addition to his £20 a year Tim also had the fees of the scholars, twelve of whom only were taught gratis, so not only was he able to afford an assistant, but also to give up his night school. Twenty pounds a year in those up nine children, Tim considered himself rich.

It was about the time that he became

days went as far as fifty or sixty pounds at the present time ; it is no wonder, therefore, that with an income—not counting the extras—only ten pounds less than that upon which his father had supported himself and his wife and brought head-master that Tim began to write both in prose and verse, one of his earliest productions being a satire in rhyme upon a magistrate, Edward Chetham of Castleton, called "The Blackbird," and during the next five years not only did he continue to use his pen, but he made a serious study of drawing, for which he had a natural bent. This he developed into drawing likenesses of his friends and neighbours, but in these, as in his writings, Tim's quick perception of the ridiculous made itself manifest, and his portraits were generally caricatures of the person represented, but it was such good-humoured caricature that the person portrayed joined in the laugh against himself. He also taught himself to play "the hautboy and the common flute, and upon the former he very much excelled." As Mr. Espinasse very truly says, although the expression "self-culture" was unknown in Tim Bobbin's days, it was familiar to him as a fact.

No young school-master could have been happier than Tim, his witty conversation, the ease with which he dashed off a squib or a caricature, his flute-playing, and above all his geniality and good humour made him a welcome guest wherever he chose to go. He was constantly at the Townleys at Belfield, and at the houses of the neighbouring gentry. "Tim," says Mr. Espinasse, "seems to have been a bit of a buck, too, and what with his village dandyism, his talents and accomplishments, and the twenty pounds a year of certain income, he was looked upon as a desirable match by the lasses of Milnrow and its neighbourhood." But Tim, probably with the remembrance of his father's struggles and miseries as a married man upon thirty pounds a year, was in no haste to take to himself a partner, and he was thirty-five when he married Mary Clay, a handsome young Yorkshire-woman, who had come upon a visit to her aunt, Mrs. Butterworth, at Milnrow. It is easy to suppose that Tim with his scholarly accomplishment, and his interest in art and music would not be attracted by the average country girl; he would look for somebody with a wider outlook upon life, a woman who could sympathize in his many interests. This woman he found in Mary Clay, who made him the most devoted wife. She had spent several years in London with another aunt, a Mrs Pitt, "a woman of property, and married to Mr. Pitt, an officer in the Tower," and therefore had received a "metropolitan polish." They were married April 1, 1744, Tim being fourteen years older than his bride, and settled down in a house close to the school.

Milnrow was then a mile and a half from Rochdale, and was described by Edwin Waugh (Tim's worthy successor in the delineation of Lancashire folk) as lying "on the ground not unlike a tall tree laid lengthwise, in a valley, by a river side. At the bridge its roots spread themselves out in clots and fibrous shoots in all directions, while the almost branchless trunk runs up, with a little bend above half a mile, towards Oldham, where it again spreads itself out in an umbrageous way at the little fold called Butterworth Hall." From the west end of the bridge "a lane leads between the ends of the dwelling houses, down to the water-side. There still stands the quaint substantial cottage of John Collier in the old garden by the river" (this was many years ago). The house was of fair size and had remains of a fine oak staircase. But the garden was Tim's chief delight. Here he "had a roomy green arbour, with a smooth stone table in the middle, on which lay his books, his flute, or his meals, as he was in the mood. He would stretch himself out here, and muse for hours together. The lads used to bring their tasks from the school behind the house, to this arbour for Tim to examine. He had a green shaded walk from the school into the garden. When in the school, or about the house, he wore a silk velvet skull-cap."

But for the spur of necessity it is highly probable that this life of ease and comfort with its musing "for hours together" would have robbed Lancashire of its most characteristic literature. The spur was provided by Tim's own folly. Upon her marriage, together with "several silk gowns and other elegant articles of female attire," his wife brought a portion of three hundred pounds, which, in place of investing, Tim proceeded to spend in what one of his biographers calls "irregular joviality." They were days of heavy drinking, and Tim seems to have had a fair share of the failing of his period; at any rate the three hundred pounds disappeared in feasting all and sundry at the inns for miles round, feasts that were accompanied by lavish potations.

When the money was all gone, Tim

realized his folly, and his repentance was so sincere that his wife, in place of reproaching him, said she was "heartily glad that the money was all spent." Tim now turned his talents in painting and with his pen to account, in order to meet the increasing expenditure of his family. At first he relied solely upon his brush, painting altar-pieces for country churches and sign-boards for inns. At Shaw Chapel two large figures of Aaron and Moses on each side of the east window, painted in oils on boards, were his work, as was also the figure of an angel at Milnrow, with a trumpet at its mouth and holding a scroll in which the psalm was announced from the singing-loft. When the demand for sign-boards and altar-pieces was exhausted, Tim tried his powers of caricature—and with considerable success. He painted

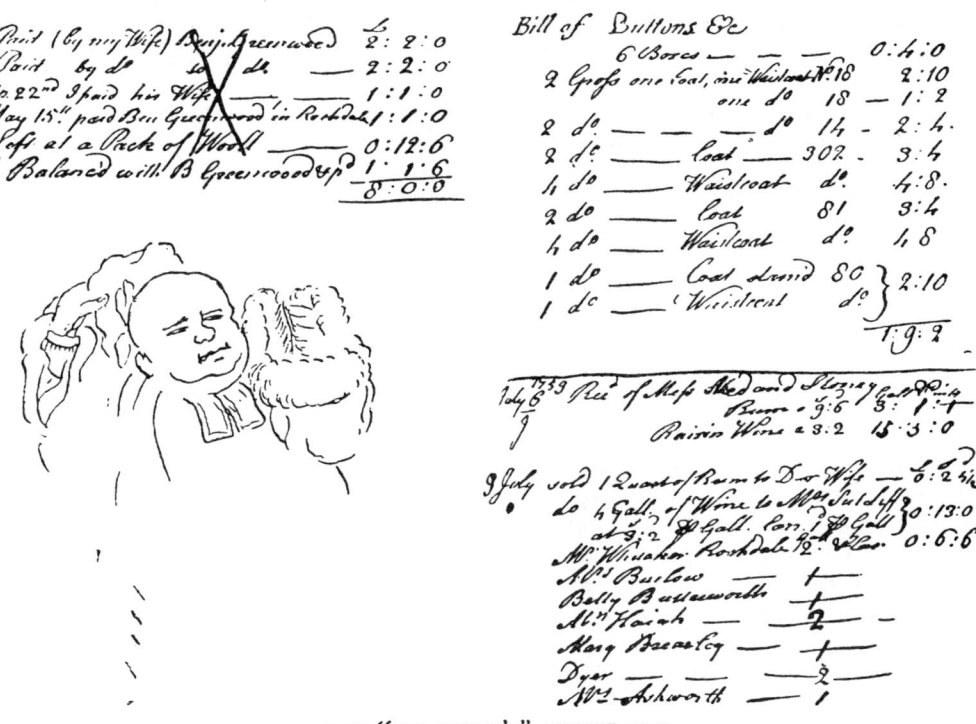

A PAGE IN "TIM BOBBIN'S" ACCOUNT BOOK

−A

quickly, and could, " when he chose, turn out a head in a day or two, and a group in a week." These pictures he carried to one of the much-frequented inns at Rochdale, or on the road into Yorkshire. The landlords, to whom alas! Tim was only too well known as a customer, were always pleased to take the part of salesmen, sometimes even advancing money to the painter. Commercial travellers in those days were called " riders " because they rode from town to town with samples and patterns in their saddle-bags, and it was amongst the " riders " that Tim's " grotesques " found a ready sale at the inns, being either bought for their own pleasure, or else with a view to being re-sold at a higher price. A little later, Tim learned to etch, and was thus able to command a wider market. A series of his etchings called " The Human Passions Delineated " had a considerable success: it was full of spirit and humour. As an artist it must be confessed that Tim had no sense of beauty, it was only strong personality or physical peculiarities that appealed to him, and these he portrayed with a strong touch of humour, giving curious reality and strength to his portraits of " ugly, grinning old fellows, and mumbling old crones on broomsticks," as Colonel Townley described his work.

Notwithstanding his painting and his etching, Tim's pen was not idle, and in the intervals between using the brush and the burin, he found time to write many satires both in prose and verse. Two years after his marriage he published *Tummas and Meary*, the dialogue in dialect which made him famous, and which has been described as " the first genuine Lancashire classic." It was signed " Tim Bobbin," and so popular did it become throughout the whole county that Tim Bobbin was a household name from the Mersey to the Lune, and

from the sea to the Yorkshire border, thousands of the readers of *Tummas and Meary* never knowing that " Tim Bobbin " was John Collier. Tim himself always used his pseudonym in preference to his real name.

Tummas and Meary had an instant success, but Tim was robbed of a large portion of his profits by printers and booksellers; he was compensated, however, by bringing out many editions himself; the dialogue became a steady source of income to him throughout the rest of his life.

" Teaching, toping, painting, writing," says Mr. Espinasse, " a welcome guest in inn and hall, journeying sometimes as far as Newcastle and Liverpool to enjoy the hospitality of distant admirers, but ever keeping an eye to business and the sale of his heads, Tim Bobbin passed the remainder of his days with few vicissitudes more striking than the arrival of a new child, or an illness brought on by over-potations and otherwise punished, very properly, by a sound rating from his wife." But there was one episode which shows the character of this son of Lancashire.

Five years after the publication of *Tummas and Meary*, when Tim was at the height of his fame, he received an offer from Mr. Hill of Kilbroyd and Halifax in Yorkshire to become his head clerk. It was an unusual offer to be made to a school-master without any commercial education, but Mr. Hill was led to offer the appointment, it was said, partly because he wished to enjoy Tim's droll conversation, and partly because he wrote a hand like print: Tim was famous for his handwriting. Although it meant severing himself from his beloved Milnrow, Tim accepted the offer, as he told Colonel Townley, " because of his wife and children," but he did so reluctantly, and when he went to Belfield Hall to take his leave of his patron, the latter says that he wept and "entreated me not to be too hasty in filling up the vacancy in that school, where he had lived so many years contented and happy; for he had already some foreboding that he should never relish his new situation and new occupation."

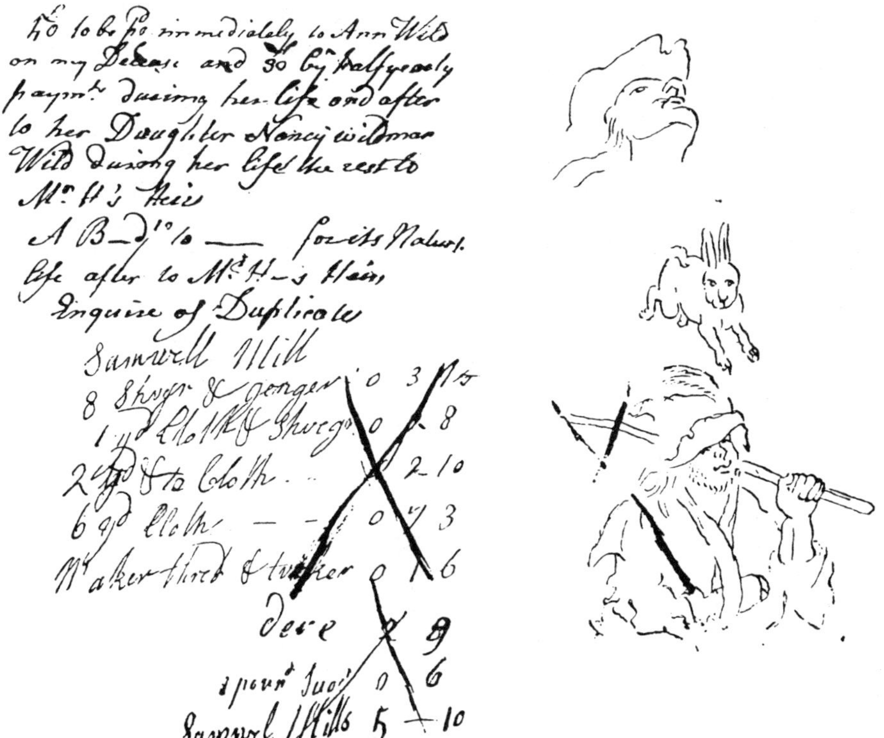

sweet calm and contentment? I must now take my farewell of all that made life worth preserving; I must give up my painting, my rhyming, my bowling, my tippling, and every inviting nonsense." Kilbroyd, he says, is "a fresh scene which has brought me to my senses"; and instead of being "a little monarch," he has become "a kind of slave." His dis-

A PAGE IN "TIM BOBBIN'S" NOTE BOOK

Tim, with his wife and children and all his belongings, set out for Yorkshire on June 12, 1751; but although his agreement with Mr. Hill was for several years, at the end of a few months he grew weary of being chained to a desk. "It is true I have more than double the salary" (than at Milnrow), he wrote to a friend, "and a good house rent free: ah, my friend! what are these to pleasing liberty, to

taste for his new life and its irksomeness is bitterly expressed in another letter. "They are conspiring to make me rich," he says. "I am almost sick when I hear two sixpences jingle together, and ready to swear at the sight of a guinea. By what I have seen here I have seen enough to satisfy me that he who has a bare competency, and can sleep soundly at night with his door open and never fear thieves, is the only happy man, and goes through life with the easiest burden. Such happy days have I seen at my old habitation in Lancashire, and I hope to see again, when, if you'll come and see me, your old favourite repast, mull'd ale and toast, shall be at your service."

Poor Tim was like a caged wild bird as the head clerk of Mr. Hill, "then one of the greatest cloth merchants, and also one of the most considerable manufacturers of baizes and shalloons in the north of England," and it is not surprising, therefore, that ere the first year of his engagement had passed, the agreement was cancelled, and he returned joyfully to Milnrow to his little cottage and his school. Restored to his old position Tim used all his talents to earn money. He painted heads, and went even so far as Chester to paint the panels of carriages for a coachbuilder; he acted as his own bookseller, carrying his *Tummas and Meary*, books of his etchings, his satires and poems, in his wallet, and offering them for sale, sometimes receiving payment for them in kind, as witness these three entries from his account book: " Delivered a book of prints to coz. John Hulme to have a hat for it. Exchanged a book of *Human Passions* for 3 lbs. of thread at 3s. a lb.; blue tape ½d. yard; tape a 1d. a knot; a gross of laces. Paid

John Kenyon, a book for a wig." He likewise turned his wonderful handwriting to account, writing the Lord's Prayer at two shillings a time: " Mr. Aspinell, Burnley—12 Lord's Prayers at 2s. each, *very small.*"

And so passed the remainder of his happy life, across which drink had thrown the only shadow. He had six children, the eldest of whom, Charles, settled at Kendal, and, succeeding in his business, bought the old cottage at Milnrow and gave it to his parents for their lives. The last letter that Tim wrote was to this son. " Things remain as you left 'em," he says, " they are all well except your poor mother . . . Rich and Sal drive on, but my old peepers cannot pierce far into futurity. I have painted a good deal of things since you left, and drunk punch betimes as customers came in. Make sure to keep sober, which is more than he could do who is, dear Charles, your loving Father."

Tim died in July 1786, being then seventy-seven, only a few weeks after his faithful and devoted wife. They were buried in the churchyard at Rochdale; and to Tim's honour it should be said that the doggerel epitaph upon their tombstone, which refers to his taste for punch, was not written by him, as is generally supposed.

JOHN BRADSHAW, THE REGICIDE

THE STORY

OF THE

LANCASHIRE MAN

WHO CONDEMNED

HIS KING TO

DEATH

JOHN BRADSHAW,
President of the High Court of Justice, Died
Nov. 22, 1659.

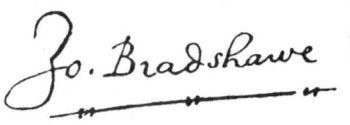

A MONGST the many old halls which are gradually being swallowed up by the ever stretching suburbs of Manchester is Marple Hall, the ancient home of the Bradshaws, and famous as the birthplace of John Bradshaw, whose name stands first upon the death warrant of King Charles I. No man's character has been so diversely painted as John Bradshaw's. By the more extreme Parliamentarians and Puritans he was regarded as a demi-god; by the Royalists he was regarded as a demon for the part he had played in the trial of the unfortunate monarch.

Bradshaw was born at Marple in 1602,

his father, Henry Bradshaw, being a member of the old Lancashire family of that name. John was baptized at Stockport on December 18 in the same year, and against the entry of his birth in the register of the parish church is still to be seen the awful word, "traitor," written by some outraged Royalist. He was the third son of his father and received his first education at the grammar school at Middleton, and afterwards at Bunbury, a fact which he afterwards remembered by bequeathing to each school the sum of five hundred pounds for " 'amending the charges of the master and ushers as part of his thankful acknowledgments." It is also said that Bradshaw spent some time at the grammar school at Macclesfield, and tradition has it that whilst there he scribbled these lines on a stone in the church wall—

" My brother Henry must heir the land,
My brother Frank must be at his command;
Whilst I, poor Jack, will do that
That all the world will wonder at."

This boyish scribbling has been regarded by many as a prophetic utterance as to the part Bradshaw was destined to play in his country's history; by others as merely boyish boasting. But John Bradshaw was no ordinary boy. He was possessed of self-confidence and energy in their highest degree, and it is not improbable that under their influence he voiced this ambition, and that when in the course of time he had done that which " all the world " was wondering at, his boyish doggerel was at once remembered by his family and ascribed to prophecy. There are many prophecies that are only remembered when their predictions have been fulfilled. Be that as it may, the Bradshaw family treasured these words, and a member of a later generation had

them inscribed in a window at Marple Hall, where they may still be seen. Marple Hall itself, with its beautiful staircase and wainscoted rooms, has remained absolutely unchanged since John Bradshaw lived there as a small boy. That he was ever at Middleton grammar school has been a matter for dispute, but it was the nearest place of any importance to Marple, and in the bequest of five hundred pounds to the schools at Middleton and Bunbury, Bradshaw particularly speaks of them as " schools in which I had *part* of my educac'on."

His school-days done, Bradshaw served his clerkship in the office of an attorney in Congleton, but the drudgery of office-work and the quiet life of a country town were ill-suited to his active disposition, and seeking a larger field for his energies he went to London, where he was called to the Bar at Gray's Inn in 1627. " All his early life," writes Bradshaw's relative, the poet John Milton, " he was sedulously improving in making himself acquainted with the laws of his country ; " he then practised with singular success and reputation at the Bar. He returned to Congleton, where, in 1637, he was Mayor and also held the post of High Steward of the borough for several years. But whatever success he may have attained, and whatever influence he possessed at Congleton, the brilliancy and prosperity of his career did not begin until his forty-first year, when he left the town and once more settled in London.

At first he seemed to have kept clear of the political controversies which at that time were distracting the country, although he had never made any disguise of his Republican principles. The government was in the hands of the Parliament, and it was by the Parliament that Bradshaw was appointed to his first office as one of the counsel for the prosecution, on behalf of the State, of two Irish rebels, Lord Maguire of Fermanagh and Hugh Macmahon, for their part in the Irish rebellion of 1641 ; the other counsel were Mr. Prynne and Mr. Newdigate. It was at this trial that Bradshaw's profound knowledge of the law was first made manifest, and it was by his elaborate arguments, proving that Irish peers were amenable to English juries, that Lord Maguire was convicted. The brilliance of his legal talents, his known Republican sympathies, and the austerity of his life, all marked him as one who might be extremely useful to the Parliament, and two years later he was appointed to hold the Great Seal of England, with Sir Rowland Wandsworth and Sir Thomas Bedingfield, for the term of six months. Meanwhile the struggle between the King and the Parliament was approaching its tragical close.

In January 1647, the Scotch handed over Charles I. to the Army of the Parliament, and from that time until November 10, he was virtually a prisoner in various country houses and finally at Hampton Court. On November 10, an understanding was arrived at between the Army—which had taken possession of London and, under Cromwell, had assumed the direction of national affairs — and the Parliament. The next day the King escaped to Carisbrooke Castle in the Isle of Wight, where he was made prisoner. Two months later, when Charles refused to give his assent to four bills passed by the Parliament, the House of Commons resolved that they would not again address the monarch.

Here comes in one of the most sinister proofs that the death of the King had been determined upon by Cromwell and the Army. In October 1648, it was ordered by the Parliament that there should be a new corps of Serjeants-at-Law, and the first name upon the list was that of John Bradshaw. There is no direct evidence of the fact—that is scarcely to be expected, since such designs would never be put into writing—but from the manner in which Bradshaw was rewarded, and contemporary references after the tragedy of the King's execution, it was believed that there was a special object in this promotion of Bradshaw, and that, it being intended to bring the King to trial, Cromwell saw the necessity of " securing an efficient instrument " for the conduct of the trial. A month after the appointment of Bradshaw as Serjeant-at-Law, a council of the officers of the Army, on November 16, demanded " that the capital and grand author of our trouble, the person of the king, by whose commissions, commands, or pronouncements, and in whose behalf and for whose interest only, of will and power, all our wars and troubles have been, with all the miseries attending them, may be speedily brought to justice for the treason, blood and mischief he is therein guilty of." In December Charles was removed from Carisbrooke Castle to Hurst Castle, and thence to Windsor, where he spent his last Christmas.

On January 2, 1649, the House of Lords rejected an ordinance of the Commons for bringing the King to trial before a Parliamentary Commission, whereupon the House of Commons decided to act upon its own authority. Certain peers and judges had already been appointed Commissioners, but the names of the peers were now removed, and those of Bradshaw, Nicholas and Steele, all lawyers with no seat in the House, were appointed in their stead. At neither of the first two meetings of the Commission, held privately in the Painted Chamber at Westminster, to discuss the procedure of the trial, was Bradshaw present. Yet in his absence the Commissioners elected him as their President. Bradshaw appeared at the third meeting and "enlarged upon his own want of abilities to undergo so important a charge." He was strongly urged by his fellow Commissioners to accept the charge, but required time to consider it. The next day he accepted the office "with every sign of humility." The Commission decided that he should bear the title of Lord President. There would appear to be considerable evidence to show that the appointment of Bradshaw as Lord President of the Commission which was to try the King, was a carefully arranged affair, and not a matter—as it would seem from the proceedings of the Commission—of their unbiassed choice. Bradshaw's position did not warrant the choice, for there were many others of much higher reputation, both in Parliament and at the Bar, upon whom so important a duty should have fallen. But the trial demanded the most careful observance of legal formalities, and Cromwell, and those who supported him, were in a difficult position. Men of greater eminence than Bradshaw, such as Whitlocke and Widdrington—who had been named Serjeants-at-Law at the same time—both refused to serve on the Commission. Serjeant Nicholas, who had been nominated to the Commission, refused to take part in the trial at all. The Parliamentary judges, St. John, Wylde and Rolle, denounced the proceedings as irregular, and Edmund Prideaux, who had been appointed Solicitor-General on the same day that Bradshaw was made a Serjeant, declined to appear against the King. This would go to show that the appointment was based upon Bradshaw's profound knowledge of legal procedure and his Republican sentiments.

The Parliament did everything in its power to invest the office of the Lord President with state and dignity. Bradshaw was given the Deanery of Westminster for his life, but it was arranged that during the trial he should stay at a house in Palace Yard in order to be near Westminster Hall. He was given a strong bodyguard, and wore scarlet robes. Bradshaw's admirers have insisted upon his indifference to danger, but it is clear he went in fear of personal violence, for "besides for defence he had a high crowned beaver hat, lined with plated steel to ward off blows." The hat is shown in our illustration.

During the week preceding the trial of the King, the most memorable and tragic trial in our history, the Commission held private meetings every day, meetings that were attended by only one-half of its members, for as the tragedy drew near its fulfilment the more faint-hearted lost courage, or were influenced by the horror which was steadily gaining ground amongst the less rabid Parliamentarians and Republicans, against the demand of the Army. As it has been written, "To depose Charles was one thing, to execute him was another. In hurrying on to the latter action the Army only exposed the radical injustice of its proceeding by the self-deception with which it clothed an act of violence with informal forms of law." Whatever Bradshaw's own personal convictions may have been, it is beyond all question that he was appointed Lord President in order that his knowledge of the law might give specious aid to these "informal forms of law."

In January 1649, Charles was brought from Windsor to St. James's Palace, and on the twentieth of the month was taken to Westminster Hall to be tried. The proceedings were invested with great pomp and solemnity. The Lord President Bradshaw, clad in his scarlet robes and wearing his steel protected hat, entered

A fac-simile

of the

DEATH WARRANT of KING CHARLES 1st;

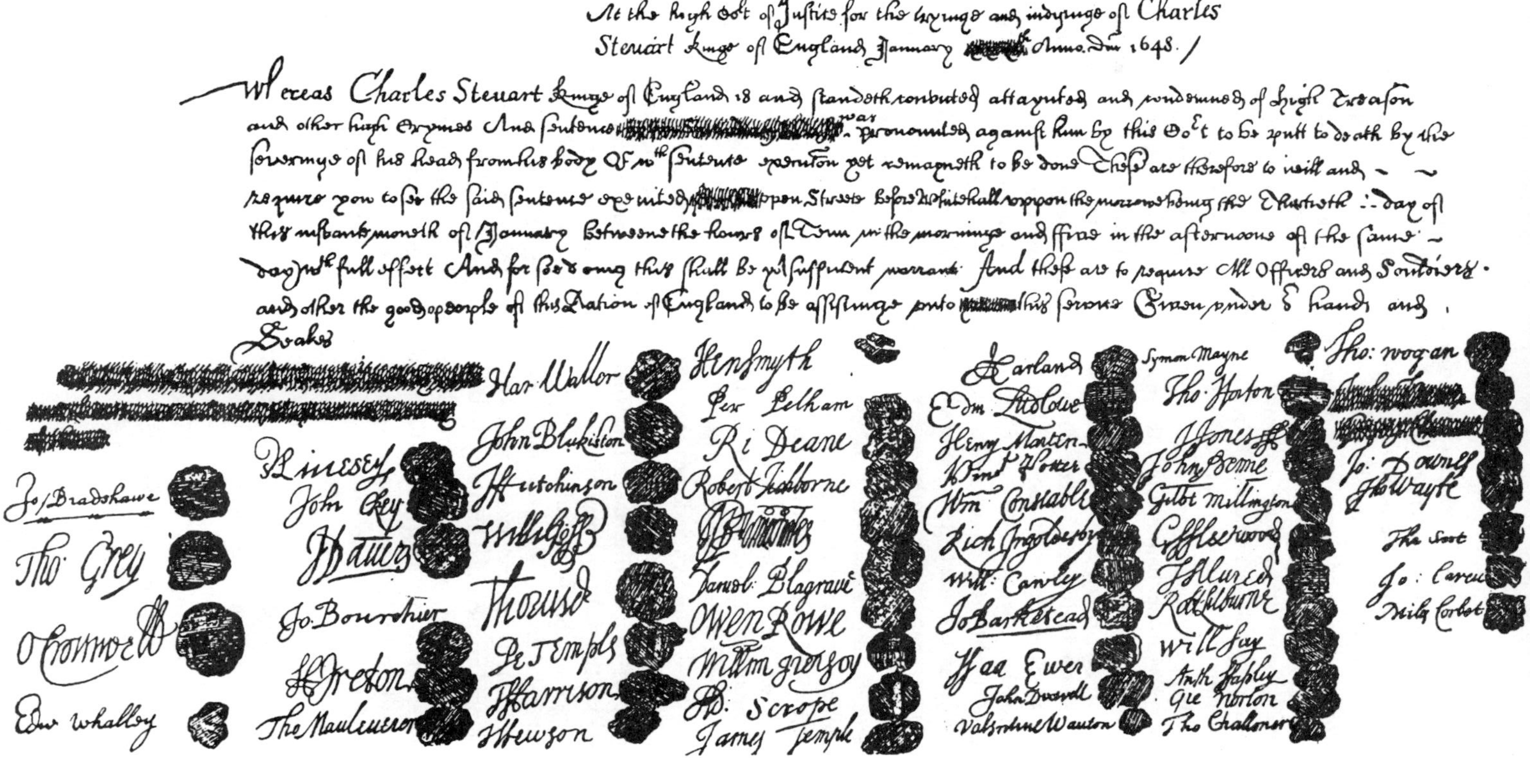

At the high Co[ur]t of Justice for the tryinge and iudginge of Charles Steuart Kinge of England Ianuary xxix Anno Dni 1648/

Whereas Charles Steuart Kinge of England is and standeth convicted attaynted and condemned of High Treason and other high Crymes And Sentence vppon Saturday last was pronounced against him by this Co[ur]t to be putt to death by the severinge of his head from his body Of w[hi]ch Sentence execucon yet remayneth to be done These are therefore to will and require you to see the said Sentence executed In the open Streete before Whitehall vppon the morrowe being the Thirtieth day of this instante moneth of Ianuary betweene the houres of Tenn in the morninge and Five in the afternoone of the same day w[i]th full effecte And for soe doing this shall be yo[ur] sufficient warrant And these are to require All Officers and Souldiers and other the good people of this Nation of England to be assisting vnto you in this Service Given vnder our hands and Seales

Jo Bradshawe
Tho: Grey
O Cromwell
Edw Whalley

Ha: Mallever
John Blakiston
J Hutchinson
Willi Goffe
Tho Pride
Pe. Temple
T Harrison
J Hewson

Henr: Smyth
Per. Pelham
Ri. Deane
Robert Tichborne
H Edwardes
Daniel Blagrave
Owen Rowe
Willi Purefoy
Ad. Scrope
James Temple

M Livesey
John Okey
J Danvers
Jo: Bourchier
H Ireton
Tho Mauleverer

Isaa Ewer
John Dixwell
Valentine Wauton

Sym: Mayne
Tho Horton
J Iones
John Moore
Gilbt Millington
G Fleetwood
J Alured
Robt Lilburne
Will Say

Tho Wogan
Antho Stapley
Greg Norton
Tho Challoner
Tho Wayte
Jo Venn
Gregory Clement
Jo Downes
Thomas Wogan
Vinct Potter
Wm Constable
Rich Ingoldesby
Willi Cawley
Jo Barkstead
Isaa Pennington
Adrian Scrope

Edm Ludlowe
Henry Marten
Jo Hutchinson
Willi Goffe

the Hall preceded by the sword and mace of the Parliament, attended by a guard of twenty gentlemen armed with partisans, and followed by the members of the Commission. Silence was proclaimed, and then the Act of the House of Commons constituting the Commission was read; Bradshaw's name was called out and he took his seat upon a crimson velvet chair, "having a desk with a crimson velvet cushion before him," the members of the Commission taking their places upon his right and left. Behind him stood the bodyguard. The King, dressed in black satin with lace ruffles at his throat and wrists, and the Order of the Garter glittering upon his doublet, faced his judges, his hat upon his head.

In a harsh and imperious voice the Lord President called upon "Charles Stuart, king of England" to plead to the indictment against him. Charles resolutely refused, declaring that the Commission had no legal right to try him. Thereupon ensued a dispute between the King and Bradshaw as to the validity of his trial; undignified on the part of Charles: hectoring and bullying on the part of the Lord President. Unable to shake the King in his determination not to plead, Bradshaw adjourned the trial for two days. This hearing was a repetition of the first, except that Bradshaw showed an increased brutality to the King, who resolutely refused to acknowledge the jurisdiction of the Commission, or to plead to the charges made against him, saying "it was not his case alone that he stood for, but the freedom of all the people of England; for if power without law can make or alter law, no subject can be safe for his life or anything that he calls his own." Throughout the whole of this hearing the Lord President frequently rebuked the King—and in no measured language—for his freedom of

language, yet at the same time would not allow him to make a speech. His attitude to the King during that second day's hearing is one of the blackest charges against Bradshaw.

Three days later twenty-nine witnesses were hurriedly examined, in proof of the charges brought against the King by Cromwell and the Army. On the following day Bradshaw and the Commissioners drew up a sentence of death at a private sitting of the Commission. This sentence was read over to them on the morning of January 27, 1649, after which, led by Bradshaw in his steel protected hat and his scarlet robes, the Commission, wearing "their best habits," went in procession to Westminster Hall.

Once more there was an undignified dispute between the King and the Lord President, which ended in Bradshaw "making a large speech of the king's misgovernment, and that by law kings were accountable to their people and to the law, which was their superior; and he instanced several kings which had been deposed and imprisoned by their subjects, especially in the king's native country (Scotland), where, of one hundred and nine kings, most were deposed, imprisoned, or proceeded against for misgovernment, and his own grandmother (Mary Stuart) removed, and his father, an infant, crowned." At the conclusion of a long harangue, in which vilification played an ugly part, the sentence of death was read.

Before Bradshaw spoke the King had made a touching appeal to be heard in his own defence, and although several of the Commission were anxious to grant his request Bradshaw would not allow him to speak. Again, after the sentence of death had been pronounced, the King demanded to be heard, whereupon the Lord President "roughly told him to be quiet and ordered the guards to remove him."

It is our first duty towards our fellowmen to respect their convictions, a duty we owe equally to the dead as to the living. But whatever John Bradshaw's belief may have been as to the virtues of Republicanism and the evils wrought by King Charles, a sinister shadow must lie for ever upon his name. Whether he was the tool of Cromwell and the Army, or the victim of the inflamed political passions of his time, cannot now be determined, but the fact remains, he condemned a man to death to whom he refused all defence. King Charles was absolutely within his right when he protested against the validity of the Commission, and refused to plead before it.

It has ever been one of the laws of England that a sovereign may not plead in person ; the sovereign is above the law. In our own time we have proof of this. Early in the reign of King George V., a foul calumny was published against his Majesty, a calumny which was proved beyond any manner of doubt in a court of law to be a malicious invention. Our King was anxious to give evidence, but because of the law he could not go into the witness-box.

The ordinance of the Parliament that appointed the Commission to try King Charles I., was a technical breach of the constitution, and " not only was the sentence technically illegal,but on the grounds alleged it was substantially unjust. The Civil War was neither a levy of arms by the King against the Parliament, nor by the Parliament against the King, it had been a conflict between one section of the kingdom and the other." The date of execution was fixed for January 30, and on that day the Commission held its last private meeting, and signed the death warrant which ordered that " Charles

Stuart, King of England should be putte to death by the severinge of his head from his body." Fifty-eight members of the Commission signed the warrant, Bradshaw's signature heading the list.

The scaffold was erected outside one of the windows of the Banqueting House at Whitehall, and as the King passed to his doom not a sound was heard save the outcries of the soldiers who had been directed to shout against him. "The dignity which he had failed to preserve in his long wrangling with Bradshaw and the judges returned at the call of death," and " He nothing common did nor mean upon that memorable scene." The streets and roofs were thronged with people, the scaffold being guarded by a strong body of soldiers drawn up around it. Charles's head fell at the first blow, and as the executioner, according to custom, picked up the head and showed it to the people, calling out "This is the head of a traitor," a groan of pity and horror burst forth from the hitherto silent throng.

A thrill of horror likewise ran through Europe at the news of the King's death, and both abroad and in England with that horror, the name of John Bradshaw as the King's judge was indissolubly connected. In England he was called a " viper of hell," and " a monster of men." Immediately after the King's judicial murder, there was a flood of pamphlets denouncing Bradshaw for his overbearing and brutal behaviour towards the dead monarch at his trial. He showed the same brutality to the leading Royalists who were tried for high treason before the Lord President's Court, when it was re-established a few days after the King's execution. The chief prisoners were the Duke of Hamilton, Lord Capel, and the Earl of Holland, upon each of whom Bradshaw pronounced sentence of death.

Honours and rewards were heaped upon

Bradshaw by the Parliament. After a thousand pounds had been voted to him for his services, two thousand a year was settled upon him out of the estates of the Earl of St. Albans and Lord Cottington, and at the same time he was appointed Chancellor of the Duchy of Lancaster, and selected as one of the thirty-eight persons who composed the Council of State.

By the Royalists Bradshaw was regarded with especial abhorrence, and when he was " held up " by a noted highwayman, Captain James Hind, and relieved of all his money, there was widespread rejoicing. Hind had fought on the Royalist side at the Battle of Worcester, and on one occasion narrowly escaped capture when attempting to rob Cromwell himself. When he was ultimately caught, however, his highway robberies could not be proved against him, and he was hanged for the part he had played at Worcester. The following is the story of Hind and Serjeant Bradshaw :—

" The place where this rencontre happened was upon the road between Sherborne and Shaftesbury. The Serjeant was in much state in a travelling chariot drawn by six horses. Hind rode up to the side of the carriage and demanded the Serjeant's money, who, supposing his name would carry terror with it, told him who he was. Quoth Hind, ' I fear neither you nor any king-killing villain alive. I have now as much power over you as you lately had over the king, and I should do God and my country good service if I made the same use of it ; but live, villain, to suffer the pangs of thine own conscience, till justice shall lay her iron hand upon thee, and require an answer for thy crimes, in a way more proper for such a monster, who art unworthy to die by any hands, but those of the common hangman, and at any other place than Tyburn. Nevertheless, although I spare thy life as a regicide, be assured that unless thou deliverest thy money immediately thou shalt die for thy obstinacy.'

" Bradshaw began to be sensible that the case was not now with him, as it had been when he sat at Westminster Hall attended with the whole strength of the Parliament. He put his hand into his pocket and pulled out about forty shillings in silver which he presented to the Captain, who swore he would that minute shoot him through the heart if he did not find coin of another specie. The Serjeant at last gave the Captain a purse full of Jacobuses.

" Hind having thus got possession of the cash, he made Bradshaw yet wait a considerable time longer, while he made the following eulogium upon money.

" ' This, sir, is the metal that wins my heart for ever. O precious gold, I admire and adore thee as much as either Bradshaw, Pryn, or any other villain of the same stamp who for sake of thee would sell their Redeemer again, were He now upon earth. This is that incomparable medicament which the Republican physicians call the wonder-working plaister. It is truly catholic in operation, and somewhat of a kin to the Jesuit's Powder, but more effectual. The virtues of it are strange and various, it makes justice deaf as well as blind, and takes out spots of the deepest treason as easily as Castile soap does common stains ; it alters men's constitutions in two or three days more than the virtuoso's tranfusion of blood can do in seven years. It is a great Alexispharmick, and helps poisonous principles of rebellion, and those that use them. It miraculously exalts and purifies the eyesight and makes traitors behold nothing but innocence in the blackest malefactor. It is a mighty cordial for a declining cause ; it helps faction and schism as certainly as the itch is destroyed by butter and brimstone. In a word, it makes fools wise men and wise men fools, and both of them knaves. The very colour of this precious balm is bright and dazzling. If it be properly applied to the fist, that is, in a decent manner, and a confidential dose, it infallibly performs all the above-mentioned cures and many others too numerous to be here mentioned.'

money and the means of continuing his journey."

Whatever judgment may be passed upon Bradshaw for his conduct of the trial of King Charles and the Royalists, there is abundant proof that he was no mere time-server. When Oliver Cromwell, in 1658, in his usual abrupt and savage manner, dismissed the Council of State

BRADSHAW HALL

"Having finished, he pulled out his pistol, and said, ' You and your infernal crew have a long while run on, like Jehu, in a career of blood and impiety, pretending that zeal for the Lord of Hosts has been your only motive. How long you may be suffered to continue in the same course, God only knows. I will, however, for this time stop your race in the literal sense of the words.'

"With that he shot the six horses in Bradshaw's chariot and left him minus

after having dissolved the Parliament, " swearing by the living God that they should not sit a moment longer," Bradshaw said to him :—

"Sir, we have heard what you did at the House this morning, and before many hours all England will know it ; but, Sir, you are mistaken to think that the Parliament is dissolved. No power under heaven can dissolve them but themselves ; therefore take you notice of that."

The following year Bradshaw died of

45

a quartan ague at the Deanery at Westminster, which had been one of his many rewards for his conduct at the King's trial.

When lying on his deathbed he was besought to review his past life and particularly "to examine himself touching the King's death."

He answered, "Had it to be done again I would be the first man in England to do it."

Bradshaw was buried in Westminster Abbey, but on the restoration of King Charles II. his body, and those of Cromwell and Ireton, were dragged from their tombs. "The carcase of John Bradshaw, President of the High Court of Justice . . . was carried in a cart to Holbourn also; and the next day following, that which was the 30th January the day on which King Charles I. was beheaded in 1649, from there drawn to Tyburn in three several sledges, followed by the universal outcry of the people. Afterwards they being pulled out from their coffins, were hanged up at the several angles of that triple tree, where they hung till the sun was set; after which they were taken down, their heads cut off, to be set on Westminster Hall . . . their loathsome trunks thrown in a deep hole under the gallows where they now remain." If Bradshaw had lived to see the restoration of Charles II. he would have met the same fate as that king's father, for in a proclamation issued in 1654, from Holland by King Charles II. Bradshaw was exempted from any hope of pardon. His property was confiscated to the Crown.

But in spite of his high-handed conduct as Lord President, Bradshaw was not of an unkindly nature. A few years ago a document was discovered which proves that Bradshaw, after having been granted the estates of a royalist named Richard Green, discovered that this grant left Green's three daughters absolutely destitute, whereupon he ordered his agent to collect the rents from the estate and pay them direct to the three ladies. Bradshaw owned estates in Berkshire, Wiltshire, Somerset and Middlesex, as well as in Lancashire and Cheshire.

It is often erroneously believed that the Lord President was the owner of Bradshaw Hall, near Bolton, which now belongs to his collateral descendants, but the first owner of Bradshaw Hall was his nephew Henry, son of that elder brother who "must heir the land." The younger Henry Bradshaw purchased the Hall in 1693. The arms of the family can still be seen in the stained glass of the window, and cut on the stone over the hall door. The representative of the Lord President's family is Mr. Bradshaw-Isherwood, who owns Marple Hall and Bradshaw Hall, a Bradshaw heiress having married an Isherwood of Bowdon.

JOHN BRADFORD
THE MARTYR

" IN Manchester was I born," wrote John Bradford in a farewell address to his native county when he had been condemned to die, and the stake was already looming before him. He was the first " Manchester man " to earn a lasting name in our country's history. Froude, the historian, has called him the " illustrious Bradford." He was generally believed to have been born at Blackley, but this local tradition may have arisen from an incident which will be described later on. " Born in Lancastershire, in Manchester, a notable town of that county," says a friend, who wrote four years after Bradford's martyrdom, " was of his gentle parents brought up in virtue and good learning even from his very childhood, and among other praises of his good education, he obtained as a chief gift, the cunning and readiness of writing, which knowledge was not only an ornament with him, but also an help to the necessary sustentation of his living." According to Baines, Bradford " received a liberal education in the Free Grammar School of his native town, founded by Bishop Oldham, and stood in high estimation for his proficiency in the Latin language and his extensive knowledge of Arithmetic." The Manchester Grammar School was founded by the worthy Bishop in 1515, and as Bradford was supposed to have been born in 1510, it may reasonably be taken he was one of its earliest pupils.

His " cunningness and readiness of writing " gained him the secretaryship to Sir John Harrington, a Rutlandshire knight who was Treasurer of the King's Camps and Buildings, a poet of considerable importance in the reigns of King Henry VIII. and Edward VI. And such was Bradford's " activity in writings " and " expertness in the art of auditors," that Sir John made him paymaster of the siege of Montreuil in 1544, when that place was invested by the Duke of Norfolk and a small English force as a trick, whilst Henry VIII. in person invested and took Boulogne. The life of a secretary, however, does not appear to have satisfied John Bradford, and at the age of thirty-seven, shortly after the accession of Edward VI., he entered the Inner Temple as a student of common law with the intention of going to the Bar. One of Sir John Harrington's sons shared his chambers, and on this account his old master gave him a small allowance; Bradford had also saved money, and he was certain of Sir John's powerful influence in his new career. But although his prospects were so bright, Bradford was not happy. During the time he was paymaster to the army before Montreuil he had overcharged an article in his accounts, a fraud by which the King was a considerable loser. His conscience had pricked him ever afterwards, and he became both melancholy and restless. At that time the doctrines of the Reformation were being preached with burning fervour and eloquence, and the Church of England became Protestant. Now, a great friend of Bradford, a law student like himself, called Thomas Sampson, became so firm a believer in the new faith that he resolved to leave the law and enter the Church. He had great influence upon Bradford, and a year after the latter had entered the Temple we find him writing to a friend in Blackley in terms which show unmistakably that he too had embraced the doctrine of the Reformed faith. "After that God had touched his heart," Sampson wrote, "with that holy and effectual calling, he sold his chains, rings, brooches and jewels of gold, which before he used to wear, and did bestow the price of this his former vanity in the necessary relief of Christ's poor members, which he could hear of, or find lying sick, or pining in poverty." But Bradford could not forget his fraud, "even in this mean time," says Sampson, "he heard a sermon which that notable preacher Master Latimer made before King Edward VI., in which he did earnestly speak of restitution to be made for things falsely gotten, which did strike Bradford so to the heart, for with one dash with a pen, which he had made without the knowledge of his master (as full often I have heard him confess with plenty of tears), being clerk to the Treasurer of the King's Camp beyond the seas, and was to the deceiving of the King, that he could never be quiet till, by the advice of the same Master Latimer, a restitution was made."

Bradford thereupon wrote to Sir John Harrington confessing his fraud and desiring to refund the money to the Government. But Sir John made many difficulties and excuses. He may have been fearful that he might be accused of complicity or, failing that, of negligence in not having detected the false entry ; but whatever the reason his continual delays made it clear that he wished to have nothing to do with the restitution. Henry VIII. was dead, and very naturally Sir John may not have wished to put himself in the bad graces of the new King Edward VI. and of his uncle the Lord Protector. Bradford could not rest and therefore, as he wrote to his friend Mr. Travis, the minister of Blackley : "Since my coming to London I was with Master Latimer, whose counsel is as you shall hear, which I purpose, by God's grace, to obey. He willed me, as I have done, to write to my master (Sir John Harrington), who is in the country, and to shew him that, if within a certain time, which I have appointed, fourteen days, he do not go about to make restitution I will submit myself to my lord protector and the king's majesty's council, and confess the fault and ask pardon. This life is uncertain and frail, and when time is it must not be deferred ; and what should it profit me to win the whole world and lose my own soul ?" This determination to go to the Lord Protector frightened Sir John into giving a receipt for the repayment of the money under his own hand and seal in terms arranged by Latimer ; but he was so deeply offended that he never saw Bradford again.

It was immediately after this restitution, and upon Latimer's persuasion, that Bradford gave up his study of the law and prepared himself for ministry in the Reformed Church by entering Catharine Hall, Cambridge. His knowledge and deep piety were instantly recognized and within a year he was invited by Bishop Ridley, Bishop of Rochester and Master of Pembroke Hall, to become a Fellow of that College. According to a letter to his friend at Blackley, his own College had proffered a similar honour. "I am now a Fellow of Pembroke Hall," he wrote in 1549, "for the which neither I

thirty-three shillings and fourpence a year; besides my chamber, launder, barber, &c., and I am bound to nothing, but once or twice a year to keep a problem."

In the following year Bradford was ordained a deacon by Ridley, who, when he became Bishop of London, sent for him at once, and making him one of his own

JOHN BRADFORD

nor any other for me, did ever make any suit. Yea, there was a contention between the Master of Catharine Hall and the Bishop of Rochester, who is Master of Pembroke Hall, whether should have me. Thus you may see the Lord's carefulness for me. My Fellowship is worth seven pounds a year; for I have allowed me eighteenpence a week, and as good as

chaplains lodged him in his own house. Bishop Ridley wrote of him, " Mr. Bradforde, a man by whom, as I am assuredly informed, God hath and doth work wonders, in setting forth his words." Shortly afterwards, in order to give full scope to his wonderful powers of preaching, he was made Prebendary of St. Paul's Cathedral, where " he so constantly laboured to engraft the true principles of religion in the hearts and minds of the people, to reform the vicious, reclaim the perverted, and fix the wavering, that no preacher of his time was better attended, or more famed for his doctrine and example." By reason of the soundness of his doctrine and the eloquence of his preaching, Bradford was appointed one of the six chaplains in ordinary to the boy-king, Edward VI. Two of these chaplains were always in attendance on the King, whilst the other four preached throughout the country. The portion allotted to Bradford included Lancashire and Cheshire, and in his native county his piety and fervour, and his winning character, created as much enthusiasm for his preaching as they had in London.

"The fervour, which earned for Bradford's denunciation of sin in high places and in low, the praise of the terrible Reformer of Scotland,[1] seems to have been accompanied by a sweetness of temper that made even his enemies look upon him with favour," says Mr. L'Espinasse. "A blameless purity, not to say austerity of life, severity to himself greater than to others in combination with fine intellectual gifts and the utmost gentleness of disposition, point out Bradford as approaching the ideal of the Protestant saint." Fuller places him amongst his "Worthies," and says: "It is a demonstration to me that he was of a sweet nature, because Parsons (a Jesuit) who will hardly afford a good word to a Protestant, saith that he seemed to be of a more soft and mild nature than many of his fellows." It was also said of Bradford, "Foes as well as friends have borne testimony to his lovableness."

Mr. Aubrey Townsend in the biographical notice written for an edition of *The*

[1] John Knox had written and published his approval of some of Bradford's sermons.

Writings of John Bradford in 1853, tells a story which shows how the tradition arose that Blackley was the birthplace of this Lancashire martyr: "Local tradition," he says, "even yet points to the spot in Blackley where the country people say that Bradford, during that last visit to Manchester, knelt down and made solemn supplication to Almighty God. His request at the throne of grace was that the everlasting gospel might be preached in Blackley to the end of time by ministers divinely taught to feed the flock with wisdom and knowledge. The martyr's prayer, it is alleged, has been answered in the continuance, with scarcely an exception, of faithful men in that place."

Unlike so many men who receive the "call" after the first flush of youth is over, Bradford never became self-righteous, and ever had a remembrance of his own fraud before him. When he saw criminals being led to punishment he used to say, "But for the grace of God there goes John Bradford."

In July, 1553, King Edward VI. died. The Duke of Northumberland proclaimed his daughter-in-law, the hapless Lady Jane Grey, Queen, but on August 3rd Mary Tudor rode triumphantly into London as Queen of England, and one of the blackest periods in our history began. The services of the Reformed Church were swept away and Roman Catholicism was again established as the national religion. So ruthless and sudden was the change that within nine days of Mary's triumphant entry into her capital, the threatening attitude of the Londoners caused her to retire to Richmond. On the very next day a priest called Bourne, who had left the Reformed Church for the Roman Church, and had been made a chaplain to Queen Mary as a reward, preached before the Lord Mayor and the Corporation of London from the great open pulpit of

St. Paul's Cross. A large crowd had assembled, a crowd simmering with anger and resentment at the threatened change in religion, and filled with indignation that a man upon whom the majority looked as a renegade should be deputed to preach to the City Fathers. Bishop Bonner, who was hated by the Londoners, was present at this sermon. Bonner had been the Roman Catholic Bishop of London, and because he would not enforce the use of the prayer-book known as the King Edward VI. Prayer-Book, and would not preach that the King's authority was as great during his minority as if he were thirty or forty years old, had been condemned " to remain in perpetual prison at the King's pleasure, and to lose all his spiritual promotions and dignities for ever." Two days after the entry of Queen Mary Tudor he was liberated from prison and restored to the see of London, Bradford's friend Ridley, who had been made Bishop in his place, being regarded by Mary and her Council as only an interloper.

So it was as Roman Catholic Bishop of London that Bonner sat with the Lord Mayor and Corporation to listen to Bourne's sermon. As it has been said he was detested by the Londoners, and the fulsome praise lavished upon him by the preacher was the signal for an outbreak. The crowd yelled with fury. Bradford, it is believed, because he had some knowledge of what would happen, had placed himself in the pulpit behind the preacher. As the crowd of angry people seethed and yelled round the pulpit, the terrified Bourne implored Bradford to pacify them. Instantly he stepped forward, and as he did so, a dagger which had been thrown at the renegade Bourne, passed close by his head.

" Bradford! Bradford! God save thy life, Bradford!" was the universal cry as he stepped to the front of the pulpit. With winning words he exhorted the crowd to be patient, and to abstain from all violence; having thus completely pacified them he covered Bourne with his gown and took him into St. Paul's School near by.

" Ah, Bradford! Bradford!" cried some one in the crowd as he and Bourne descended the pulpit stairs, " thou savest him that will help to burn thee!"

Never was there a truer prophecy. Three days later Bradford was arrested and taken before the Privy Council. The charge against him was of " sedition " in rescuing Bourne from the fury of the mob, and for preaching heresy. He was sent to the Tower, where he remained until January 1554, when he underwent his first examination. To the charge of sedition he answered—

" My lords, I confess that I have been long imprisoned and unjustly, for that I did nothing seditiously, falsely, or arrogantly, in word or fact, by preaching or otherwise, but sought peace as an obedient and dutiful subject; both in attempting to save the present Bishop of Bath, then Master Bourne, the preacher at the Cross, and in preaching for quietness accordingly."

Gardiner, the Bishop of Winchester, here interrupted saying that Bradford spoke falsely, " The fact was seditious," he said, " as you, my lord of London, can bear witness."

" You say true," answered Bonner, " I saw him with my own eyes when he took upon him to rule and lead the people malapertly; thereby declaring that he was the author of sedition."

There can be little doubt in Bradford's case that the Council was anxious to fix a charge upon him, no matter how unjust. A man who, after only three years in the Church, and a considerable portion of that time spent in Lancashire, could control an infuriated London mob, was a force not to be ignored. Even Gardiner, during his examination, said to him, " I know thou hast a glorious tongue."

His defence, therefore, availed him nothing, and he was sent back to the Tower, where by that time all the heads of the Reformed Church were imprisoned. " The Providence of God," wrote Latimer, the aged Bishop of Worcester, " did bring this to pass that when these famous men, viz. Master Cranmer, Archbishop of Canterbury, Master Ridley, Bishop of London, and I, old Hugh Latimer, were imprisoned in the Tower for Christ's gospel preaching, and for because we would not go a-massing, every one in close prison together ; the same Tower being so full of other prisoners, that we four were thrust into one chamber, as men not to be accounted of, but, God be thanked, to our great joy and comfort ; there we did read together over the New Testament with great deliberation and painful study."

After a while Bradford was removed from the crowded Tower to the King's Bench prison, where " his benign and saintly disposition won over even his gaolers, and he preached and prayed without stint to those that flocked to hear him." He also helped the ordinary criminals of the prison out of his own purse, prisoners in those days being obliged to find their own food or else be nearly starved to death on the meagre fare given to them. So for fifteen months he went on preaching and praying and enduring all the miseries of a Tudor prison. In January, 1555, he was once more brought before Gardiner and Bonner, and indignantly refusing Bonner's suggestion that he should recant and become a Roman Catholic— " If you will with us return ; if you will do so as we have

done, you shall find as we have found," said Bonner—he was condemned to death as a heretic. In February the first of the martyrs under Mary's persecution, Rogers, suffered death by burning at Smithfield, but in order to make this legal an Act of Parliament had to be passed reviving the penal statutes against the Lollards in the reign of Henry IV. Bradford therefore expected his own end to follow shortly, and wrote to Cranmer, Ridley and Latimer rejoicing that Rogers, their "dear brother," had " broken the ice so valiantly." Death had no terrors for him, and he spoke of being their " gentleman-usher " going before, and to show the way.

Convinced that the end was near, the saintly Bradford wrote a " Farewell to Lancashire and Cheshire," in which occurs the famous passage—

" Turn once more unto the Lord, yet once more I heartily beseech thee, thou Manchester, thou Ashton-under-Lyne—thou Bolton, Bury, Wigan, Liverpool, Mottrine (Mottram), Stepport (Stockport), Winsley (Winstanley), Eccles, Prestwich, Middleton, Radcliff, and thou City of West Chester (Chester), where I have truly taught and preached the Word of God." In the same " Farewell " he says, " I hear it reported creditably, my dearly loved in the Lord, that my heavenly Father hath thought it good to provide that as I have preached his true gospel and doctrine amongst you by word, so I shall testify the same by deed, that is, I shall with you leave my life, which by His Providence I first received there (for in Manchester was I born), for a seal to the doctrine I have taught with you and amongst you ; so that if from henceforth you waver in the same you have none excuse at all."

This refers to the original intention of the Council to burn him in Lancashire as an example to the " heretics " of his native county. But whether it was from a fear that the veneration in which Bradford was regarded, especially round about Manchester, might cause his barbarous execution to have a different effect, or whether they hoped that he might eventually recant, and so bring a powerful preacher and a man with a large following into the Roman Catholic fold, has never been made clear. Whatever the reason, he was kept lingering on in prison until the summer of 1555. In May of that year Mary Tudor's confident hopes of a child were disappointed. Her fanatical husband, Philip of Spain, her confessor, and many of those about her urged that her childlessness was a direct sign of the anger of Heaven, that "heresy" must be exterminated before the Divine Power would be appeased. Mary was already bigoted; her bitter disappointment made her half insane, and under the influence of the fanatics around her she issued that terrible circular to the Bishops urging them to greater zeal against "heretics," and amongst other executions that of Bradford was specially ordered to take place.

The Queen's command was carried out on July 1, 1555. On the previous night Bradford was taken to Newgate prison, purposely at a late hour as his popularity was feared, and it was thought "the city would be a-bed." But word had got abroad, "and there was in Cheapside and other places between the Compter and Newgate a great multitude of people, that came to see him, which most gently bade him farewell, praying for him with most lamentable and pitiable tears; and he again as gently bade them farewell, praying most heartily for them and their welfare."

A great concourse of people waited at Smithfield all night, expecting the execution would take place at daybreak, but it was nine o'clock before he was brought "with a great company of weaponed men to conduct him hither, as the like was not seen at no man's burning; for in every corner of Smithfield there were some besides those who stood about the stake." This carefulness suggests that an attempt at rescue was feared. A tallow chandler's apprentice, named John Leaf, a boy of nineteen who would not admit the Real Presence in the Sacrament, was condemned to die with Bradford. Both knelt by the stake and began to pray, but one of the Sheriffs, apparently alarmed by the threatening attitude of the crowd, interrupted their devotions, saying: "Arise and make an end, for the press of the people is great!"

"At that word," says Foxe in his *Book of Martyrs*, "they both stood upon their feet, and Master Bradford took a faggot in his hand and kissed it, and so likewise the stake. And when he had so done, he desired of the sheriffs that his servant might have his raiment: 'For,' said he, 'I have nothing else to give him, and besides that he is a poor man.' And the sheriff said he should have it. And so forthwith Master Bradford did put off his raiment, and went to the stake; and holding up his arms and casting his countenance up to heaven, he said thus:—'O England, England, repent thee of thy sins! Beware of idolatry, beware of false antichrists! Take heed they do not deceive you!' And as he was speaking these words the sheriff bade tie his hands if he would not be quiet. 'O, Master Sheriff!' said Master Bradford, 'I am quiet; God forgive you this, Master Sheriff!' And one of the officers which made the fire, hearing Master Bradford so speaking to the Sheriff said, 'If you have no better learning than that, you are but a fool, and it were best to hold your peace.' To which words Master Bradford gave no answer, but asked all the world's forgiveness, and forgave all the world, and prayed the world to pray for him. Then embracing the reeds said thus:—'Straight is the way, and narrow is the gate that leadeth to eternal salvation, and few be they who find it.'"

The finest trait in John Bradford's saintlike character was his thought for others, and at the supreme moment when the cruel flames began to hiss and lick about him, his last words were for the poor boy suffering beside him, "Be of good comfort, brother," he cried, "for we shall have a merry supper with the Lord this night."

"He endured the flames," said Fuller, "as a fresh gale of wind on a summer's day."

Mary Tudor, counselled by evil and fanatical men who deliberately worked upon her bigotry, and upon a disposition soured by a life of misery, triumphed in the death of John Bradford. She had silencèd his tongue; but in Lancashire his martyrdom raised a spirit of endurance which filled the Collegiate Church at Manchester—turned into a prison—with "heretics," whose allegiance to the Reformed Church and all that John Bradford had taught, neither threats, promises nor the terrors of death itself, could shake.

The defcription of the burning of M. Iohn Bradford preacher, and Iohn Leafe a Prentife.

JOHN BYROM

JOHN BYROM was the inventor of a shorthand upon which nearly all the modern systems have been founded; he was also a poet, and in his later life a prominent figure in Manchester.

The Byroms of Kersall were small squires, who were called in the eighteenth century a "genteel family." Like many of their neighbours they had gone into trade by a process the reverse of that which takes place to-day. Now, the successful merchant or manufacturer, having made his fortune, seeks to become a landed proprietor, and found a county family; but towards the end of the seventeenth century many of the Lancashire landed proprietors sought to become merchants. The reason was that the cotton trade was growing so rapidly that any one with capital to invest had an excellent chance of making a comfortable fortune. Thus, long before the inventions of Hargreaves, Arkwright, and Crompton had given the trade such enormous impetus, "many country gentlemen began to send their sons as apprentices to Manchester." Byrom's father had been thus apprenticed, and, at the time of his second son's birth in 1691, was what was then called "a linen draper," but which would be now described as "a Manchester warehouseman." He had prospered in the

trade, for he had a place of business in London as well as in Manchester, and in addition held the family estates at Kersall. From his earliest childhood John Byrom gave evidence of cleverness and high intelligence, and it was therefore decided that he should take up a professional career, whilst his elder brother, Edward, should follow the father in the business. He was accordingly sent to school at Chester, and, later, to the Merchant Taylors' School in London, where he distinguished himself so highly that he was admitted a pensioner of Trinity College, Cambridge.

In those days (1709) wigs were worn by men, not the powdered ones which came in later, but wigs with long curls and in natural-coloured hair. Writing to his son at Cambridge old Mr. Byrom says, "As for your wig, let us know whether you will have it a natural one, or wherein you would have it differ from such as Mr. Banks wears, or Mr. Edwardson, or Mr. Worsley's tutor. I took it as a piece of extravagancy, the giving of a guinea for altering the last in London, and no doubt but you were cheated, and worse hair for your own put in. So I say, write to us when you have noted these gentlemen's wigs, wherein you would have yours differ, and we will venture it, and so you may be sure of your sister's good hair and no cheat, as you will certainly be if made in London." Sisters in the days of Queen Anne must have been of much meeker temperament than those of to-day; it is difficult to imagine the most devoted and generous sister nowadays, giving her hair to make alterations in her brother's wig! The elder Byrom was evidently a very careful man, and it is not surprising that he should consider the guinea spent in London for altering a wig as an "extravagancy," when the material could be supplied for nothing—from his daughter's head!

Byrom had a happy and successful university career, making many friends and being universally popular for his kindness of heart and merry wit. His sister, in a letter to a friend, gives a vivid picture of his lively disposition at Kersall during one of his vacations. "Brother John is most at Kersall; he goes every morning to the water-side, and bawls out one of Tully's orations in Latin so loud they can hear him a mile off; so that all the neighbourhood think he is mad, and you would think so too, if you saw him. Sometimes he threshes corn with John Rigby's men, and helps them to get potatoes, and works as hard as any of them. He is very good company, and we shall miss him when he is gone."

At that time shorthand, which is now associated with commercial and newspaper work, was one of the accomplishments of the scholar and the student, and for this reason: books were very dear and mostly of unwieldy size, and scholars and students were therefore obliged to copy from them all the facts they needed; it was also the fashion for every man with any pretension to learning to have a collection of manuscripts, copied by himself, for the purpose of reference. Shorthand lessened the trouble of the endless copying. And not only was shorthand a help to the scholar and the student, it was a safeguard to those who were politically inclined. Politics from the days of James II. to those of George II.—a period of five reigns—were based upon one fact, the succession to the throne. Throughout the reigns of William and Mary, Queen Anne, George I., and George II., there were countless plots and intrigues for the restoration of the Stuarts. In self-defence it behoved the authorities to keep a watchful eye upon those suspected of Stuart leanings. At any moment such suspected persons, especially if they were of high rank, ran the risk of their houses being searched, and any incriminating papers being seized; shorthand, therefore, was useful as a private cipher in which the most dangerous political sentiments could be expressed with safety. It was likewise a period in which diary-keeping was universal, and if the entries were made in shorthand, it would be impossible for any stranger into whose hands the diaries might fall to read them. An example of this was the diary of Samuel Pepys, which gives us a most vivid picture of life in the reign of Charles II. This valuable historical document lay in the library of Magdalen College, Oxford, to which it had been left by Pepys, for one hundred and twenty-five years before it was deciphered. Pepys had left a transcript in longhand of the shorthand account he had written of the escape of Charles II., and this served as the basis for deciphering of the famous diary. There were many systems of shorthand in vogue when Byrom was at Cambridge, but when he came to study them he found they were all very cumbrous and difficult. He therefore began to invent one of his own, which he elaborated and practised constantly throughout his university career. His academical studies, and his shorthand, however, did not occupy all his time; and before he left Cambridge he was a valued contributor to the *Spectator*, the famous journal run by Steele and Addison. At the age of twenty-three Byrom found himself famous. His pastoral poem of "Colin and Phœbe" was published in

pride and delight at Kersall on the publication of "Brother John's" verses in the great London journal can be imagined. They were said to have been inspired by the daughter of the master of his college, the great Dr. Bentley, whose biographer described them as being "celebrated as one of the most exquisite specimens in existence of playful poetry."

JOHN BYROM

the *Spectator* in October, 1714, a poem "which thrilled the hearts of the young ladies and gentlemen of England." Writing of Byrom between 1800 and 1810, his biographer said that "Colin and Phœbe" was the poem "which brought him into general notice, and which was, as it continues to be, universally admired." The poem may not be "universally admired" now, but it certainly had a wide popularity during a hundred years. The

My time, O ye Muses, was happily spent,
When Phœbe went with me wherever I went,
Ten thousand sweet pleasures I felt in my breast;
Sure never fond shepherd like Colin was blest!
But now she has gone, and has left me behind,
What a marvellous change on a sudden I find!
When things were as fine as could possibly be,

57

I thought 'twas the Spring, but alas! it was
 she.

When walking with Phœbe what sights
 have I seen,
How fair was the flower, how fresh was the
 green!
What a lively appearance the trees and the
 shade,
The cornfields and hedges and everything
 made!
But now she has left me, though all are still
 there,
They none of them now so delightful
 appear:
'Twas nought but the magic, I find, of her
 eyes,
Made so many beautiful prospects arise.

Sweet music went with us both all the
 wood through,
The lark, linnet, throstle and nightingale
 too;
Winds over us whispered, flocks by us did
 bleat,
And chirp went the grasshopper under our
 feet.
But now she is absent, though still they sing
 on,
The woods are but lonely, the melody's
 gone:
Her voice in the concert, as now I have
 found,
Gave everything else its agreeable sound.

Rose, what is become of thy delicate hue?
And where is the violet's beautiful blue?
Does aught of its sweetness the blossom
 beguile?
That meadow, those daisies, why do they
 now smile?
Ah! rivals, I see what it was that you drest
And made yourselves fine for—a place in
 her breast:
You put on your colours to pleasure her eye,
To be plucked by her hand, on her bosom
 to die.

Notwithstanding this brilliant university career Byrom seemed to have no
bent for any particular profession, although
he seems to have made perfunctory studies
in medicine at Montpelier in France. He
had hopes of a fellowship at his college,
but as he wrote would have preferred the
librarianship of the Chetham library, which
was then vacant. "I should be very willing," he said, "to have the library. . . .
It would be better worth while than staying on for a doubtful fellowship, where a
profit will be slow a-coming: besides, 'tis
in Manchester, which place I love
entirely." But neither fellowship nor
librarianship came to him, and he therefore determined to earn his living by
teaching his system of shorthand. A
graduate of Trinity College, Cambridge,
who set up as a teacher of shorthand in
these days, would find his only pupils
amongst those who wished to be clerks or
newspaper reporters, but, as it has been
shown, shorthand was used for different
purposes in Byrom's time, and by the
upper classes. Amongst his pupils were
the Duke of Devonshire, the Earl of
Chesterfield, Horace Walpole, Lord
Camden, Bishop Hoadley, Hartley the
metaphysician, and many other noblemen, politicians, and men of science. His
system was regarded as being so valuable
and important that he was made a member
of the Royal Society.

At the age of thirty Byrom made a
romantic marriage. He had long been
in love with his cousin, but her father
opposed the match because of his nephew's
lack of profession or prospects; finally,
however, won over by the constancy of the
two lovers, he gave a reluctant consent
and they were married in 1721. The
husband's shorthand lessons necessitated
that he should be in London during those
months when his aristocratic and fashionable pupils were resident there; but the
wife preferred to live in her native town,
consequently for many years Byrom
divided his time between the capital and
Manchester. They were a devoted couple,
and when he was away a constant stream
of letters came from him addressed to
"Mrs. Byrom, near the Old Church,

Manchester." Every detail of his busy London life was described, his lessons, the friends he visited, the meetings of the Royal Society, the poetry he wrote, and in one letter he added, " And this you see is how I go on, dull enough for me to be obliged to such an absence, but so it must be. I would give twopence-halfpenny for a moment's talk with thee and my little wench." The journey from Manchester coach in which he was travelling was held up by a highwayman near Epping Forest " in a red rug upon a high horse, who came out of the bushes, and presenting a pistol first at the coachman, and then at the corporation within, with a volley of oaths demanded money—and got it."

In addition to the invention of his system of shorthand, and his position as a poet, Byrom had another claim to con-

BEDROOM AT KERSALL CELL, FORMERLY JOHN BYROM'S LIBRARY

to London was no mean undertaking, for it occupied more days than it now takes hours to perform. Leaving Manchester at noon on the Monday on horseback, Byrom " lay " at Lichfield on the Tuesday, and jogging on by Oswestry, Daventry, Towcester, Stony Stratford, Barnet and Highgate, did not reach London until the Friday night. On one of his journeys to Cambridge, Byrom experienced a common enough adventure in those times. The sideration: he invented a phrase which will last as long as the English language is spoken—" The difference between Tweedle-dum and Tweedle-dee." There was great rivalry in London between the Italian composer Buononcini and the German Handel, their partisans took sides and the battle raged hotly, pamphlets, lampoons, verses, and personal attacks upon the two composers raining from the press. Byrom turned the absurd con-

H 2

troversy into ridicule by the following epigram—

"Some say, compared to Buononcini,
  That Mynheer Handel's but a ninny,
  Others aver that he to Handel
  Is scarcely fit to hold a candle:
  Strange all this difference should be
  'Twixt Tweedle-dum and Tweedle-dee!"

The methods of the two men were so similar that Byrom's phrase was an exact description of the controversy. Buononcini's name would have been forgotten but for this famous epigram, which for many years was attributed to Dean Swift.

Byrom had a happy knack of writing what are called "occasional verses," upon any conceivable subject; these gained many friends for him in high and cultivated society, and by this means he obtained many pupils, for, with true Lancashire energy and "push," he never lost an opportunity. He was also a good conversationalist and quick at repartee. It is said of him, "Men of worth with whom he differed he could respect, and he gave them the go-by when it was necessary with an amiable ingenuity. 'Mr. Wesley' —the Rev. John—he records once in his diary, 'preaches at Moorfields and Kennington on Sunday morning and night; he asked me if he should invite me to come and hear him; 'Shall I invite you to stay at home?' said I. 'No,' said he. 'Then,' says I, 'don't invite me to come.'"

By the death of his elder brother, Edward Byrom, without issue, John succeeded to the family estates at Kersall, and quitted London with joy for his beloved Manchester, and for the rest of his life lived in ease and comfort. Only once was the serenity of his later days disturbed. This was in 1745 when the Young Pretender took Manchester. In his young days Byrom had been an ardent supporter of the Stuart cause, but he was now a landowner, and remembering the heavy fines and punishments inflicted upon those who had openly sympathized with the Young Pretender's father, thirty years before, Byrom now acted with great discretion. His daughter wrote, "My papa and my uncle are gone to consult with Mr. Croxton, Mr. Fielden, and others how to keep out of any scrape and yet behave civilly." As a result of this conference Byrom did not wait upon the Prince, and after his daughter and sister had kissed the royal hand at Mr. Fletcher's house, where the Pretender was staying, the former says: "My papa was fetched a prisoner to do the same." However, when all the troubles were over, and Whig and Jacobite had become only political terms, Byrom showed his Jacobite leanings by so many squibs and poems that he was called "The Poet Laureate of the Jacobites," and it was at this time he wrote the famous lines—

"God bless the King! I mean our Faith's defender,
God bless—no harm in blessing—the Pretender!
But who Pretender is, or who is King,
God bless us all, that's quite another thing!"

Some of his later poems, amongst them "The Three Black Crows," were written to be spoken at the annual breaking-up of the Manchester Free Grammar School. Byrom lived to the ripe age of seventy-two, dying in 1763, and was buried in the Byrom Chapel of the Cathedral Church, one of the worthiest of Manchester's worthies.

A curious incident happened after his death, "The Constables of the Township of Manchester" were directed by "John Gee Booth Esqre one of His Majesty's Justices of the Peace to levy the sum of five pounds by distress and sale of the goods and chattels" which "John Byrom had at the time of his death, one moiety to go to the poor of the township, and the other to the informer." Byrom had been buried " in a shirt, shift, sheet or shroud, not made of sheep's wool." This was an offence against an old law—made when woollen goods were the staple manufacture of England—in order to protect the woollen trade from the encroachments of silk and linen. The penalty for being buried in a linen shirt or shroud was five pounds!

CARELESS CONTENT

By John Byrom

I AM content, I do not care,
   Wag as it will the world for me;
When fuss and fret was all my fare,
   It got no ground as I did see:
So when away my caring went,
I counted cost, and was content.

With more of thanks and less of thought,
   I strive to make my matters meet;
To seek what ancient sages sought,
   Physic and food in sour and sweet;
To take what passes in good part,
And keep the hiccups from my heart.

With good and gentle humour'd hearts,
   I choose to chat where'er I come;
Whate'er the subject be that starts;
   But if I get among the glum,
I hold my tongue to tell the troth,
And keep my breath to cool my broth.

For chance or change, of peace or pain,
   For Fortune's favour or her frown,
For lack or glut, for loss or gain,
   I never dodge, nor up, nor down;
But swing what way the ship shall swim,
Or tack about with equal trim.

I suit [1] not where I shall not speed,
   Nor trace the turn of ev'ry tide;
If simple sense will not succeed,
   I make no bustling but abide:
For shining wealth or scaring woe,
I force no friend, I fear no foe.
Of ups and downs, of ins and outs,
   Of "they are wrong," and "we are right,"
I shun the rancours and the routs,
   And, wishing well to every wight,
Whatever turn the matter takes,
I deem it all but ducks and drakes.

[1] I follow or sue.

With whom I feast I do not fawn,
   Nor, if the folks should flout me, faint;
If wonted welcome be withdrawn,
   I cook no kind of a complaint;
With none disposed to disagree,
But like them best, who best like me.

Not that I rate myself the rule
   How all my betters should behave;
But Fame shall find me no man's fool,
   Nor to a set of men a slave;
I love a friendship free and frank,
And hate to hang upon a bank.

Fond of a true and trusty tie,
   I never lose where'er I link;
Though if a business budges by,
   I talk thereon just as I think;
My word, my work, my heart, my hand,
Still on a side together stand.

If names or notions make a noise,
   Whatever hap the question hath,
The point impartially I poise,
   And read or write, but without wrath;
For should I burn or break my brains,
Pray who will pay me for my pains?

I love my neighbour as myself,
   Myself like him, too, by his leave;
Nor to his pleasure, pow'r, or pelf,
   Came I to crouch, as I conceive:
Dame Nature doubtless has design'd
A man—the monarch of his mind.

Now taste and try this temper, sirs,
   Mood it, and brood it, in your breast;
Or if you ween, for worldly stirs,
   That man does right to mar his rest;
Let me be deft and debonair,
I am content, I do not care.

HUMPHREY CHETHAM

OF all the men who filled the stage in Manchester during the momentous days of Charles I., one only conferred an abiding benefit upon his native place—Humphrey Chetham; and of him there are fewer records than of many men who did far less. But for Fuller, who included Humphrey Chetham in his *Worthies*, there would be little known of this benefactor to Manchester. He was the first to set the example of devoting a portion of the wealth he had gained in his native town, to the benefit of the people, an example which has been most nobly followed.

Humphrey Chetham was a descendant of the family of Chethams of Nuthurst, which was an offshoot of the Chethams of Chetham, whose founder, Geffrey de Chetham, had been "a man of considerable consequence, and several times Sheriff of Lancashire in the reign of King Henry III." As was very common, the family took their name from the little village of Chetham, which is now one of the suburbs of Manchester. The "said Sir Geffrey falling in troublous times incurred the king's displeasure, his family (in fact) was ruinated, but it seems his posterity was unwilling to fly from their old but destroyed Nest, and got themselves a handsome habitation at Crumpsall hard by," says the chronicler. Another account states that the Chetham family was "ruinated" at a much later period, owing to their having sided with Richard III. against Henry VII. As Sir William Stanley, Henry VII.'s stepfather, had paramount influence in Lancashire, this would seem to be the more likely story, since he would naturally visit any support of the "crookbacked" king with the utmost severity. However, whether the family was "ruinated" in the reign of Henry III. or of Richard III., at the close of the sixteenth century there was a Henry Chetham living at Crumpsall Hall, a prosperous merchant and a man of substance. To him Humphrey Chetham was born in 1580, and on the 10th July was baptized at the Collegiate Church in Manchester. Like all Manchester youths he received his education at Bishop Oldham's grammar school, and at the age of seventeen was apprenticed to a Manchester linen-draper named Tipping. When he had served his apprenticeship he entered into partnership with his brother George, who was a citizen and grocer of London, a partnership which lasted until George Chetham's death in 1626. The trade of the two brothers was that of merchants and manufacturers of woollen cloth or fustian.

Manchester had been famous since the reign of Henry VIII. for a thriving trade in weaving what were called "cottons," but which were in reality woollen and linen yarn, for cotton was then unknown, although it may have been imported into England towards the close of the sixteenth century; and that it was worked in Manchester during the lifetime of Humphrey Chetham is shown by Lewis Roberts's *Treasure of Traffic*, which was published in 1641 :—

"The town of Manchester in Lancashire must be also herein remembered, and "the glory of its *woollen* cloths which they call Manchester *cottons*." As showing that the weaving trade was the one in which Manchester was then principally engaged, Fuller says: "Other commodities made in Manchester are so small in themselves, and various in their kinds, they will fill the shop of an *Haberdasher of small wares*. Being, therefore, too many for me to reckon up or remember, it will be the safest way to wrap them all together in some Manchester *Tickin*, and

CRUMPSALL HALL

worthily for their encouragement commended, who buy the yarn of the Irish in great quantity and weave it, returning the same again into Ireland, still neither doth their industry rest here, for they buy *cotton wool* in London that comes first from Cyprus and Smyrna, and in time work the same, and perfect it into *fustians, vermillions, dimities* and other such stuffs." But the import of cotton was very small, and we have the authority of the historian Camden who, writing of Manchester as it was ten years after Humphrey Chetham's birth, speaks of to fasten them with the *Pinns* (to prevent their falling out and scattering), or tie them with the *Tape*, and also (because 'sure bind sure find') to bind them about with *Points* and *Laces*, all met in the same place."

As we think of the endless variety of the manufactures of present-day Lancashire, it is very curious to find Fuller in his introduction to his account of the *Worthies of Lancashire*, writing at considerable length upon its production of horn. Under the heading of "Oxen" he says: "The fairest in England are bred (or if you will, made) in this county, the tips of whose horns are sometimes distanced five foot asunder. Horns are a commodity not to be slighted, since I cannot call to mind any other substance so hard that it will not break, so solid that it will hold made of Horns to garnish houses? I mean artificial flowers of all colours. And besides what is spent in England, many thousand-weight are shaven down into leaves for Lanthorns, and sent over daily into France. In a word, the very

HUMPHREY CHETHAM

liquor within it, and yet so clear that light will pass through it. No mechanick trade but hath some utensil made thereof, and even now I recruit my pen with ink from a vessel of the same. Yea, it is useful *cap-à-pie*, from combs to shoe-horns. What shall I speak of the many Gardens shavings of Horns are profitable, sold by the sack, and sent many miles from London for the manuring of ground. . . . The best Horns in all England, and freest to work without flaws, are what are brought out of this County to London, the Shop General of English Industry."

A considerable portion of the fustian manufactured by Humphrey Chetham was sent up to be sold by his brother in London, with marked profit to them both. In addition, Humphrey was in the habit of advancing a portion of the money made in his business at interest to needy gentlemen and traders, and in many ways seems to have performed the work of money-changer and banker. As well as manufacturing fustian he bought a considerable quantity in the neighbouring markets, of which Bolton was the chief. In all his dealings Humphrey Chetham was remarkable for his integrity. He was a distinctly " canny " young man, and, as was written of him, kept " one eye firmly fixed on the main chance, and the other on the kingdom of Heaven." He had a strong leaning to the growing Puritanism of the time, and was of the "strictest walk and conversation."

Dr. Aikin gives us a striking instance of Chetham's honourable dealings : " Fustians," he says, " were manufactured about Bolton, Leigh and the places adjacent; but Bolton was the principal market for them, where they were bought in the grey by the Manchester chapmen who finished and sold them in the country. Fustians were made as early as the middle of the last century, when Mr. Chetham, who founded the Bluecoat Hospital, was the principal buyer at Bolton. When he had made his markets, the remainder was purchased by Mr. Cooke, a much less honourable dealer, who took the advantage of calling the pieces what length he pleased, and giving his own price." Speaking of fustian, there is a passage in Fuller which is more eloquent than many lectures upon the change that has come about in public opinion as to the relationship of the classes. " The making of fustian in Lancashire," he says, " is to the good Injoyment of the Poor and great *improvement* of the Rich therein, serving *mean* people for their *outsides*, and their *betters* for the Lineings of their garments."

By the time Chetham had reached the age of forty, his prosperity in business and the judicious investment of his money in loans, enabled him to share with his brother George in buying Clayton Hall, the ancient seat of the Byron family near Manchester. In 1628 he purchased Turton Tower, near Bolton, from the knightly family of Orrell. Although Chetham's one desire in life was to live quietly and " neither to achieve honour nor have honour thrust upon him," his increasing wealth began to attract the attention of unscrupulous courtiers, ever ready to find money to meet the growing embarrassments of King Charles I. The order of baronetage had been created by James I., and an ever-profitable source of income it had proved to the Court. Charles I. had continued the system by which men paid for honours, and to the baronetage he added knighthoods. In the seventeenth century prosperous men of the middle classes avoided knighthoods and baronetcies as eagerly as they seek them now; the reason was obvious. Not only did it mean that the honour was accorded solely as a means of mulcting them of a large sum of money, but the social conditions of the time being entirely different from our own, the possession of a knighthood or a baronetcy, whilst it did not give them the means of satisfying any social aspirations they might have, put them above the world in which they had been brought up. In those days the aristocracy and the gentry were a class apart ; then came the merchants and the manufacturers, who were equally a class by themselves. There was no merging of the classes as there is now.

Baffled in their attempts to gain money

by the creation of knighthoods and baronetcies, the official advisers of King Charles hit upon a happy expedient. When either honour was offered and refused, a heavy fine was inflicted. Thus Chetham was summoned to London to be knighted, and disobeying the summons was called upon to pay a fine for non-attendance at His Majesty's "crownea-tion," to "take upon him the honour of knighthood." Chetham was undoubtedly a very modest and retiring man, and when shortly afterwards he heard that he was likely to be appointed High Sheriff of Lancashire, he was in a great state of alarm, and tried to avoid the honour as one "whereby I shall be made more popular and thereby more subject to the perils of the times." The sense in which Chetham uses the word "popular" is that of prominent or conspicuous. His modesty and his reluctance, however, were unavail-

ing. In November 1634, he was appointed to the office "discharging the place," says Fuller, "with great honour, insomuch that very good gentlemen of birth and estate did wear his cloth at the Assizes to testify their unfeigned affection to him."

This wearing of the cloth was a common custom in Lancashire upon occasions of circumstance, and consisted of wearing the livery of a friend or neighbour when he was engaged in some ceremony or office. Thus, for instance, when Henry VII. paid his historic visit to Lord Derby at Knowsley, all the Lancashire and Cheshire gentlemen, who accompanied the Earl when he rode forth to meet the King, wore the Stanley livery. Again, when James I. paid his visit to Hoghton Tower, the squires and gentlemen from the neighbourhood all wore the Hoghton livery.

Chetham's earliest official duty was to

CLAYTON HALL

levy the ship-money, that unjust tax which was one of the direct causes of the bloody quarrel between Charles and the Parliament. In raising the money Chetham found that he was considerably out of pocket; he seems to have endeavoured to make good his loss in a manner which nearly brought him before the Star Chamber. He had considerable trouble with the authorities over the matter, and at the same time he was charged with having taken another man's coat-of-arms. On being appointed Sheriff he had thought it essential that he should display a coat-of-arms, and apparently had laid hold of one to which he was in no way entitled. There was a long correspondence between Chetham and the Heralds' College, which ended in a coat-of-arms being granted to him upon the payment of " ten pieces " to Norroy King-at-Arms. Chetham accepted this arrangement, but that he had a sense of humour is shown by the letter which accompanied the payment : " They—the coat-of-arms to be paid for— are not depicted in soe good mettall as those armes we gave for them ; but when the herald meets with a novice he will double the gayn."

Rarely has there been a case of a man of so retiring a disposition upon whom offices and appointments were continually thrust by the authorities. When the Parliament assumed the government of the country Chetham was appointed High Collector of Subsidies within the county of Lancaster ; and again, later, " General Treasurer for the County," although he pleaded to be excused " on account of his many infirmities." These offices soured the last years of his life, for they involved him in ceaseless trouble and vexation, there being times when it was impossible to satisfy the Puritan commanders whom he had to supply with money.

When King Charles was executed Hum-phrey Chetham was nearly seventy ; he was unmarried, he was very rich, and his relations were well provided for. He therefore decided to found a school—or hospital as they were then called—for the education of poor boys of his native county ; and for this purpose he entered into negotiations to buy the " College " at Manchester, which had originally been built as a residence for the ecclesiastics of the Collegiate Church. At the time Chetham wished to buy it, the College was in the hands of the sequestrators, having been a portion of the estates of James, Earl of Derby, which had been confiscated after his execution. The negotiations, however, came to nothing, and it was not until after Humphrey Chetham's death that the College was bought with the money he had provided for the purpose.

Although he was unable to acquire the " College " at Manchester, Humphrey Chetham did not abandon his idea of educating poor boys. In the same year in which he opened negotiations for the College he began to choose fitting objects for his charity, and between then and 1651 had " taken up and maintained fourteen poor boys of the town of Manchester, six of the town of Salford, and two of the town of Droylsden, being in all twenty-two." There being no building in which they could be housed and educated, he boarded these boys with deserving people, to whom the money for their support would be a help—thus achieving a double charity. Humphrey Chetham kept a note-book in which he entered the various payments made for the boys. The prices paid for linen, work, and board afford an interesting contrast with those of to-day. Thus, in 1649, " 65 yards of linen cloth " cost £2 14s., " 18 dozens of thread buttons," 1s. 6d. George Walker was paid one guinea " for sixty days worke of himself, and his men

HUMPHREY CHETHAM'S MONUMENT IN MANCHESTER CATHEDRAL

at 4d. per diem and XIId. over all for making the Hospital Boyes cloathes." A guinea also provided " yr. dyate [the diet] at 6d. per diem every man." A board of the " boyes " in their various homes cost 6s. 8d. a month each. Not only did the good Humphrey feed and clothe the " boyes," but he also had them educated at his expense, as is shown by the entries, such as " a Psalter, 10d." "a Latin book, 2d.," "construing book, 1d.," and an " accidence " and " a testament, 1s. 5d."

For four years Chetham carried on this good work of educating and bringing up the twenty-two poor boys, and when he died at Clayton Hall on October 12, 1653, aged seventy-three, it was found that he had left complete provision for the establishment and maintenance of a " hospital." He had settled Turton Tower and Clayton Hall upon two of his nephews during his lifetime, and after leaving generous legacies to relatives, friends, and servants in his will, he bequeathed seven thousand pounds for the purchase of a fee-simple estate, the income of which was to be devoted to " the relief, maintenance, education, bringing up, and binding apprentice, or other preferment of poor boys and male children;" eighteen of whom from Droylsden, Crumpsall, Bolton and Turton were to be added to the twenty-two already being educated. Humphrey Chetham's " will and mind " was that these boys should be " children of honest, industrious and painful parents [that is poor parents] and not of wandering idle beggars or rogues, nor that any of the said boys should be bastards, nor such as are lame, infirm, or diseased at the time of their election." He ordained that they should be " well and sufficiently maintained, and kept with meat, drink, lodging, and apparel, and also educated and brought up to learning or labour in the towns of Manchester and Salford." In addition to the seven thou-sand pounds he left to purchase an estate for the maintenance of his " hospital," Humphrey Chetham bequeathed a further five hundred pounds to buy a house for the boys, " the College it may be."

Two hundred pounds were also left for the buying of " godly English books, such as Calvin, Preston's and Perkins's works, comments, or annotations on the Bible," or such books as his executors should " think most proper for the edification of the common people." These books were to be " chained up on desks, or to be fixed to the pillars, or in other convenient places in the parish churches of Manchester and Bolton-in-the-Moors, and in the chapels of Turton, Walmsley and Gorton." The books were duly bought, and at Turton they were at one time much read between the Sunday services, particularly during the summer months, and the usual place for reading them was the window-sill of the chapel. Books and bookcases have vanished from Bolton and Manchester, but more than two centuries after Humphrey Chetham's death it was said " the Gorton bookcase is in good preservation, and still contains fifty-six volumes chained to an iron rail."

In addition to his munificence in founding the Chetham Hospital, the good Humphrey left a further bequest of one thousand pounds " towards a Library within the town of Manchester, for the use of scholars and others well-affected . . . the same books there to remain as a public library for ever," his " mind and will " being " that care be taken that none of the said books be taken out of the said Library at any time. . . . The same books be fixed or chained, as well as may be within the said Library for the better preservation thereof." An extra hundred pounds was left to provide a place for the books, the residue of Chetham's personalty being left for their increase. Thus, not only did this son of Manchester create a school which for over two hundred and fifty years has been the means of educating thousands of poor boys and placing them in good positions in life, but he founded the first Free Library in England.

His executors were able to secure the College, and his school and library were placed there, happily remaining to this day, a living witness of his benevolence, and a quaint example of the architecture of an earlier Manchester.

TURTON TOWER

SAMUEL CROMPTON
& his Spinning Mule

IN all the history of invention there is no sadder story than that of Samuel Crompton, whose spinning mule more than any other machine contributed to the expansion and the prosperity of the cotton manufacture. Invention has been called the poetry of labour, and certainly Crompton, with his shrinking and sensitive nature, his lack of practicality, evinces all the characteristics which are generally associated with poets. His temperament utterly unfitted him for the struggle in the industrial world to which his inventive genius committed him.

His father was a small farmer at Firwood, near Bolton, and, as was then the general rule, he and his family combined spinning, weaving and carding with farming, selling the produce of their looms in Bolton, side by side with the produce of their land. When Crompton was born in 1753, Bolton was a very small place, known under the name of "Bolton-in-the-Moors," because of the marshy waste by which it was surrounded. It is owing to Crompton that this marsh is now covered with mills and houses. Writing of Bolton some forty years after Crompton's birth, Dr. Aikin says: "In the memory of some persons now living not more than one cow used to be killed weekly in Bolton; or if two, the unsold beef used to be sent to Bury market."

Under Crompton's father there seems to have been a decline in the family fortunes, for Firwood farm had once belonged to them, but being mortgaged by his grandfather was sold by his father, who remained in it as a tenant only. But shortly after Samuel's birth a further change for the worse in their circumstances caused the removal of the family to a small cottage, and later to Hall-i'-th'-Wood. The purchaser of Firwood was also the owner of this old mansion, which was untenanted. It is more than probable that wishing to assist Crompton's parents, who were hard-working, honest, and religious people, he offered them rooms in the old house at a small rental in order that they might look after it. The beautiful old house is thus described—

"An interesting specimen of the old rural mansion before Lancashire had become manufacturing—it is Elizabethan in style, small compared with modern mansions, but commodious and snug; and shows the advancing wealth of the owners by the successive additions which have from time to time been made in its accommodation: first, the roomy kitchen or hall, with sleeping apartments above, lit by latticed windows; then the addition of a dining-hall and drawing-room, with their large oriel windows of stained glass. The situation is very fine, on a plateau once covered with timber, from which it derived its name. The little river Eagley, a tributary of the Irwell, runs deep in the valley beneath, the high land descending precipitously in some places almost to the banks of the stream."

Shortly after they settled at Hall-i'-th'-Wood, when Crompton was a child of five, his father died, and his mother was left to bring him up with his two sisters as best she might. She was a woman of considerable character, and instantly set to work to carry on her husband's farming and weaving. Her butter was famous, and to this she added the sale of honey, the old garden of the Hall giving her this opportunity. Mrs. Crompton was much appreciated by her neighbours, who—a most unusual thing in those days—made her overseer of the poor.

Crompton was naturally very shy and sensitive, and the rigorous up-bringing which was then given to children, and in which the rod played a prominent part, did not tend to lessen these difficulties. He was sent to a good day-school, but oddly enough seems to have made no friends. He spent a very lonely childhood, his only companion besides his mother and sisters being an old uncle, called Alexander, who was so crippled that he could not leave his room where he left his bed to work at his loom, and left his loom to go to his bed. Uncle Alexander, like the rest of the Crompton family, was very religious, and there is a touching picture of the poor old man on Sunday morning and evening. When Mrs. Crompton and her children had gone to All Saints' Church at Bolton, the old man stayed in his lonely room waiting to hear the church bells. Before they ceased ringing he took off his ordinary working-day coat, and put on one which was specially kept for Sundays. Then he read to himself the whole of the Morning Service and a sermon. When the dismissal bell of the church began ringing he took off his Sunday coat, putting it on again in the evening when he read the Evening Service and another sermon.

Crompton began to help his mother very early in her hardworking life, and "probably his little legs became accustomed to the loom almost as soon as they were long enough to reach the treddles." In addition to his school work and weaving, his mother made him do a certain amount of spinning every day. When Hargreaves, in 1767, had perfected the spinning jenny, so that even a child could work eight spindles at once, Crompton was a boy of fourteen. Two years later the jenny was in general use, and at the age of sixteen it was said of Crompton that he "span on one of these machines with eight spindles the yarn which he afterwards wove into quilting, and thus was he occupied for the five following years." But the spinning jenny which Crompton used during those five years was apparently a poor one, or there was something wrong in its construction, for much of his time was passed "mending the ever breaking ends of his miserable yarn," a cause of constant delay, and which brought down upon him his mother's reproaches for not having accomplished the daily task.

There is little wonder that Crompton, with his already somewhat morbid temperament, grew up a self-contained yet irritable young man, for not only his childhood but the whole of his youth was spent in ceaseless drudgery, with no companionship save that of his family, and, it must also be added, in the constant fear of his mother's reproaches. His only consolation was his love of music. His father had been engaged upon the building of an organ in what is now All Saints' Church, Little Bolton, at the time he died, and it was from him that Crompton inherited this passion of his life, which found its first expression in making a fiddle. This was the first kitchen fire or thrifty lamp; and in many a summer twilight he wandered contemplatively among the green lanes, or by the margin of the pleasant brook that swept round her romantic old residence."

The making of this fiddle doubtless set Crompton's thoughts running in another channel. Whatever might be the superiority of Hargreaves' spinning jenny over the old one-thread spinning wheel,

Harwood

T Dixon

HALL-I'-TH'-WOOD

evidence of the mechanical genius he possessed, and he not only made the instrument but he taught himself to play upon it. "He soon scraped a very intimate acquaintance with his fiddle, which became to him truly a bosom friend, proving in after-life the consolation of many a solitary hour, and a source of consolation after many a bitter disappointment. With this mechanical friend he, on winter nights, practised the homely tunes of the time by the dim light of his mother's it had many imperfections, one of which was the brittleness and incessant breaking of the thread. In order to protect the Lancashire spinning trade, an Act had been passed in 1721, which made the importation or the use of Indian calicos, plain or printed, a penal matter. But this Act did not prohibit the importation of Indian muslins, and try as they would the English manufacturers could not produce anything that could touch them. Considerable quantities of English calicoes, in which the warp was furnished by Arkwright's rollers, and the weft by Hargreaves' jenny, were being made, and an attempt was made both in Lancashire and in Glasgow to manufacture delicate and beautiful muslins with weft spun by the jenny. But it failed entirely owing to the coarseness of the yarn. Muslin certainly had been woven in England, and in Bolton itself, but this could only be done from hand-spun material or from fine yarn, which from time to time was imported from the East Indies. But the hand-spun yarn and the fine Indian yarn were equally dear to produce or import; the price, therefore, at which this home-made muslin had to be sold gave it no chance in the market against the Indian muslins.

As Crompton worked at his loom for ever mending his broken threads, an idea gradually shaped itself in his brain, and that was to enable the English spinner to produce a yarn from which the most delicate muslin could be woven, a muslin which should not only compete with, but supersede, the products of the Indian looms, and from this idea came the mule.

For five years—that is from the time he was twenty-two until he was twenty-seven—Crompton brooded and worked over this wonder-working machine. He never seems to have had any idea of using his invention as a means of fortune, or of even patenting it; his only thought seems to have been that by its means he would be able to turn out for his own loom a finer and more valuable yarn than the one produced by the jenny; and all along he was determined that if the machine turned out a success he would keep it a close secret, which would account for Crompton's shrinking, as he did at this time, from the society of the few acquaintances that he had. His tools were very few, being in fact those used by his father in building the unfinished organ. But the most important and the most useful was a clasp-knife of his own. In order to buy others which were absolutely essential, he had no means save what he could spare from his very slender earnings, and it was partly to gain the wherewithal to buy tools, and partly to satisfy his love of music that he took a place in the orchestra of the Bolton theatre for the magnificent sum of eighteenpence a night.

But even when Crompton had secured his tools he had to set to work to teach himself how to use them, for he ran the risk of betraying his secret if he asked help or instruction. In order to keep his secret, and because his work for his bread gave him no time in the day, Crompton worked at his machine during the night. "Indeed, this it was which first called the attention of his family and neighbours to his proceedings. Strange and unaccountable sounds were heard in the old Hall at most untimely hours; lights were seen in unusual places; and a rumour became current that the place was haunted. Samuel, however, was soon discovered to be himself the embodied *spirit (of invention)*, which had caused such fears and troubles to his family. Even when relieved from the alarm of a ghost, they yet found that they had among them a *conjurer!*—for such was the term applied in contempt to inventors in those days, and indeed for a long time afterwards."

But just as his experiments were approaching success something more serious than the gibes and jeers of his ignorant neighbours threatened Crompton's work of five years. It was in the year 1774, that he had begun to work upon his machine, and until 1779, night after night with the most elementary of tools, inexperienced and alone, he had worked steadily on, devoting all his thoughts to this one great object which he himself described as "a continual endeavour to realize a more perfect principle of spinning. Though often baffled," he said, "I as often renewed the attempt, and at last succeeded to my utmost desire, at the expense of every shilling I had in the world."

The perfecting of his invention coincided with the terrible outbreak of the Lancashire working classes against machinery. In this same year, 1779, and in the very moment of success Crompton was threatened with the sweeping away of his five years' work and ceaseless sacrifices. The spinning jenny was the main object of the machine-breakers, and nowhere did they carry out their work of destruction more thoroughly than in the neighbourhood of Bolton. It had become generally known that Crompton was inventing some piece of machinery, and the mob being seen and heard quite close to Hall-i'-th'-Wood busily destroying all the jennys they could find, Crompton very wisely took precautions. "Crompton was well aware that his invention would be still more obnoxious to the rioters than Hargreaves' jenny, and appears to have taken careful measures for its protection or concealment, should they have paid a domiciliary visit to the Hall-i'-th'-Wood. The ceiling of the room in which he worked is cut through, as well as a corresponding part of the clay floor of the room above, the aperture being covered by replacing the part cut away. This opening was recently detected by two visitors who were investigating the mysteries of the old mansion; but they could not imagine any use for a secret trap door until, on pointing it out to Mr. Bromerley, the present tenant, he recalled to his memory a conversation he had had with Samuel Crompton during one of his latest visits to the Hall many years ago.

Mr. Crompton informed Mr. Bromerley that once, when he was at work on the mule, he heard the rioters shouting at the destruction of a building at Folds (an adjoining hamlet) where there was a carding engine. Fearing that they would come to the Hall-i'-th'-Wood and destroy his mule, he took it to pieces and put it into a skip which he hoisted through the cealing into the attic by the trap-door, which had, doubtless, been prepared in anticipation of such a visit, and now offers a curious evidence of the insecurity of manufacturing inventions in their early infancy. The various parts were concealed in the loft or garret near the cockloft, and there they remained concealed for many weeks ere he dared to put them together again, but in the course of the same year the Hall-i'-th'-Wood wheel was completed and the yarn spun upon it used for the manufacture of muslins of an extremely fine and delicate texture."

Crompton's invention was originally called the Hall-i'-th'-Wood wheel, because of the fine quality of the yarn spun upon it, but ultimately it became known as the "mule," because of its combination of the principle of Arkwright's rollers with the principle of Hargreaves' spinning jenny. The value of this invention is thus summed up by one of Crompton's biographers: "In this machine was accomplished for the first time the action of the spinner's left arm and finger and thumb, which consisted in holding and elongating the sliver as the spindle was twisting it into the yarn."

When Crompton had satisfied himself that he had succeeded in perfecting his invention he got married, his wife being a daughter of a West Indian merchant, a Mr. Pimlott, who had lived at New Heys Hall, near Warrington; but having had money losses his daughter was forced to work for her living. She, therefore, left Warrington for Turton, near Bolton, because "ample and profitable employment could be obtained by spinning on Hargreaves' jenny," which had been taken up much more warmly in that place than elsewhere. It is said that it was her expertness in spinning that first attracted Crompton's attention to her. The young Mrs. Crompton was described as "a very handsome, dark-haired woman, of middle size and erect carriage, while Crompton, then aged twenty-seven, was said to be a singularly handsome and prepossessing young man; all his limbs, particularly his hands, were elegantly formed and possessed great muscular power." The young people started housekeeping in a cottage close to Hall-i'-th'-Wood, where Crompton continued his spinning. Husband and wife worked at the mule together in the greatest secrecy. Compared with any of its later forms this outcome of Crompton's inventive genius was both rude and imperfect, but it turned out a yarn of a fineness and strength hitherto unknown.

The first consignment offered for sale in the market caused a sensation amongst the Bolton manufacturers. There arose an immediate and pressing demand, to meet which Crompton gave up weaving, and with his wife devoted himself to spinning. As he went on he was able to produce finer and finer yarn, with the result that he could obtain his own price for the very small quantities which he was able to produce. Crompton himself said that on the invention of his machine, " he obtained fourteen shillings per pound for the spinning and preparation of No. 40 (this yarn weighing forty hanks to the pound), but a short time after he got twenty-five shillings a pound for the spinning and preparation of No. 60, and he then span a small quantity of No. 80

to show that it was not impossible, as was supposed, to spin yarn, of that fineness, with the greatest ease, and for the spinning and preparation of this he got forty-two shillings a pound."

For the first time in his life Crompton was happy, for not only was his wife a perfect helpmate to him, but, thanks to his own genius and dogged perseverance, their future seemed assured. But his happiness did not last long. Keep the secret of his mule as carefully as he might, it was impossible to conceal the fact that the wonderful new yarn which was causing so much excitement in Bolton market came from the Hall-i'-th'-Wood, and when this discovery was made it was only a step to finding out that it was being produced by a machine of Crompton's own invention. Public curiosity was aroused, and with it came the end of Crompton's peace and quiet. He was not only beset by purchasers of the yarn, but his life was made a misery by the spying of his neighbours, who were all eager to see the wonder-working machine. People even went so far as to climb ladders and to look at him through the window, so that he was compelled to work behind a screen. To such lengths did this curiosity go that "one inquisitive adventurer is said to have ensconced himself for some days in the cockloft, where he watched Samuel at work through a gimlet hole pierced through the ceiling." There is a story that Arkwright, then at the height of his success, came over from Cromford to inquire into this new machine. The two inventors did not meet, for Crompton was out collecting poor rates for his mother. There was something a little underhand in this visit of Arkwright's, for whilst he pretended that it was a friendly visit because of some slender relationship existing between his first wife and Crompton's wife, all the time he had come to spy out what was happening. Seeing the fate that afterwards befell Crompton's mule it is unfortunate that the two men did not meet, for it is more than possible that the pushing and practical Arkwright, on realising the value of the mule, would have entered into some sort of partnership with Crompton.

Unhappily Crompton was entirely deficient in "push," a strange lack in a Lancashire man and a Lancashire worker; a man even of ordinary energy would have tried to secure a patent for his machine. He himself says that he had not the means to procure a patent, but the possibilities and the value of the mule having been proved beyond all manner of doubt, there must have been many people in Bolton who would only have been too pleased to subscribe to the necessary expenses and so enjoy a portion of the profits. But such an idea does not seem to have occurred either to Crompton or his wife. The unceasing annoyance of being spied upon began to prey upon his mind, and writing years afterwards he said: "During this time I married and commenced spinner altogether. But a few months reduced me to the cruel necessity either of destroying my machine altogether, or giving it up to the public. To destroy

SAMUEL CROMPTON

it I could not think of; to give up that for which I had laboured so long was cruel. I had no patent, nor the means of purchasing one. In preference to destroying I gave it to the public."

We now come to that incident in Crompton's life which is without parallel in the history of invention. Crompton, tormented by his spies, too shy or too proud to approach people for the money, consulted a Mr. Pilkington, who was a manufacturer of some standing in Bolton, showing him the machine and describing the principle of its operation. His advice seems incredible from a business man; he advised Crompton to give the mule to the public, and equally incredible to relate, Crompton accepted his advice. He not only gave the principle of the invention, but the actual machine on which he was working. The only return he received for these gifts was a paper which, as a point of fact, had no legal value, in which some eighty firms and individual manufacturers agreed to pay certain sums of money, the whole total of which amounted to £67 6s. 6d. Of this sum Crompton never received more than fifty or sixty pounds. He himself says: "I received as much by way of subscription as built me a new machine with only four spindles more than the one I had given up; the old one having forty-eight, the new one fifty-two, spindles."

The copy of the agreement is in existence with the list of subscribers in Crompton's own handwriting: "There are fifty-five subscribers of one guinea each, twenty-seven of half-a-guinea, one of seven-and-sixpence, and one of five-and-sixpence, making altogether £67 6s. 6d.; but it is known that several did not pay at all, and that he was at considerable expense of time and money in personally collecting the subscriptions of others, it may be assumed that the amount did not exceed sixty pounds. The list is curiously interesting, as containing among the half-guinea subscribers the names of many Bolton firms (in 1860) of great wealth and eminence as mule subscribers, whose colossal fortunes may be said to have been based upon this singularly small investment."

But no sooner was the mule given to the public than a bitter deception awaited poor Crompton. He says: "From many subscribers, who would not pay the sums they had set opposite their names when I applied to them for it, I got nothing but abusive language, given me to drive me from them, *which was easily done*, for I never till then could think it possible that any man (in such situation of life and circumstance) could pretend one thing and act the direct opposite. I then found it was possible, having had proof positive."

This treatment was the turning-point in Crompton's career. Himself the most upright of men, the meanness and treachery with which he was treated influenced his point of view for the rest of his life. His temper became soured, and unfortunately for himself he was henceforth too prone to take offence where none was intended. And this was exemplified by his attitude to the first Sir Robert Peel. Sir Robert was one of the signatories of the agreement by which the mule was given to the public, the terms of the agreement being that all subscribers should have the right to inspect and copy its mechanism. Accordingly Sir Robert Peel came from Bury to Hall-i'-th'-Wood, bringing with him some mechanics to inspect the mule and take the details of its construction and working. When he was leaving Sir Robert Peel gave Crompton a small sum of money —sixpence for each of the mechanics—as some payment for the time he had lost during the inspection of the mule. The first Sir Robert Peel was a good judge of character, but on this occasion he had entirely mistaken his man; Crompton declined to take the money and looked upon it as an insult which, to his own hurt, he never forgot or forgave.

Even after the mule was given to the public, curious visitors still continued to stream to Hall-i'-th'-Wood, and with the hope therefore of ridding himself of these tiresome attentions Crompton removed to a farmhouse at Oldhams, about two miles out of Bolton. But here, rumours that he had invented all sorts of improvements to the machine, brought both the interested and the merely curious in large numbers, and in order to escape from these pestering attentions, Crompton contrived a secret fastening to the door in the upper storey where he worked at the mule. Sir Robert Peel paid two visits to Oldhams—of the first, George Crompton, Crompton's eldest son, had a vivid recollection: "On his first visit Crompton was absent, but Mr. Peel chatted with his wife and gave young George half-a-guinea. Mrs. Crompton going into her dairy to bring her guest a bowl of milk, Mr. Peel took the opportunity to ask the boy where his father worked. George was pointing out the nail head which on being pressed, lifted the concealed latch of the door leading to the upper storey, when his mother returned with the milk and by a look warned him that he had committed an error. On his second visit Sir Robert offered to give Crompton a highly paid position in his firm which was to lead to a partnership. Both these offers Crompton declined, partly it was said from a morbid desire for independence, but more especially because of the insult he believed Sir Robert had offered him when he came to inspect his mule at Hall-i'-th'-Wood."

At Oldhams Crompton continued to live much as he had done at Hall-i'-th'-Wood, by spinning and a little agriculture. His children, almost as soon as they could walk, were pressed into the service of spinning. His eldest son gives us a vivid impression of the little home ; he says: "When I was quite a child my father removed from Hall-i'-th'-Wood to Oldhams. . . . I recollect that soon after I was able to walk I was employed in the cotton manufacture. My mother used to batt the cotton wool on a wire riddle. It was then put into a deep brown mug with a strong ley of soap-suds. My mother then tucked up my petticoats about my waist, and put me in the mug to tread upon the cotton at the bottom. When a second riddleful was batted I was lifted out, and it was placed in the mug, and I again trod it down. This process was continued until the mug became so full that I could no longer safely stand in it, when a chair

HANDLOOM WEAVING

was placed beside it, and I held on by the back. When the mug was quite full, the soap-suds were poured off, and each separate *dollop* of wool well squeezed to free it from moisture. They were then placed on the bread rack under the beams of the kitchen loft to dry. My mother and my grandmother curled the cotton wool by hand, taking one of the *dollops* at a time on the simple hand cards. When carded they were put aside in separate parcels ready for spinning."

Crompton's failure in life was solely owing to his lack of business faculty, and as he himself wrote : "I found to my sorrow I was not calculated to contend with men of the world, neither did I know there was such a thing as protection for me on earth! I found I was as unfitted for the task that was before me, as a child of two years old to contend with a disciplined army." Shy and sensitive in an extreme degree, he would frequently return from Manchester without having attempted to transact any business, because he had observed himself being pointed out to strangers as a remarkable man. His yarn was the finest and his muslins were the most delicate on the market; " but," says one of his biographers, " when he attended the Manchester Exchange to sell his yarn or muslins, and any rough-and-ready manufacturer ventured to offer him a less price than he had asked, he would invariably wrap up his samples, put them in his pocket and quietly walk away."

The remainder of Crompton's life was passed in sorrow and repeated disappointments. On several occasions the Government was petitioned to give a pension or a money grant to the man who had revolutionised the spinning trade and thus brought untold wealth into the country, but without success. Once, poor Crompton was within sight of recognition when the bullet of an assassin deprived him of a comfortable future. He was talking to Sir Robert Peel and Mr. Blackburne, a Lancashire Member of Parliament, who was a strong supporter of his claim, in the lobby of the House of Commons on the 11th May 1812 when Mr. Perceval, the Premier and Chancellor of the Exchequer, joined the little group.

" You will be glad to know that we mean to propose twenty thousand pounds for Crompton. Do you think that will be satisfactory?" he said.

Crompton, prompted by motives of delicacy, moved away, and therefore did not hear the reply. He was just leaving the Lobby when he heard the sound of many people running, and some one near him called out that Mr. Perceval had been shot. The Prime Minister had been murdered by a man called Bellingham.

A month after, Parliament voted Crompton a grant of five thousand pounds —a bitter disappointment to the inventor, who had spent a considerable sum of money in laying his claims before the authorities. The larger part of the grant he lost in starting some bleaching-works and in joining a firm of cotton merchants and spinners. Finally, he was reduced to such poverty that, unknown to him, a subscription was raised amongst the firms using the mule, and with it an annuity of sixty-three pounds was bought. In 1827 Crompton died, having enjoyed his annuity for only two years.

His whole life had been one of struggle and sorrow, thousands had benefited by his inventions, hundreds had become rich. Some of the most prosperous firms in Bolton owed their existence and their fortunes to Crompton; but whilst others had prospered by the children of his brain they had allowed him to die in poverty. Thirty-five years later the consciences of the sons and grandsons of many who had benefited by Crompton's rash gift of the patent of his mule, were awakened, and Crompton being dead, a statue costing some two thousand pounds was erected to his memory in Nelson Square at Bolton. That which the fathers withheld from Crompton living, honour and fair reward, the sons gave to Crompton dead.

JOHN DALTON

— Father of Chemistry

ALTHOUGH John Dalton was a Cumberland man by birth, fifty of the seventy-eight years of his life were spent in Manchester, and it was there that he made the great discovery which established chemistry as a science, and incidentally made the fortunes of many Lancashire manufacturers. Manchester has honoured his memory with statues, and by calling one of her principal streets after his name, which is further perpetuated by Dalton scholarships and Dalton prizes at Owens College.

Like so many of the men who have brought world-wide renown to the County Palatine, Dalton was of humble birth. His father, who came of a Cumberland yeoman family, was himself a woollen weaver at Eaglesfield, a village some three miles from Cockermouth. But he was an indifferent worker and gained only a scanty livelihood. He was a Quaker, and the future scientist and his elder brother Jonathan were educated at a Quaker school kept by Mr. John Fletcher at Pardshaw Hall. Whilst still attending school, at the age of ten Dalton entered the service of Mr. Elihu Robinson, a well-to-do Quaker at Eaglesfield, who had a taste for science. Struck by the boy's intelligence and his love of study, Mr. Robinson gave him lessons in mathematics in the evening, and it was amongst this worthy Quaker's books and scientific apparatus that Dalton gained the first rudiments of a knowledge which in later years resulted in the most remarkable discoveries.

By the time he was twelve, Dalton had made such progress under Mr. Robinson's tuition and by his own studies, that when Mr. Fletcher gave up the Quaker school in 1778, he became its master. His first schoolroom was a barn, but later he held his classes in the Friends' Meeting House at Eaglesfield. His pupils were boys and girls of all ages, some so young that he had to hold them on his knees whilst he taught them their letters, some older than himself who challenged him to fight when he called them to order. The reward of this teaching was some five shillings weekly. At the end of two years the school was closed, and for a time Dalton had to work in the fields for his living. But all the time he was steadily pursuing his own studies. From his earliest years he showed a dogged perseverance and an independence of character which never wavered.

The elder brother, Jonathan, had likewise taken to school-mastering, and was an assistant in a school belonging to one of their cousins at Kendal, and in 1781 the fifteen-year-old John was given the post of assistant in the same school.

Here again the fates were kind to John Dalton. Living at Kendal was a Mr. Gough, who, although he had been blind from childhood, was " a zealous and instructed cultivator of science, and possessed of means, apparatus and leisure for scientific study and investigation." The poet Wordsworth described Gough as " a most extraordinary person," and introduced him into *The Excursion*.

From this " blind philosopher," as he was called, young Dalton learnt many things—a little Greek, Latin and French, the higher mathematics, and how to make meteorological observations. In addition, he had the run of Gough's library, which was remarkable amongst the private collections in the country for its scientific works and apparatus. Under Gough's guidance he began to keep a meteorological journal, the first entry being on March 24, 1787. He continued it regularly until his death in 1844, and during the fifty-seven years between these two dates, entered no less than two hundred thousand observations in it.

Four years after Dalton joined his brother as assistant at their cousin's school, the latter retired, and the two brothers carried on the establishment by themselves. Their success, however, was only qualified. Both brothers were uncouth in manner, their discipline was very severe, and Jonathan gave the school an unenviable reputation by reason of the drastic punishments he administered. John was too much absorbed in his own mathematical and scientific studies during school-hours to notice the shortcomings of his pupils. His duty was to hold the boys whilst his brother applied the birch, which was done with such thoroughness that even in those days, when corporal punishment was part of the curriculum in every school, the parents protested.

Dalton remained at the school at Kendal for eight years, and during that time he made barometers and thermometers of his own invention for his meteorological observations; he collected butterflies; studied zoology and botany; and gave subscription lectures in the town on mechanics, optics, pneumatics, astronomy, and the use of the globe—a marvellous range of knowledge for a young man of twenty-two. This was in 1787. In 1789, firmly convinced that his talents fitted him for a wider field than that of the schoolmaster, he ventured to hint at his ambition to study law or medicine to a Quaker uncle, his mother's brother, Thomas Greenup. " Law and physic are totally out of the reach of a person in thy circumstances," was the crusty reply. " If thou art tired of being a teacher, and wishest to change it for some more lucrative and agreeable employment, and couldst be content, instead of becoming a physician or a barrister, to move in the humble sphere of apothecary or attorney, thou mightest perhaps be able, with a little capital and great industry, to establish thyself in one of these." This was by no means encouraging. Dalton had no inclination to become either an apothecary or an attorney.

But three years later he had his chance. The famous Warrington Academy had been removed to Manchester, where it was called the Manchester New College. In 1793 it was a flourishing institution, providing the youth of the town with what would now be called " higher education." A tutor for mathematics and natural philosophy being required, Gough was asked if he could recommend some one for the post. Unhesitatingly he suggested Dalton, who was forthwith appointed, and with the acceptance of the post Dalton's fifty-one years of residence in Manchester began.

Amongst the humble luggage Dalton

took with him from Kendal to Manchester, were the proofs of his first book, *Meteorological Discoveries and Essays*, the fruit of many years' close observation of Nature. Forty years later Dalton said that this book contained the germ of most of the ideas which he afterwards expanded into discoveries. A year after his arrival in Manchester he was elected a member of the Manchester Literary and Philosophical Society, reading his first paper in the month of his election. The subject was colour-blindness, from which both his brother Jonathan and himself suffered. Dalton was the first to draw attention to this peculiarity of vision. The paper attracted universal attention, and on the Continent the complaint was called Daltonism. In the course of time he became successively secretary, vice-president, and president of the Literary and Philosophical Society, which very early in his membership gave him a room as a laboratory. To one in Dalton's poor circumstances this was an inestimable boon, and he showed his appreciation of the Society's kindness by communicating all his researches and discoveries to its members. These papers were published in the Memoirs of the Society, and, as a result, Dalton's name became known not only to all the scientists in his own country, but on the Continent also.

For six years Dalton taught mathematics, natural philosophy, and chemistry at the New College; then the number of pupils fell off, and ultimately it was removed to York. Dalton was therefore obliged to support himself by private tuition, and also by making analyses. He was the first man to make chemical analyses in Manchester, charging a fee of half-a-guinea, where ten guineas or more would be charged to-day. For his tuition he charged one-and-sixpence and two-and-sixpence a lesson, according to the subject. His gains, therefore, must have been small, but he was extremely frugal in his habits, and whatever he earned he always contrived to save something towards a provision for his old age.

Dalton's discovery of the effect of heat upon gases in the atmosphere led to meteorology being constituted a science, but his greatest discovery was the atomic theory. The first suggestion of the discovery was given by Dalton in a paper read to the Literary and Philosophical Society on October 21, 1803, dealing with " the absorption of gases by water and other liquids," but the actual theory itself was communicated by him in conversation to Dr. Thomson, by whom it was first published to the world. The smallest boy in a chemistry class now knows that wherever water is found it consists of exactly the same weight of oxygen in combination with the same weight of hydrogen, that these component gases are invariable. This was Dalton's discovery, and it applies throughout Nature. The scientific result of the discovery is only interesting to those with a knowledge of chemistry; its practical result is thus given by Professor Roscoe :—

" Of the scientific importance of this discovery there can be no question ; indeed chemistry could hardly be said to exist as a science before the establishment of the laws of combination in multiple proportions, and the subsequent progress of chemical science materially depended upon the determination of these combined proportions or atomic weights of the elements, first set up by Dalton. So that amongst the founders of our science, next to the name of the great French philosopher, Lavoisier, will stand in future ages the name of John Dalton of Manchester. Even from a practical and business point of view the discovery of these combining proportions is of the greatest value. Thus, for instance, in the manufacture of oil of vitriol, a substance which is required in thousands and thousands of tons every year for different industrial purposes, before John Dalton had determined how much sulphur and how much oxygen and how much hydrogen combine together to form this sulphuric acid, or oil of vitriol, no manufacturer could tell, except by rule of thumb, how much of each particular constituent had to be brought together. It was necessary, in order that the chemical manufacturer should be able to prepare this substance economically, that he should be able to ascertain, with the greatest precision, how much sulphur he should burn, how much air he must use, and how much water he must add, in order, with the greatest economy, to produce this product for the market. It is the same with every chemical action that occurs, and it is to John Dalton—who made his living by giving private lessons at half-a-crown each—that we owe this knowledge which has made the fortune of thousands, because he first told us the laws which govern these chemical actions."

This wonderful discovery made no difference to Dalton's way of life. He rose very early in the morning and went from his lodging in George Street to the room provided for him by the Literary and Philosophical Society, where he dusted his pupils' desks and lighted the fire. Then he went back to George Street for breakfast. At nine o'clock he was ready for his pupils, whom he taught " mathematics, science, cyphering, anything and everything," until twelve or one o'clock. Dinner was punctually at one o'clock, and if he had a few minutes to spare between lessons and this time he went to the Portico and read the newspapers. After dinner he returned to his laboratory; at five o'clock came tea, and from six to nine he worked at his researches. At nine he took a light supper, and at ten o'clock went to bed. Year in year out his routine went like clockwork, his only recreation being a game of bowls every Thursday afternoon at the " Dog and Partridge," and an annual visit to Cumberland, where mountain climbing was his great pleasure. He is said to have ascended Helvellyn between thirty and forty times.

Dalton's choice of his lodging in George Street was characteristic. One of his colleagues at the New College was the Rev. W. Johns, and one day in the autumn of 1804, seeing Dalton pass the door, Mrs. Johns asked him why he never went to see them.

" I do not know," Dalton replied, " but I will come and live with you if you will let me."

He took the only spare bedroom and lived with the Johns for twenty-six years. So methodical and regular was Dalton in his habits that the neighbours could tell the hour to a minute by seeing him read the thermometer outside his window each morning.

For many years his discoveries in science brought him nothing except European fame. And we have this description of a visit paid him by a French admirer :—

" Mons. Pelletan, of Paris, visited Manchester in 1820, for the sole purpose of paying his respects to the founder of the atomic theory. He fancied that Dalton would be occupying a Professor's Chair, surrounded by adepts in science and hundreds of ingenuous youths ; residing in a handsome square in the city, or enjoying his *otium cum dignitate* in a suburban villa, with roses embellishing its porch; in short, the great representative man of Manchester, and well known and appreciated by every citizen. Judge of his surprise when *Monsieur Dalton le philosophe* could only be found after much inquiry, and when found was engaged in looking over the shoulders of a boy figuring sums on a slate. The Frenchman, doubting his senses, asked the grey-headed gentleman if he really had the honour of addressing Monsieur Dalton. 'Yes,' replied Dalton; 'will you sit down till I put this lad right about his arithmetic?'"

In 1822 Dalton paid a visit to Paris, where he was received with great honour in the scientific world. This recognition in France seems to have stirred the English scientists to a sense of their lack of appreciation of their fellow-countryman, for in the same year he was elected a member of the Royal Society. Honours then fell thickly upon the "Manchester Philosopher." The Royal Society gave him the first of the gold medals which had been founded by George IV., as scientific prizes; the French Academy of Science elected him one of its eight foreign associates, and in 1832 the University of Oxford conferred upon him the degree of D.C.L. Dalton was now sixty-six and still dependent upon his earnings as a teacher for his livelihood. This was felt to be not only an injustice to the man, but a reflection upon the country, and he was given a Civil List pension of one hundred and fifty pounds a year, which was increased to three hundred a year in 1836. In the meantime Dalton's recognition as a great man in London and on the Continent led his friends and admirers to start a subscription for a statue of him by the great sculptor Chantrey. This statue was placed in the entrance hall of the Manchester Royal Institution.

Whilst he was in London giving sit-tings for the statue he was persuaded to allow himself to be presented at Court. But, being a Quaker, he would not wear a sword; the difficulty was got over by his wearing his scarlet robes as a D.C.L. of Oxford over his sombre Quaker dress.

Babbage, the inventor of the calculating machine, was the instigator of this attendance at Court, and it was he who coached the still uncouth Dalton in the necessary bows and movements. The "Manchester Philosopher" was received with marked attention by King William IV., and Babbage relates with friendly pride: "I heard one officer say to another: 'Who the d——l is that fellow whom the King keeps talking to so long?'"

In the autumn of the year in which Dalton made his bow at Court his brother Jonathan died, leaving him everything he possessed. With this small inheritance, his own savings, and his pension, Dalton was placed beyond any monetary anxiety, and "considered himself rich enough to buy a full set of silver spoons for dinner, dessert, and tea service." But he had only enjoyed his modest competence for three years when he was struck down by paralysis. He grew weaker and weaker, and when the British Association held its meeting at Manchester in 1842 he was not able to discharge his duties as its President, an office to which he had been appointed. The then Earl of Ellesmere took his place. In May 1844 he had another paralytic stroke. On the 26th of July he made his last feeble record of the barometer; the next morning he was found lifeless upon the floor of his bedroom.

His death brought this somewhat cynical remark from Dr. Angus Smith: "As is usually the case on the death of an eminent man, the first proof was furnished to many persons that he was once alive." In his death Dalton was certainly more famous in Manchester than in his lifetime. Despite the protests of the Society of Friends, the Corporation gave him a public funeral. His body, in a "beautiful mahogany coffin," was placed in the Town Hall, and during the five days of the lying-in-state over forty thousand people passed before it. On the 12th of August the funeral took place at Ardwick Cemetery, followed by a procession a mile long, in which were a hundred carriages, all business being suspended in the streets through which it passed. A bronze replica of the Chantrey statue was placed in front of the Manchester Infirmary, and a sum of three thousand pounds was raised to perpetuate his memory by the foundation of the Dalton scholarships and Dalton prizes in Owens College.

Throughout his life Dalton wore the Quaker dress—knee-breeches, dark grey stockings, and buckled shoes. His broad-brimmed beaver hat was of the finest quality; his white neckcloth was always spotless, and he invariably carried a gold or silver-headed cane.

Dr. Davy, the brother of Sir Humphrey Davy, the inventor of the miner's lamp, thus described the great scientist in 1810 :—

"Mr. Dalton's aspect and manner were repulsive. There was no gracefulness belonging to him. His voice was harsh and brawling; his gait stiff and awkward; his style of writing and conversation dry, and almost crabbed. In person he was tall, bony, and slender. . . . Independence and simplicity of manner and originality were his best qualities. Though in comparatively humble circumstances, he maintained the dignity of the philosophical character." Dalton did not shine in society, and it is related of him that he had the habit of cutting short any importunate questionings with regard to his discoveries with a gruff, "I have written a book on that subject, and if thou wishest to inform thyself about the matter, thou canst buy my book for three-and-sixpence."

Yet, notwithstanding his bad manner and uncouthness, Dalton was one of the kindest and most lovable of men. Once he had given his friendship he never changed or wavered, and those who really knew the man loved him devotedly. He was kind and most painstaking with his pupils, and an anecdote was told which is a happy example of that kindness and his strict regard for the truth. "A student who missed one lecture of a course applied to him for a certificate of full attendance. Dalton at first declined to give it, but, after thinking a little, replied : 'If thou wilt come to-morrow, I will go over the lecture thou hast missed.'"

Dalton never married, and when asked, later in life, the reason, answered : "I never had time." But this answer was characteristic of the man. Throughout his whole life he cherished the memory of a hopeless attachment.

JAMES, Earl of Derby

FOR nearly two hundred years—from the reign of the seventh Henry to that of the first Charles—Fortune showered all her gifts upon the Stanleys, Earls of Derby. They became the largest landowners in the country; in Lancashire their slightest wish was law: son, and whose three daughters were his coheiresses. Earl William disputed the will, which alienated a large portion of the Stanley property from the title for the benefit of Earl Ferdinando's three daughters. Their mother, Countess Alice, daughter of that Sir John Spencer who

JAMES STANLEY, SEVENTH EARL OF DERBY

in the Isle of Man they exercised the rights of sovereign princes. But with the accession of William, the sixth earl, the smiles of Fortune were turned to frowns, and both he and his son paid dearly for the prosperity of their ancestors.

Earl William succeeded his brother Ferdinando, the fifth earl, who had no was the ancestor of the great Duke of Marlborough, stoutly defended her daughters' rights, and by marrying the famous Lord Chancellor Ellesmere a few years after Earl Ferdinando's death, obtained the " best legal advice in England. " The result of this marriage was a series of lawsuits between Earl William and his sister-in-law and nieces, which ended in complete triumph for the ladies and Earl Ferdinando's will being upheld by the Courts. Earl William was to retain Knowsley and Lathom and other large possessions, but he lost "the Baronies of Strange, of Mohun, Barnewell, Basset and Lacy, with all the houses, castles, manors and lands thereto belonging, with several other manors and large estates lying in most counties of England and many in Wales." He even had to buy back the lordship of the Isle of Man from Countess Alice and her daughters.

The "martyr" Earl of Derby, James, was the eldest son of Earl William, and was born at Knowsley in 1607, thirteen years after his father's succession to the title. Lord Strange, as he was called in his father's lifetime, was what we should call in these days a "serious young man," of profound religious feeling not untouched with Puritanism. This was probably due to his tutors, one of whom, Charles Erle, was a Presbyterian and afterwards one of the two representatives of Lancashire at the Westminister Assembly of Divines. The other tutor, George Murray, was the brother of Richard Murray whom James I. appointed Warden of Manchester College. Richard Murray was "a careless, easygoing ecclesiastic, of whom his royal patron had so accurately taken the measure, that, it is said, once having given for his text, 'I am not ashamed of the Gospel of Christ,' the King made the audible comment—'spiced with an oath'—'But the Gospel may well be ashamed of thee!'"

At the age of eighteen Lord Strange was elected Member of Parliament for Liverpool—in the year of Charles I.'s accession—and shortly afterwards set out for The Hague avowedly to pay a visit to the Dutch Court, but in reality to see Charlotte de la Trémouille, the daughter of the great French Duc de la Tremouille,

his marriage with whom had been suggested by James I.'s daughter Elizabeth, Queen of Bohemia, then an exile in Holland. The cost of the long litigation with the Countess Alice and the loss of a large portion of his estates had so crippled Earl William that his son was obliged to borrow the money necessary for him to make his appearance at The Hague befitting his high rank. Charlotte de la Trémouille was paying a visit to her great-uncle the Stadtholder-Prince of Nassau, brother of William the Silent, who was the father of the Duchess de la Trémouille. The young couple—the lady was six years older than Lord Strange—fell in love with one another and in June 1626, were married "in a palace of the Prince of Orange at The Hague in the presence of the King and Queen of Bohemia and many royal and noble personages," the bride having a dowry of twenty thousand pounds, a very large sum for those days. This, however, was never fully paid. The settlement of the dowry had somewhat delayed the wedding, for the Duchesse de la Trémouille would not agree to a clause which stated that upon the death of the husband the wife's marriage portion was to be given up to his relatives. Such was the English law at the time.

Many years afterwards, writing to his son, Lord Strange said: "If your estate be good, match near home and at leisure, but if weak or encumbered marry afar and quickly"—a counsel clearly based upon his own experience.

Shortly after Lord and Lady Strange arrived in England his mother the Countess of Derby died, and Earl William gave up the family estates to his son. "My father," wrote Lord Strange, "upon the death of my mother, growing infirm and disconsolate, and willing to repose himself from the troubles of the world, purchased a house on the side of the river

Dee, near Chester, and retired to it; reserving to himself a thousand pounds a year for life, and put the rest of his estate and revenue into my hands."

But although Lord Strange had entire charge of the Stanley fortune he seems to have been in some straits for ready money. Only a year after their marriage we find Lady Strange writing from Lathom to her duchess-mother, and asking for an instalment of her dowry: "The time of our stay here is not yet determined, but if the twenty thousand crowns do not come, it will be a hard matter to get away." In another letter she describes a visit she and her husband had paid to old Earl William: "I wrote you word, madame, that I had seen my father-in-law at Chester, where he always lives—never desiring to go to any of his other houses; he has been there now three or four years. He spoke to me in French and said very kind things to me, calling me lady and mistress of the house—a position which he said he wished no other woman to hold; that I had the law in my own hands entirely. We were very well received in the town; though we were not expected many people came to meet us. I told you also, madame, how much I liked Lathom House, and that I had every reason to thank God and you for having married me so happily. I do not doubt, madame, that you will do everything in your power with regard to my money; indeed I expect this from you, and certes, madame, necessity constrains me to importune you in the matter more than I ought; your goodness emboldens me to do so, and truly my happiness partly depends on it, that I may be able to shut the mouths of some people who do not love foreigners, though, thank God, the best of these wish me no harm."

The troubles that twenty years later brought King Charles to the block were already beginning. Lord Strange was given a seat in the House of Peers, and for some time he and his wife were notable figures at Court; and his house in London, which had been built by his father, was "the resort of distinguished statesmen, foreigners and scholars; his hospitality, like his fortune, being almost regal." At this time he was only twenty-three, and was described as "possessing a tall and graceful figure, regular and handsome features, a florid complexion, with a forehead probably capacious and lofty, but which is in all his portraits concealed by overhanging dark hair." Despite his power in Lancashire, and his great hospitality Lord Strange was not popular with King Charles's chief courtiers and advisers; nor were he and his wife viewed with very kindly eyes by Queen Henrietta Maria. The Queen was a rigid Roman Catholic, and although obliged to hide her opinions as to what she considered "heresy" where the English ladies of the Court were concerned, felt herself at liberty to show that opinion towards a countrywoman of her own. She openly slighted the daughter of her father's— Henri IV. of France—staunchest and oldest friend, the Duc de la Trémouille, because she was a Protestant. Lord Strange may have been too straightforward to please the shifty counsellors by whom Charles was surrounded, Lady Strange may have found the Queen's attitude unbearable, but whatever the cause, when they retired to Lancashire it was said that they had been "disobliged by the Court."

During the next seven years Lord Strange lived upon his estates, devoting his time to their management, employing his leisure in studying philosophy and composing anthems. When Scotland rose in rebellion against Charles in 1639, Lord Strange was one of the first to obey the King's summons to a Council at York. Any personal feelings he may have had as to the treatment of himself and his wife in London were completely forgotten in the danger threatening the monarchy. Before setting out for York he " addressed a stirring appeal without any delay to his deputy-lieutenants for military aid, magnificent offer both of men and money. But his suggestion was regarded with distrust, and Nottingham was decided upon. If Lord Strange's advice had been followed a different history might have been written of the Civil War, for Lancashire at that time was strongly Royalist.

Lancashire first took sides in the

THE EARL AND COUNTESS OF DERBY AND THEIR DAUGHTER, LADY CATHARINE STANLEY
(AFTER VANDYCK)

and the service was promptly rendered." Three years later, and he was once more with King Charles at York. But a graver danger loomed ahead. The Civil War was imminent. The Cavaliers were arming for the King, and the Roundheads for the Parliament. Lord Strange urged the raising of the Royal Standard at Warrington, at the same time making a struggle at a county meeting held on Preston Moor in 1642. The High Sheriff, a stout Royalist, took advantage of the occasion to read a proclamation for King Charles, ordering a "commission of array," as the military organization of each county was called. Instantly there were wild shouts of " For the King! For the King!" from the Lancashire

Royalists, and counter-shouts of "For the King and Parliament" from those who then believed that the rebellion was only against Charles's councillors, and not against himself. In a very short time they were undeceived, and their cry was only for the Parliament.

If Charles's advisers had doubted the loyalty of Lord Strange when they refused his offer of men and money for the raising of the King's standard at Warrington, they must now have seen their mistake. Placing himself at the head of the Lancashire Cavaliers the young nobleman marched to Manchester, and demanded that all the gunpowder and ammunition stored in the town, which had already shown strong inclination towards the Parliamentarian party, should be yielded up to him. Not only was the demand refused, but such an array of force was mustered that he withdrew. Thereupon the Royalists of Manchester invited Lord Strange to a banquet. It was this banquet that brought the smoking embers of civil war to a flame. It is thought that the large number of armed followers attending Lord Strange and his Royalist friends to the feast, aroused the suspicions of the Manchester Parliamentarians as to its actual object. Halley tells us that—

"Sir Thomas Stanley of Bickerstaff and Captain Birch of Birch, who happened to be in the town at the time, beat up the train-bands by the sound of the drum, and led them to the front of the house where the Royalists were feasting. The accounts differ as to the party which actually began the fray. The Royalists say that the attack was commenced by Sir Thomas Stanley,[1] who fired a pistol at his relative, Lord Strange. The Parliamentarians say that Lord Strange ordered his horsemen to attack the train-bands who were preserving order in the street. On the one side or the other a Stanley seems to have begun the fight, in which Richard Percival, a weaver, was shot by the Royalists—the first person in Lancashire, and probably in England, who was killed in the Civil War."

A few weeks later Lord Strange was impeached for "levying war against the king, parliament and kingdom, in that he entered Manchester maliciously and treacherously, with force and arms and in a hostile and warlike manner; and that he did kill, murder and destroy Richard Percival, linen webster." His reply to this impeachment was to lay siege to Manchester.

The town made itself ready for defence both spiritually and materially. "A spirit of devotion in prayers and singing of psalms rested generally upon persons and families; yea, upon taverns and inns where it might not put its head formerly"; and whilst the prayers and singing went on the walls were fortified, and the citizens drilled by a soldier of fortune, Lieutenant-Colonel John Rosworm. Military adventurers of all kinds flocked into England when it became clear that the Civil War was inevitable, and amongst them came Rosworm, who had made a considerable reputation on the Continent. War being the trade of these adventurers, it was a matter of indifference to them which side they served, their swords and their talents going to the highest bidder. At this time Rosworm happened to be in Manchester and was promptly engaged by the

---

[1] This Sir Thomas Stanley, like Lord Strange, was descended from the eldest son of the first Earl of Derby who died in his father's lifetime. The present Earl of Derby is descended from this Sir Thomas, as in 1736, James, Lord Strange's grandson died without a male heir, and the earldom passed to the younger branch of the family, to "Sir Edward Stanley of Bickerstaff, in Lancashire, Bart.," the great-grandson of the Parliamentarian Sir Thomas.

Parliamentarians. Rosworm's anger knew no bounds when, a few days later, Lord Strange made him an offer to serve the Royalists at a far higher price, but although he denounced Manchester for what he considered its "shabby treatment" of him, he served the town faithfully, and it was owing to him that when Lord Strange answered his impeachment by appearing before Manchester with "two thousand foot, three hundred horse, and six pieces of ordnance," and the majority of the Royalist gentlemen in Lancashire, the place was in a state of defence. Lord Strange's little army marched into Salford with their drums beating, their colours flying, and the multitude shouting "For the King! For the King!" Salford Bridge and Deansgate were the points attacked by the Royalists, but they were successfully repulsed by the Manchester men. This was on September 25, 1642. Five days afterwards Earl William died in his retreat at Chester, and Lord Strange became the seventh Earl of Derby. But he was not able to go to his father's death-bed or to attend his funeral, for he had received an urgent summons from the King to come to his aid at Shrewsbury. Withdrawing his troops, after only a week's siege of Manchester, the new Lord Derby pressed with all haste to his royal master, leaving the Parliamentarians triumphant and the Royalists disgusted. His forces had been raised for the defence of Lancashire, and their withdrawal was so deeply resented by the Royalists that it is said to have cost King Charles the loss of the county.

On his return from Shrewsbury Lord Derby made valiant efforts for the King. Manchester and Bolton were Parliamentary strongholds, Wigan and Warrington were Royalist, and the first six months of 1643 saw a series of incessant fightings, marches, and countermarches. Lancashire was deep in the horrors of civil war. In January the Parliamentarians captured Preston; in February Lord Derby made an unsuccessful attack on Bolton; in March he laid successful siege to Lancaster. The bitterness with which the war was waged is shown by this quotation from one of his letters :—

"When I came before the town (Lancaster) I summoned it in His Majesty's name, and the Mayor (as I heard), counselled by the commanders for the Parliament, made me so slight an answer, after I expecting it for a whole day, that I, enraged to see their sauciness against so good a Prince, made bold to burn the greater part of the town, and in it many of their soldiers who defended it very sharply for two hours. But we beat them into the Castle, and I, seeing the town clear from all but smoke, spared the remainder of that town, and laid siege unto the Castle. There was no woman or child suffered, or any but those who did bear arms, for so I gave directions to my soldiers, except some three or four that I think as likely to be killed by them. Having got some advantage (which was the first that I had ever had since these unhappy times) I thought well to slip on to Preston."

The Earl recaptured Preston from the Parliamentarians, but was again repulsed at Bolton. Then an attack by the Parliamentarians upon Wigan was defeated, but this was the last of the Royalist successes, for Colonel Assheton of Middleton, driving Lord Derby out of the hundred of Blackburn, captured Wigan and retook Preston; and pursuing the Royalists in their retreat to the north, drove them into Westmorland. Warrington, the last Royalist stronghold in

Lancashire, speedily fell, and by Midsummer "all the fortified towns and houses of Lancashire, except Lathom, were in possession of the Parliamentarians."

The heaviest of the many anxieties Lord Derby had borne so loyally for his King was now laid upon him. He was ordered by Queen Henrietta Maria to go to the Isle of Man in order to prevent a proposed landing of the Scottish army there, on its way to join the forces of the Parliament. In his absence Lady Derby was besieged in Lathom House. Her heroic resistance, and the raising of the siege by Prince Rupert and her husband, are told in the story, "The Siege of Lathom House."

The taking of Bolton, prior to the raising the siege of his beautiful old home, roused the strongest feelings among the Lancashire Parliamentarians against the Earl, and the " Bolton Massacre " was one of the causes that brought him to the scaffold and the block. When husband and wife were reunited they crossed to the Isle of Man, where, eighteen months later, they heard of the taking of Lathom House and its utter destruction. During the next four or five years Lord Derby enjoyed comparative peace and quiet in his island-kingdom. He did his utmost to improve the island and the condition of the people; but as the Parliament had sequestrated his estates in England, and had also publicly excepted his name from any act of amnesty, he was practically without means.

Lord and Lady Derby kept their court at Rushen Castle, but being cut off from all communication with the mainland, except of a secret and dangerous kind, they and their children and household were at times reduced to sore straits, even for clothing. On one occasion—in June 1650—a bark belonging to the Commonwealth was captured, and the evidence of two of the crew, which was given when the owners petitioned Parliament for compensation for their losses, throws an interesting side light upon the distress to which a great nobleman was reduced after the fall of the monarchy. Amongst the cargo of the captured vessel was a large quantity of draper's goods, belonging to a man called Massey of Warrington : " The cloths, silks, and taffetas, and other goods found in the ship, were soon disposed of in the Earl's own house or made into garments for the commander's gentlewomen. " Further " in the house, or castle, wherein the said Earl lives and keeps his court of guard he "—the witness—" saw about twenty tailors all busy at work, making garments out of Massey's goods, for the half-naked servants and others of the household."

Lord Derby was a deeply religious man, and imbued with a piety which gained him the respect even of his enemies. He kept a journal of " Private Devotions" in which he recorded his reasons for thankfulness. One of these prayers referred to the refuge given him by his island-kingdom. It ran : " O Lord, I thank Thee for this island, which hath been to me a very blessed and happy place of retreat from the storms and inconveniences of war, which many better than myself have suffered in the three kingdoms about us. I give Thee thanks, O Lord—I never enough can thank Thee, O Lord—for preserving my soul from the trouble and danger of taking the many oaths that have been pressed on very many against their consciences, and for which divers of Thy servants have suffered martyrdom. O Lord, I thank Thee for the plentiful seasons we have had, by which I have not only clothed and fed myself and family, but have relieved many strangers which have been distressed. O Lord, Thou hast given me much honour here, therefore whilst I live and have a being I will, to the utmost of my power, give Thee glory. Let me never forget Thy great goodness, O my God, in having made me so exceedingly happy with a blessed wife and with many sweet and hopeful children."

It was owing to Lady Derby's unceasing efforts that the Parliament agreed that a fifth part of the income from the Earl's estates, which had passed into other hands, should be given to his wife and children, and charged on the Manor of Knowsley. Probably with the object of protecting Knowsley from destruction or partial ruin, and to prevent the Parliament holding back this income on the ground that mother and daughters were sharing the exile of one whom they declared to be a rebel, Lord Derby sent his two daughters, Catherine and Amelia, to occupy their old home. Upon their arrival Sir Thomas Fairfax ordered the military officer who had charge of Knowsley for the Parliament to leave it. In the following year King Charles was executed at Whitehall; and Oliver Cromwell was acknowledged as the head of the country, everywhere except in Ireland and the Isle of Man. Seven months after King Charles's execution Lord Derby was summoned to surrender his island-kingdom by Ireton, Cromwell's son-in-law, being promised as a reward " the peaceable possession of half his estate."

His reply breathes a splendid spirit of loyalty to his king, personal courage, and scathing contempt for those whom ne regarded as regicides, despoilers and oppressors. It was directed to " Commissary-General Ireton," and ran: " Castletown, July 12, 1649. Sir—I have received your letter with indignation and scorn, and return you this answer, that I cannot but wonder whence you should gather any hopes from me that I should, like you, prove treacherous to my Sovereign, since you cannot but be sensible of my former actings in his late Majesty's service; from which principles of loyalty I am no whit departed. I scorn your proffers, disclaim your favour, and abhor your treason, and am so far from delivering up this island to your advantage that I will keep it to the utmost of my power and your destruction. Take this for your final answer, and forbear any further solicitations, for if you trouble me with any more messages on this occasion I will burn the paper and hang the messenger. This is the immutable resolution, and shall be the undoubted practice, of him who accounts it his chiefest glory to be His Majesty's most loyal and obedient servant, Derby."

Another offer made by Sir Thomas Fairfax was based on a condition which comes under the heading of refined torture. The Commonwealth tried to force Lord Derby to give up the Isle of Man by seizing his two daughters at Knowsley, and throwing them into prison at Liverpool. Writing to her sister-in-

LIEUT.-COLONEL ROSWORM

law, the Duchesse de la Trémouille in France, Lady Derby says: " No reason is given for this, but we hear it is because they are thought to be too much liked, and that people were beginning to make application to the Parliament in the hope that their father might come to terms, of which I see no chance. . . . We hear that they are bearing it bravely, and I have no doubt this is true of the eldest; but my daughter Amelia is delicate and timid and is undergoing medical treatment. They are in a wretched place, ill-lodged, and in a bad air; but these barbarians think of nothing but carrying out their damnable designs, which could not be worse if all Hell had invented them." Fairfax had always behaved with the greatest courtesy and consideration to the two girls, and complaints of their cruel treatment were made to him. His reply shows the design of the Parliament. In throwing the daughters into prison they wished to force the distracted father to come to terms. Fairfax said that if Lord Derby would deliver up the Isle of Man " to the Parliament's commands, his children should not only be set at liberty but he should peaceably return to England and enjoy one moiety of all his estates." Lord Derby's answer was in the same spirit as his letter to Ireton: " That he was greatly afflicted for the suffering of his children; that it was not the course of great and noble minds to punish innocent children for their father's offences; that it would be a clemency in Sir Thomas Fairfax either to send them back to him or to Holland or to France; but if he could do none of these things, his children must submit to the mercy of God Almighty, but should never be redeemed by his disloyalty."

In addition to this anxiety about their daughters, Lord and Lady Derby were sorely distressed by the conduct of their eldest son, Lord Strange, who, slipping away from the Isle of Man, had gone to France and thence to The Hague. His conduct was most unsatisfactory to his parents, and he put the crowning blow upon their distress by marrying a Mademoiselle de Rupa, one of the Queen of Bohemia's maids of honour, " a young German lady of good family but without fortune or rank." When the news reached the Isle of Man of the engagement Lady Derby instantly set out for Holland, by way of Scotland, with the object of breaking off what she and her husband considered a most undesirable marriage for a young man of Lord Strange's birth and connections. She got as far as Kirkcudbright when she found that the army of the Commonwealth made a passport necessary.

" I have sent to ask for one," she wrote to her sister, " and I shall wait for it in the Isle of Man, to which place I return to-day, please God. With a fair wind it is but ten hours' voyage. I have been here fifteen days, suffering every imaginable inconvenience, being reduced to eat oaten bread, and some of us to lodge in the house of the chief person of the place, though I never saw anything so dirty." Again she wrote, betraying her intense anxiety about the marriage: " I shall do my utmost to make out my journey from the island; if my passport comes, as I have reason to hope it will, I shall certainly attempt it. But if it does not, look with compassion, dear sister, on this unfortunate affair, which is of so much consequence to my poor distressed family. Have pity on an unfortunate mother distracted with grief, for I know not what to do. If my passport is refused, I see no means of bringing off this affair by personal interference, unless you would take it in hand with the prudence and skill with which you manage whatever you are pleased to undertake." But Lady Derby's passport did not come, her sister was unable to stop the marriage, which took place at The Hague, and was followed by a still heavier blow—a blow to Lord and Lady Derby's loyalty. Their son and his wife came to England in order that Lord Strange should make peace with the Parliament and thus save all that was possible of the family estates. So deeply did Lord Derby feel this disloyalty that in his will he besought King Charles II. to allow the family honours and estates to descend upon his second son. Lady Derby never forgave her eldest son, and in her will left him five pounds : " I give to my son Charles, Earl of Derby, the sum of five pounds."

But the tragedy of Lord Derby's end was approaching. In August 1651, Charles II. at the head of a Scottish army invaded England to regain his father's throne. As he passed through Lancashire Lord Derby with three hundred Manxmen and several English Royalist gentlemen, to whom he had given shelter, hastened to his aid : " We are still existing here by the goodness of God," wrote Lady Derby, " who has permitted my husband to reach the King his master in safety with a considerable force. He took with him ten ships which nothing but God's help could have brought there safely, for since his departure we have (been) harassed by the enemy's ships. He left this on Wednesday and landed in England on the 15th in a part of Lancashire called Wyrewater. I hear that the King received him with great joy and with every mark of affection." Charles marched southward, leaving Lord Derby in Lancashire to recruit men for his army. In an attempt to take possession of Wigan, Lord Derby, after fighting with the greatest courage, was badly wounded, and had to take refuge in a friend's house in the town. Thence, notwithstanding his wounds, he made his escape in disguise, and taking shelter wherever he could finally succeeded in joining King Charles at Worcester.

Three days later the battle of Worcester was fought, when again Oliver Cromwell was triumphant, and once more Charles II. was fleeing for his life. Lord Derby accompanied the King from the disastrous battlefield, and leaving him in safety [with the Penderels of Boscobel, who saved him by hiding him in an oak-tree, pressed on with Lords Lauderdale and Talbot to overtake the retreating Scottish army. But they fell into the hands of the enemy. " I escaped one great danger at Wigan," Lord Derby wrote to his wife, " and I met with a greater at Worcester. I was not so fortunate as to meet with any that would kill me, for the Lord Lauderdale and I having tired horses, we were not thought worth the killing, for we had quarter given by one Captain Edge, a Lancashire man ; and one that was so civil to me that I and all that love me are beholden to him." When Lord Derby, unable to pursue his flight because of his tired horse, had surrendered to Edge he believed that he would be entitled to the privileges of a prisoner of war. He was speedily undeceived. When it was known that Charles II. was on his way from Scotland the Parliament had hurriedly passed an Act making any " correspondence with Charles Stuart and his party high treason toward the Commonwealth," and under this Act a court-martial was summoned at Chester to try Lord Derby for his life. The trial began on September 29, but its verdict had already been determined upon, as well as the place of Lord Derby's execution—Bolton, the latter because of the " Bolton Massacre."

Oliver Cromwell himself drew up the military arrangements for the journey of the Earl from Chester to Bolton and for the execution.

Both before and after his father's condemnation Lord Strange did everything that a son could do to avert the tragedy. When the sentence was made known it is said that he, " having beforehand laid horses ready, rode post to London in one day and one night," in order to lay a petition craving mercy before Cromwell and the Parliament. But this and other petitions were useless.

A week before the date fixed for his execution — October 15, 1652 — Lord Derby, with the help of some friends, succeeded in escaping from Chester Castle, where he was imprisoned. " During the night, on some pretext, he reached the leads over his chamber, and being furnished with a long rope, by a desperate and almost incredible effort he lowered himself from the top of the Castle to the ground, and escaping from the precincts of the Castle, got out of the city. He had not proceeded far before his escape was discovered, and eager pursuers were despatched in all directions." Misfortune dogged poor Lord Derby. Thinking his pursuers were his friends, he made himself known to them, and was instantly retaken. One comfort Lord Derby had in those last days, in that he was not deprived of the society of the whole of his family. His wife and the three younger children were in the Isle of Man, but Lord Strange (whose loyal behaviour had swept all the clouds away between father and son) and his two elder daughters, Lady Catherine and Lady Amelia, were near, and were allowed to see him.

A strong guard of horse and foot took Lord Derby to Bolton, but when he was brought there it was found that the scaffold was not ready, " the people of the town and of the country generally refusing to carry so much as a plank, or strike a nail, or lend any assistance to that work." By a sinister coincidence most of the timber used for the building of the scaffold came from the ruins of Lathom House. When finally the scaffold was prepared Lord Derby was taken to it, and, as was the custom, made a lengthy speech to the assembled multitude, justifying his actions and committing himself to the Almighty.

" Good friends, I die for the King, the laws of the land, and the Protestant religion," he began.

" We will neither have king, lords, nor laws," cried out one of the troopers, and a strange sound being heard the soldiers " presently fell into a tumult, riding up and down the streets cutting and slashing the people, some being killed and many wounded. Lord Derby, looking on this sad spectacle, said thus : ' Gentlemen, it troubles me more than my own death that others are hurt, I fear, die, for me. I beseech you stay your hands ! I fly not. You pursue not me ; and here are none to pursue *you*.' "

These were the last words he was allowed to address to the weeping crowd. The soldiers shouted him down. Lord Derby, therefore, called for the executioner, and taking the axe from him said : " Friend, I will not harm it, and I am sure it cannot hurt me " ; then kissing it, " Methinks this a wedding ring, which is a sign I am to leave all the world, and eternally be married to my Saviour." Then he caused the block to be moved so that as he knelt for the death-blow he could look upon the old parish church of Bolton. Taking off his riband and Order of the Garter he gave it to a faithful servant to take to his son, then he pulled off his doublet, and asked the executioner how he should place himself.

—H

"I have been called a bloody man," he explained, "yet truly I never yet had that severe curiosity to see any man put to death in peace. Friend," he said to the executioner, "remember what I said to thee, and be no more afraid to strike than I to die, and when I put up my hand do thy work!"

Kneeling down by a chair, which is still preserved at Knowsley, Lord Derby prayed fervently, and "so, laying his neck everlasting rest.' Then saying: 'Come, Lord Jesus; come quickly,' he stretched out his arms and gave the sign, repeating the same words: 'Blessed be God's glorious Name for ever and ever. Let the whole earth be filled with His glory. Amen. Amen.' Then lifting up his hand the executioner did his work at one blow, all the people weeping and crying, and giving all expressions of grief and lamentation."

THE EXECUTION OF THE "MARTYR" EARL AT BOLTON

upon the block, and his arms stretched out, he said these words: 'Blessed be God's glorious Name for ever and ever. Amen. Let the whole earth be filled with His glory. Amen. Amen.' At which words he gave the headsman the sign; but he, either not observing it, or not being ready, stayed too long, so that his lordship rose up again, saying: 'Why do you keep me from my Saviour? What have I done that I die not, and that I may live in Him? Once more I will lay myself down in peace, and so take my

The corpse was placed in a coffin which was upon the scaffold, and conveyed to a house in the town where some one threw into it a paper with these lines—

> "Upon James Earl of Derby
> Beauty, Wit, Courage, here in one lie dead,
> A STANLEY's hand, VERE's heart, and CECIL's head."

Lord Derby's mother had been a Vere, and her mother again a Cecil.

Thus died James, Earl of Derby, "that

glorious martyr," as his wife called him, and thenceforward known to the Royalists as "The Martyr Earl." It is a curious reflection that lack of principle founded the vast fortune which this earl lost for principle's sake. The first Earl of Derby added honour to honour and estate to estate by the skill with which he always managed to be on the winning side: the seventh earl not only sacrificed his estates and worldly honours, he gave up his life for his loyalty to his King.

OLD CHAIR AND TABLE AT BOLTON HALL, CLITHEROE

FRANCIS EGERTON
The Last Duke of Bridgewater

IT is no exaggeration to say that the foundation of the present prosperity of Lancashire was laid by Francis Egerton, the last Duke of Bridgewater. And by one of those unaccountable chances which affect not only the careers of human beings but also the destinies of whole peoples, Lancashire owed the canals that first brought riches within her borders to the breaking-off of a marriage between a young man of twenty-three and the reigning beauty of her time.

The Egerton family, which had long been settled at Ridley in Cheshire, first rose to prominence in the reign of Elizabeth, but not in the person of a legitimate member of the family. Thomas Egerton, who was a handsome and most able lawyer, was the illegitimate son of Sir Richard Egerton. There is a tradition that Sir Richard so neglected the child and its mother that she was compelled to beg for her living, and that a neighbour of Sir Richard's, seeing her asking for alms, went to the father and pointed out what a disgrace he suffered by allowing his own child, " illegitimate though it was," to be carried, begging, from door to door. Sir Richard, it was said, deeply affected by the deserved reproof, acknowledged the child, gave it his name, and brought it up in a manner befitting his own station. From Thomas Egerton, the illegitimate son of the Cheshire knight and a maid-servant, the Dukes of Bridgewater descended, and also the present Earls of Ellesmere and the Lords Egerton of Tatton.

After being " well grounded in Latin and Greek," Thomas Egerton, at the age of sixteen, was sent to Brasenose College, Oxford—the college always favoured by Lancastrians—and after a brilliant University career was admitted to Lincoln's Inn and in due time called to the Bar. He early attracted the notice of Queen Elizabeth by the skill and vigour with which he conducted a case in the Court of the Exchequer against the Crown. " On my troth," the astute sovereign is reported to have said, " he shall never plead against me again," and she made him a Queen's Counsel on the spot, thus securing to the Crown his valuable eloquence and talents. His advancement was rapid, " his handsome person doing him no harm with Queen Elizabeth," and having been successively Solicitor-General and Attorney-General, at the time of Elizabeth's death he was Lord Keeper of the Privy Seal. Shortly after the accession of James I. Egerton was made Lord Chancellor and raised to the peerage as Baron Ellesmere, and when, in 1617, full of years and honours, he resigned office, he was created Viscount Brackley, the King promising him the earldom of Bridgewater. He died in his seventy-fourth year, before the earldom was conferred, but James kept his promise by bestowing it upon his son, John Egerton.

Thomas Egerton " besides being a great lawyer and a judge was an eminent orator, after the fashion of his time. The personal beauty, which he is said to have inherited from his mother he retained in old age, so that many went to the Court of Chancery to look at him. As a man, and in relation to the age in which he lived, his character stands high."

In 1598 Thomas Egerton, four years after he had been made Lord Keeper, received a great acquisition of wealth and land by the death of Richard Brereton, who had married Dorothy, the legitimate daughter of Sir Richard Egerton, and was thus Thomas Egerton's brother-in-law, save for the bar sinister. Being childless, Richard Brereton left all he possessed to the brilliant and successful half-brother of his wife, and from this bequest, nearly two hundred years later, arose the prosperity of Southern Lancashire, for Worsley was one of the Brereton estates. Thomas Egerton gained great wealth in his profession, which he invested in the purchase of estates in Lancashire, Cheshire and elsewhere, thus adding enormously to the property left him by his brother-in-law.

Three Earls of Bridgewater succeeded this famous Lord Chancellor, his son and grandson passing through the troublous times of the Rebellion and the Commonwealth without losing an acre and yet at the same time remaining loyal to the throne. When loyalty to the exiled Stuarts meant sequestration of estates, or the payment of many fines, it is difficult to understand how large landed proprietors like the Earls of Bridgewater escaped ; but escape they did, although the epitaph of the first Earl (the Lord Chancellor's son) records that " he was a dutiful son

to his mother, the Church of England, in her persecution as well as in her great splendour ; a loyal subject to his Sovereign in those worst of times when it was accounted treason not to be a traitor."

The third Earl of Bridgewater seems to have had the ambition of founding Egerton families, for during his lifetime he settled the Worsley estate upon his second son William, and the estate of Tatton upon his third son Thomas. But in his wish to found a family of the Egertons of Worsley, he was disappointed, for although William Egerton married twice he left no male heir, and the property returned to the Bridgewater earldom. Thomas Egerton, however, fulfilled his father's ambition ; and founded the family of the Egertons of Tatton, and it is from him that the present Earl Egerton is descended.

The fourth Earl of Bridgewater, Scroop, the great-great-grandson of the Lord Chancellor, was a courtier, and after holding high offices at Court during the reign of William and Mary, Queen Anne, and the two first Georges, was made Duke of Bridgewater in 1720, " in consideration of his great merits." It was his second son, Francis, who created the Bridgewater Canal.

When Scroop Egerton the first Duke of Bridgewater died in 1745 he left two sons, John and Francis. The latter passed an unhappy and neglected childhood. He was only nine years old at the time of his father's death ; the next year his mother (a daughter of the Duke of Bedford) married Sir Richard Lyttleton, and became so engrossed by her new husband that she seems to have paid no attention or given any care to the training and education of either of her sons. Francis Egerton was a sickly child and was so dull of comprehension that it was believed he was lacking in intellect, and the question was seriously mooted as to whether he should not be excluded from succession to the dukedom on this account. Before so momentous a question could be settled, however, his elder brother, John, died of consumption, and at the age of twelve Francis Egerton became the third and the last Duke of Bridgewater.

(who afterwards became Earl Gower and Marquis of Stafford), roused to a sense of their responsibilites, sent the gawky and ignorant boy abroad, on what was called in those days "the grand tour," with a hope that foreign travel would teach him manners and cultivate his mind. As a further aid in the cultivation of his

ELIZABETH GUNNING, DUCHESS OF HAMILTON AND ARGYLL

For some years it was thought he would ultimately fall a victim to the malady which had killed his brother, and no effort was made either by his mother or his step-father to repair their neglect of his education. As he grew older he threw off the sickliness of his childhood, and when it became evident he was not destined to an early death, his guardians, the Duke of Bedford and Lord Trentham

mind a famous Latin scholar and Eastern traveller, named Wood, was chosen as his tutor. Wood had but lately returned from exploring the ruins of Palmyra, his records of which are still a standard work upon the subject; and although he was a man of the world as well as a scholar, he found his task in moulding and training his "unlicked cub of a Duke" one of supreme difficulty. In Paris the seventeen-year-old Duke flatly declined to learn dancing, and although Wood persuaded him to buy antique marbles and statuary in Rome, " his unlettered and uncultivated Grace was content with paying for them," and so little did he care that " they remained in their original packing cases till after his death." The accomplished and polished tutor had a very uncomfortable time during the two years' tour ; and, as the late Lord Ellesmere remarks, " often wished himself back in the desert he had so lately left."

When the young Duke returned to England, almost as awkward and as ignorant as when he left, there were two years still wanting to the attainment of his majority ; those two years he devoted chiefly to horse-racing and to gambling, with intervals of serious plodding into the details of his vast estates. His coming-of-age was celebrated with all the pomp and circumstance due to his exalted position and great responsibilities, his guardians, the Duke of Bedford and Earl Gower (who had married Lady Louisa Egerton, the Duke's sister), rendered an account of their stewardship, and the young nobleman was his own master. Then, with all the ardour of youth, and with an intensity hitherto unsuspected in his nature, he fell in love.

The object of the young Duke's adoration, Elizabeth Gunning, had turned the heads of half London. In 1751 she and her sister, Maria, had been brought to London by their father, a poor Irish squire. Their surpassing beauty at once captivated the town ; wherever they went crowds flocked to gaze upon them. " They were mobbed at their doors by the multitude eager to catch sight of them, and theatres were crammed when it was known they were to be present." So great was the press of people when the lovely sisters walked in the Mall on Sundays, that George II. ordered a file of guards to keep the way clear for them and protect them from the pressure of the crowd. Never was beauty so triumphant, and a year after they had taken London by storm, Maria, the elder, married the Earl of Coventry, and Elizabeth, the younger, the Duke of Hamilton. The latter marriage set the gossips talking for weeks. Its romantic circumstances are thus related by Horace Walpole, the arch-gossip of his time, who did not approve of either sister, and regarded them both as adventuresses. " The Duke of Hamilton," he says, " fell in love with Elizabeth at a masquerade, and determined to marry her." " Some weeks afterwards," he continues, " his Grace one night being left alone with her, while her mother and sister were at Bedford House, he found himself so impetuous that he sent for a parson. The doctor refused to perform the ceremony without licence or ring. The Duke swore he would send for the Archbishop. At last they were married with a ring of the bed-curtains, at half-an-hour after twelve at night, at Mayfair Chapel. The Scotch are enraged, the women mad, that so much beauty has had its effect ; and what is most silly, my Lord Coventry declares he will marry the other."

When the young Duke of Bridgewater fell in love with Elizabeth Gunning, she was a widow, the Duke of Hamilton, " debauched, extravagant, and equally damaged in fortune and person," having only survived their marriage a short while. His suit was successful, and preparations were already on foot for the celebration of the marriage when the young Duke felt himself obliged to place a serious ultimatum before his betrothed. Scandal for some time had been busy with the name of Lady Coventry, and it had assumed such proportions that the Duke informed the Duchess of Hamilton she must break off all intimacy with her sister upon her marriage with him. At first the Duchess hesitated; then she refused to give up her sister, whereupon the Duke of Bridgewater ended their engagement.

The lovely widow, however, was easily consoled, for the same year she married Colonel Campbell, who ultimately became Duke of Argyll, and thus made Elizabeth Gunning a double Duchess.

Lady Coventry, for whose sake her sister had lost the Bridgewater coronet, died only a year afterwards, a victim not so much of vanity as the custom of her time. The powdered hair then in vogue was trying to the most brilliant complexion, and it was the invariable practice for the ladies of fashion to paint and rouge their faces. Lady Coventry used a pigment which gave a greatly admired whiteness to the complexion, but unhappily it was composed largely of white lead. By its constant use for years her system became impregnated with the deadly mineral, and she died literally of lead-poisoning. It was this Lady Coventry who made the famous "unfortunate" remark to George II. One day at a drawing-room this King asked the beautiful Countess what she most desired to see in the world. "A coronation, your Majesty," was the instant reply.

The news of the Duchess of Hamilton's marriage affected the Duke of Bridgewater deeply, and in order to cloak his disappointment, or to show a pretence of indifference, he gave a great ball, to which the whole world of fashion was invited. This brilliant entertainment may have been meant as a farewell to society, but whether it was given from reasons of pride or for leave-taking, it was the last time he took part in any London gaieties, thenceforward forswearing the world and all its pleasures. He retired to Worsley, not the stately palace of to-day, but an old manor-house on the outskirts of the dreary Chat Moss, surrounded by a wild and desolate country, and "never more had womenkind about him in any capacity whatever, whether social or menial."

At this period, the commerce of Liverpool, although England was in the throes of war, was expanding rapidly, because our battle-ships gave her merchants the highway of the ocean; but the trade of Manchester, which was also developing no less rapidly, was most seriously hampered by lack of means of transport and the execrable roads. The only way Manchester could send her cotton goods to the various markets, eager to buy them, was by packhorses, which went at walking pace in single file along roads that were little better than tracks. In Arthur Young's *Tour through the North of England*, published in 1770, we have an example of the means of communication between Lancashire towns in the "good old days." "I know not in the whole range of language," he says, "terms sufficiently expressive to describe this infernal road. To look over a map, and perceive that it is a principal one, not only to some towns, but even to whole counties, one would naturally conclude it to be at least decent; but let me most seriously caution all travellers who may accidentally purpose to travel this terrible country, to avoid it as they would the devil; for a thousand to one but they break their necks or their limbs by overthrows or breakings-down. They will here meet with ruts, which I actually measured, four feet deep and floating with mud, only from a wet summer. What, therefore, must it be after a winter? The only mending it in places receives is the tumbling-in of some loose stones which serve no other purpose but jolting a carriage in the most intolerable manner. These are not merely opinions but facts, for I actually passed three carts broken down in these eighteen miles of execrable memory."

These " eighteen miles of execrable memory " lay between Wigan and Preston, but the roads round Manchester were not one whit better, with the consequence that the growing trade of the city was cut off from the all-essential supply of coal; although the collieries lay only a few miles from its boundaries. Communication had already been made between Liverpool and Manchester in 1720 by the Mersey and Irwell Navigation Company, by a contrivance of locks and weirs and by cuttings across the bends of the latter river, but " the want of water in drought, and its too great abundance in floods, are circumstances under which this, as well as most other river-navigation, has laboured. It has been an expensive concern, and has at times been more burthensome to its proprietors than useful to the public." At the pit-mouth the price of coal was 10d. for a horse-load of 280 lb., but by the time it had been carried on horses' backs to the river, transferred to the boats of the Mersey and Irwell Navigation Company, slowly tugged by men, and then unloaded and carried by horses again to Manchester, the cost had been more than doubled to the consumer. And not only did the want of communication affect the price of coal, and thus hamper the growing industries of the town, but it also affected the very necessaries of life. Until 1758 there were riots every year in Manchester caused by the dearness of food.

Retiring from the world of fashion at the age of twenty-three to the then desolate region of Worsley, the young Duke naturally sought some distraction for his wounded feelings. Two years previously

his brother-in-law and former guardian Earl Gower (afterwards first Marquis of Stafford) had been keenly interested in a project to unite the rivers Trent and Mersey by a canal which would pass by Chester, Stafford, Derby, and Nottingham. But, notwithstanding Lord Gower's keen interest and his promised financial support, the scheme came to nothing. The Duke of Bridgewater was a constant visitor at Trentham, Lord Gower's stately home in Staffordshire, and there can be but little doubt that the discussion he there heard, of the scheme to unite the two great mercantile ports of Liverpool and Hull by means of a canal, first led him to consider the possibility of applying such a scheme of inland navigation upon a smaller scale. It is thought that although during his continental tour he distressed his learned tutor, Wood, by his lack of interest and appreciation, he was much struck by the system of canals in France and Italy, and that his observations abroad led to the eagerness with which, shortly after he retired to Worsley, he took up the idea of canal-making. Whatever the cause, direct or indirect, within a few months of his retiring from the world the young Duke was applying to Parliament for a Canal Act, authorizing him to build a canal from Worsley to Salford. In applying for this authority the Duke was actuated by a desire to improve his property. He owned coal-mines near the Irwell, but the expensive and cumbersome method of transportation to Manchester, by the Mersey and Irwell Navigation Company as described above, so seriously reduced the profits that at one time the abandonment of the Manchester coal supply from the Duke's estates was seriously considered.

The Duke of Bridgewater's idea was to take his canal down to the Irwell and up again on the other side, by means of locks on both banks of the river, but this scheme was abandoned for another, suggested by that mechanical genius, James Brindley, to whom Lancashire owes so much.

employed by Lord Gower to make the survey. There is little doubt that, when the Liverpool to Hull Canal fell through, Lord Gower directed the Duke of Bridgewater's attention to Brindley, for in July

THE DUKE OF BRIDGEWATER

James Brindley was the son of a poor Derbyshire cotter, a worthless scamp. He had no education, technical or otherwise, but developed his extraordinary mechanical skill with no other help than his own study and observation, and by the time the scheme for the canal between the Mersey and the Trent was being considered, his reputation was such that he was

1759 he paid a visit to the old hall at Worsley, a visit which was of the greatest importance to Lancashire.

Brindley could just read and write, but he could not spell. He had made what he described in his notes as an "ochiler survey" or "a riconnitoring" (meaning an ocular survey or a reconnoitring) of the land over which the Duke proposed to carry his canal; and he drew up a plan which perhaps would excite little or no comment in these times, but was then considered not only amazing and stupendous, but impossible. The Duke's system of locks was to be abandoned, and instead of the canal descending to the Irwell on one side and rising on the other, it was to be carried boldly across the river by stone aqueducts. This scheme aroused both contempt and amusement; it was impossible, the world said, for any navigation to be effected by means of an aqueduct passing over a stream; and the skilled engineers who were called in by the Duke to give an opinion, dismissed the scheme as the notion of an idle dreamer, a veritable castle in the air. But the young Duke believed in the plain, blunt mechanic, and when Brindley, despite the ridicule of the engineers and the proofs they brought against him—on paper—remained unshaken in all the details of the project, the Duke gave him a supreme instance of his belief by starting the works forthwith.

In the history of invention and mechanical enterprise there is no other instance of such supreme confidence, seeing that the Duke alone had to bear the entire expense and face a possible loss.

Amidst a storm of ridicule the works for this gigantic undertaking were begun, and, as they progressed, Brindley's wonderful genius made itself evident at every turn. He tunnelled the hill near Worsley in order to connect the Duke's coal-mines directly with the canal, the coal being thus literally brought by water from the seam itself—great earth embankments kept the water in the canal and when it was found there was a serious leakage, Brindley, not in the least perturbed by a circumstance over which his enemies were already beginning to triumph, applied clay puddle to the embankment and so held in the water. Serious leakage also occurred in the aqueduct itself and in the great masonry works, the water slowly but steadily filtering through the mortar. Brindley promptly invented a new lime, which rendered the mortar water-tight. Nor did his ingenuity exhaust itself upon the canal, the terminus of which at Manchester was at the foot of a hill. By means of ingenious machinery and a crane Brindley hoisted the coals from the barges, through a shaft, to the top of the hill, the buyers thus being saved the trouble and expense of having to carry their coals up the steep incline.

Two years after the work was begun, that is on July 17, 1761, the Duke was fully justified in his confidence in Brindley. On that day the first boat-load of coal passed from the Bridgewater coal-mines at Worsley along the canal until it reached the Irwell at Barton; there it sped smoothly across the much abused aqueduct and so on to Manchester.

The Duke and Brindley became the two men most talked of in the country: they had created one of the wonders of England, and from far and near thousands of people flocked to witness the amazing spectacle of boats sailing across a river. The price of coal in Manchester fell to one half of its former figure, and not only coal but provisions of all kinds. It is said that the cost of building the canal amounted to £1000 a mile.

The success of the canal from Worsley to Manchester encouraged the Duke and Brindley to attack an even more difficult problem—the connection of Liverpool and Manchester. The roads between the two towns were so bad that it cost forty shillings a ton for the transport of goods, and twelve shillings a ton when they were sent by the Mersey and Irwell Navigation Company. Both means of transit were unreliable, as sometimes the roads were impassable, and at others, floods stopped all traffic on the Mersey and Irwell "Navigation." The Duke therefore proposed to build a canal from Longford Bridge to Runcorn, but, despite the success of the first venture, there arose an outcry that Brindley's scheme for making a canal twenty-eight miles in length across bogs, through tunnels, over rivers and valleys, was absolutely impossible. Neither the Duke nor Brindley paid any heed to the false prophets, but they found themselves faced by a much more serious difficulty than the clamours of ignorance.

The Mersey and Irwell Navigation Company considered that it had vested rights in the water traffic between Liverpool and Manchester, and having failed in an attempt to bribe the Duke to abandon the scheme, they made a most determined opposition to it in Parliament. They were joined by several landowners in the district, and Lord Derby's own son led the opposition to the Bill in the House of Commons. In addition to the declared vested rights of the Navigation Company, it was solemnly asserted that the Duke's proposed canal would be a source of great danger to the country through which it would pass, as it would inevitably be the cause of constant floods. But there were many people in the region between Manchester and Liverpool who realized the advantage it would bring to their trade and manufactures, and in consequence there were quite as many petitions in favour of the Bill as there were against it. The House of Commons considered the matter very seriously, and in February 1762 Brindley was examined before a Parliamentary Committee.

Brindley was so illiterate that he could not make drawings or calculations on paper; he always made his plans in his head. He therefore had no evidence to produce before the Committee of the practicability of his scheme, and the story goes that being unable to convince the Committee by his explanations of bridge-building and "puddling," he went out and bought a large cheese which he cut in two and showed the members how he would build the semicircular arches of his bridge; he also gave them a practical demonstration with clay and water of how the water could be kept in the canal, the members learning for the first time the secrets of "puddling."

Despite the strenuous opposition the Bill passed triumphantly, but it was then that the Duke's real difficulties began. Brindley decided on having a continuous level of water until he came to the descent near Runcorn, when the canal was to be taken down by a large number of locks. These required great embankments far larger than the one which excited so much interest and speculation at Barton. Embankments cost a great deal of money, as did also the carrying of the canal over Sales Moor Moss. It was confidently predicted that the canal never would be got across the Moss, and a tall poplar at Dunham Banks to which a board had been fixed by Brindley showing the height at which the canal would run, was called "The Duke's Folly."

Whenever an engineering difficulty presented itself Brindley stayed in bed for two or three days until he had solved it, but so vast an undertaking meant the expenditure of large sums of money in wages. And money began to be very scarce. Brindley's wages were only a guinea a week! The Duke cut down his personal expenses until the whole of his establishment cost no more than four hundred a year. So convinced were all the business men that the canal was impossible, and the Duke would surely ruin himself, that he lost all credit in Manchester and Liverpool, and could not even get a bill for £500 cashed. So reduced were the Duke's credit and his resources that he gave promissory notes for £5, and his agent Gilbert (who was as enthusiastic about canals as his master and Brindley) often had to go amongst the tenantry borrowing a few pounds here and a few pounds there to pay the workmen's wages. The Duke would have been saved all this anxiety as to money for carrying on the construction of the canal, completed as far as Runcorn, but the locks leading down to the Mersey were not finished until five or six years later. These the Duke built from the profits gained by the working portion of the canal. They were opened December 1, 1772, and the *Heart of Oak,* a ship of fifty tons burden, passed from Manchester to Liverpool, amid the cheers and acclamations of thousands of people who lined the banks.

THE DUKE'S CANAL CROSSING THE IRWELL

if he had mortgaged his estates, but this he resolutely declined to do.

Matters were approaching a crisis and it seemed inevitable that the work must be stopped, when the Duke's canal from Worsley to Manchester began to pay a large annual income. The Worsley Canal had thus become a valuable asset, and the Duke, going to London, arranged with no difficulty a loan from Messrs. Child, the bankers. This loan only amounted to little over £25,000.

Five years after the passing of the opposed Bill the Bridgewater Canal was

The Duke of Bridgewater was only thirty-six when this great engineering feat was accomplished: thenceforward he occupied himself in developing the resources which his canals had created. He bought up all the land with coal seams near Worsley, and spent nearly £170,000 in building underground tunnels and canals in his coal-mines. By an ingenious system these canals, which were over forty miles in length, brought the coal from the depths of the mine to the outer world.

As he advanced in years the Duke

grew exceedingly fat, and his dress, which was usually dark brown, became slovenly. He was so careful in his personal expenditure that he gained the reputation of being parsimonious; his one indulgence was in tobacco and snuff. Indoors he smoked, but "out of doors he snuffed, and he would pull huge pinches out of his right waistcoat pocket and thrust the powder up his nose, accompanying the operation with strong snorts."

At Worsley he saw scarcely anybody except Brindley and his agent Gilbert, and on the rare occasions that he went to London "his social intercourse was limited within the circle of a few intimate friends, and for many years he avoided the trouble of maintaining an establishment suited to his station, by an agreement with one of these, who, for a stipulated sum, undertook to provide a daily dinner for his Grace and a certain number of guests. This engagement lasted till a late period of the Duke's life, when the death of the friend ended the contract."

The Duke, from being so much with his canal workmen, was as rough in his speech as they were, and thee'd and thou'd in true Lancashire fashion. He was a silent man and disliked reading, and never wrote a letter if he could possibly avoid doing so. As it has been said before, he carried his aversion to women, created by the love disappointment in his youth, to such lengths that there were no women servants either at Worsley or at his house in London. But notwithstanding his eccentricities the Duke, although he exacted a full measure of work from his people, was a kind and a just master. He was one of the first coal-owners to provide good housing for his colliers, schools for their children, and shops and markets where they could buy good food at reasonable prices. One of his great delights was to travel from Worsley to Manchester in one of the "fly-boats" as they were called, which he had established for passenger traffic along the canal. Dressed in a shabby brown or drab suit, burly, uncouth of speech, the Duke would sit among the other passengers chatting with this one and that, his keen eye meanwhile taking in all the details of the canal management. Although his name was one to conjure with in the district round about Manchester, personally he was not very well known in the towns. Dr. Smiles gives an amusing instance of this ignorance. The Duke, he says, often went to Manchester by his canal boats "to watch how the coal trade was going on. When the passengers alighted at the coal-wharf there were many poor people about, wheeling away their barrow-loads of coal. One of the Duke's regulations was, that whenever any deficiency in the supply was apprehended, those people who came with their wheel-barrows, baskets, and aprons for small quantities should be served first, and wagons, carts, and horses sent away until the supply was again abundant. The number of small customers thus resorted to the Duke's coal-yard rendered it a somewhat busy scene, and the Duke liked to look on and watch the proceedings. One day a customer of the poorer sort, having got his sack filled, looked about for some one to help it on to his back. He observed a stoutish man standing near dressed in a spencer with dark drab small clothes. 'Heigh! mester!' said the man, 'coom gi'e me a lift wi' this sack o' coal on to my shou'der!' Without any hesitation, the person in the spencer gave the man the required 'lift,' and off he trudged with the load. Some one near, who had witnessed the transaction, ran up to the man and asked, 'Dun' yo know who's that yo've been speaking tull?' 'Naw; who is he?'

'Why, it's the Duke hissen.' 'The Duke!' exclaimed the man, dropping the bag of coals from his shoulders. 'Hey! what'll he do at me? Maun a goo an' ax his pardon?' But the Duke had disappeared."

The Duke died in 1803, and with him ended the short line of the Dukes of Bridgewater. He left a certain portion of his estate to his nephew the Marquis of Stafford and first Duke of Sutherland, with a trust called the Bridgewater Trust by which the canal property was to devolve upon the Duke's second son at his father's death. The first Duke of Sutherland, whose father was the Earl Gower who had so quickened the Duke of Bridgewater's interest in canals, died in 1833, and his second son, Lord Francis Leveson-Gower, entered into possession of his great-uncle's magnificent legacy. He assumed the family name of the Bridgewaters and for thirteen years was known as Lord Francis Egerton. In 1846 he was created Earl of Ellesmere, and was the grandfather of the present owner of Worsley.

For seventy years the Bridgewater Trust was one of the most important factors in the development of the industry of South and South-east Lancashire. In 1873 it was taken over by a company.

Judging from the characteristics displayed by the Duke of Bridgewater during the brief time he led the life of a man of wealth and fashion in London, it may be justly argued that, but for the refusal of the Duchess of Hamilton to renounce the society of her sister Lady Coventry, and the Duke's consequent breaking-off of their marriage, the Worsley and Bridgewater Canals would probably never have been made, and if they had been carried out it would have been many years later. His great-nephew, the first Earl of Ellesmere wrote: "We are far from supposing, that if he had never lived England could long have remained contented with primitive modes of intercourse inadequate to her growing energies. Brindley himself might have found other patrons, or, if he had pined for want of such, Smeatons, Fultons, and Telfords might have arisen to supply his place. But for the happy conjunction, however, of such an instrument, such a hand to wield it, inland navigation might long have had to struggle with the timidity of capitalists, and for a long time, at least, would perhaps have crept along obsequious to the inequalities of surface, and the sinuosities of natural water courses. When we trace on the map the present artificial arterial system of Britain . . . when we reflect on the rapidity of the creation, how soon the junction of the Worsley coal-field with its Manchester market was followed by that of Liverpool with Hull, and Lancashire with London, we cannot but think the Duke's matrimonial disappointment ranks with other cardinal passages in the lives of eminent men—with the majority of nine which prevented the projected emigration of Cromwell, and the hurricane which scattered Admiral Christian's fleet, and drove back to the Downs the vessel freighted with Sir Arthur Wellesley and his fortune."

The benefit the Duke of Bridgewater conferred upon Manchester and Liverpool is exemplified by Dr. Smiles in a contrast between Lancashire and Wiltshire. He says that before the Duke's canal was constructed "the small quantity of Manchester woollens and cottons manufactured for exportation, was carried on horses' backs to Bewdley and Bridgnorth, on the Severn, from whence they were floated down that river to Bristol, then the chief sea-port on the west coast. No sooner, however, was the new water road opened out than the Bridgnorth pack-horses were taken off, and the whole export trade of the district concentrated in Liverpool. The additional accommodation required for the increased business of the port was promptly provided as occasion required. New harbours and docks were built; and before many years had passed Liverpool had shot far ahead of Bristol, and became the chief port on the west coast, if not in all England. Had Bristol been blest with the Duke of Bridgewater, the result might have been altogether different; and the valleys of Wilts, the coal and iron fields of Wales, and the estuary of the Severn might have been what South Lancashire and the Mersey are now. Were statues any proof of merit the Duke would long since have had the highest statue in Manchester, as well as Liverpool, erected to his memory, and that of Brindley would have been found standing by his side."

The last Duke of Bridgewater has been called " the first great Lancashire man," and, as his great-nephew said of him, he " more than any other single man contributed to lay the foundations of prosperity of Manchester, Liverpool, and the surrounding districts. The cutting of the canal from Worsley to Manchester conferred upon that town the immediate benefit of a cheap and abundant supply of coal; and when Watt's steam engine became the great motive power in manufactures, such supply became absolutely essential to its existence as a manufacturing town. Being the first to secure this great advantage Manchester thus got the start forward which she has never lost."

It is curious to reflect that the breaking off of a young man's marriage laid the foundations of a prosperity which has not only enriched millions of Lancashire men, but has enriched the whole country, and has given Lancashire the pre-eminence she holds amongst all the English counties. Few heroes or statesmen have more justly earned the title of " Great " than Francis Egerton, the third and last Duke of Bridgewater.

GEORGE FOX, THE QUAKER

QUAKERISM had its beginnings in Lancashire, where it took a very firm hold in the early years of the Commonwealth. Its founder, George Fox, was the son of a Puritan weaver, Christopher Fox—who was called "Righteous Christer"—and was born at Drayton-in-the-Clay, in Leicestershire, in 1624. His parents, who seem to have been in prosperous circum stances, intended him for the ministry of the Church of England, an avocation for which his gravity of mind and religious bent particularly suited him. "But others," he said, "persuaded to the contrary," and he was apprenticed to a shoemaker instead. At the age of nineteen an incident occurred which shaped the whole course of his after-life. His cousin and another Puritan youth wished to initiate him in the practice of

GEORGE FOX

drinking healths. Fox paid his share for the drinks and left the company. He spent the night in prayer, and felt a Divine call to leave his home. "At the command of God," he says, "on the 9th of the 7th month, 1643, I left my relations and broke off all familiarity and fellowship with old or young."

Fox was absent from his family for nearly four years, wandering about from place to place, a victim of the deepest religious melancholy. On his return, they urged him to marry or join the Parliamentary forces, but he refused both propositions, being, as he expressed it, "tender," that is, religiously affected. A prey to religious doubts of the gloomiest nature, Fox went from church to conventicle, from conventicle to church, ever seeking the truth, but finding no consolation. An old vicar, whom he consulted upon his trouble, advised him "to take tobacco and sing psalms." "Tobacco was a thing I did not love," said Fox, "and psalms I was not in a state to sing." Another advised physic and bleeding, but neither relieved Fox's doubts. Gradually out of this gloom and wrestling of the Spirit, there came the conviction to this weaver's son that he had a Divine call to go forth and spread the Word, as he interpreted it. This was the beginning of the foundation of the Society of the Children of Light, Fox's own name for his followers. Later, they were known as the Society of Friends. The name Quaker was originally a nickname applied to the new sect in contempt and derision. It came from Justice Bennett, who, when Fox was had up before him at Derby for brawling in church and had bidden him "tremble at the Name of the Lord," had retorted upon Fox with the word "Quaker."

Fox immediately began preaching his new doctrines up and down the country, in season and out of season, but he succeeded in forcing them upon the public attention. His religion was eminently practical, and took little concern in any accuracy of belief that was not accompanied by righteousness of life.

Fox's uncouthness was startling. "He was the very incarnation of plain speaking, and went right to the heart of things. To take the hat off in honour of a fellow creature seemed to him a species of idolatry, so he refused to render "hat honour" to anyone, and addressed "thee" and "thou" alike to high and low. He refused to take oaths of any kind. He refused to bear arms or pay tithes. This plain, sober-living countryman, who had no awe of dignitaries before him, was to be a trouble and a stumbling-block to the authorities. There was no common ground between them. He held the virtues of the Spirit to be higher than the rulings of the law or the letter of the Scriptures. Authority he set at naught, for he felt he had the certain word of the Lord to deliver to his fellow men. So he went into the courts of law and exhorted judges to act justly, he bade publicans not to make men drunk, he declaimed against May games and feasts, he stood in the market-place and denounced the frauds of the hucksters, he cried out against mountebanks and music, he exhorted schoolmasters and heads of families to bring up the children committed to them in the fear of the Lord. But that which chiefly excited his indignation was what he called the black, earthy spirit of the priests. The church bell had no sweet sound for his ears, but "was just like a market bell to gather people together, that the priest might expose his wares for sale."

It was in 1652 that George Fox paid his first visit to Lancashire and there formed a friendship which had great influence on Quakerism in that county. Coming from Yorkshire, Fox felt "moved by the Lord to ascend the very great and high hill of Pendle," and from there looked down upon a place which was the scene of so many striking passages in the early history of the Society of Friends—Swarthmoor Hall, on the north side of Ulverston. This ancient house belonged to Thomas Fell, a barrister of Lincoln's Inn, who had supported the Parliament throughout the Civil War, and in 1645 was one of the members for Lancaster. Later, he became a judge, and was afterwards made Chancellor of the Duchy of Lancaster. Entering the church at Newton-in-Cartmell, Fox began to preach, an interference that was neither appreciated by the clergyman nor the congregation; the latter dragged him from the church and finally threw him over a stone wall. Shortly after this we find him at Swarthmoor, again in dispute with the clergyman. Margaret Fell, the wife of the judge, was a remarkable woman; her grandmother, Anne Askew, had been burnt at the stake for her religious convictions in the reign of Henry VIII., and there was a strong religious bias in the whole family. The perpetual curate at Ulverston, William Lampitt, was what was known as a "ranter," and Mrs. Fell had fallen completely under his influence. But, by degrees, Fox's teaching exerted a regulative influence over her mind, and she became not only his ardent follower, but his right hand in the organization of his society. Judge Fell never became one of the Friends, but he always treated them with the greatest kindness.

An unseemly scene occurred in Ulverston

Church during this first visit of George Fox to Swarthmoor. This is Fox's own description of what occurred, and it shows vividly the bitter feeling he aroused in his adversaries—

"On a lecture day I was moved to go to the steeple-house at Ulverston, where there were abundance of professors, priests and people. I went up near to Priest Lampitt, who was blundering on in his preaching; and after the Lord had opened my mouth to speak, John Sawrey, the justice, came to me and said: 'If I would speak according to the Scripture I should speak.' I admired at him for speaking so to me, for I did speak according to the Scriptures, and bring the Scriptures to prove what I had to say; for I had something to speak to Lampitt and to them. Then he said that I should not speak, contradicting himself. . . . The people were quiet and heard me gladly, until this Justice Sawrey, who was the first stirrer-up of cruel persecution in the north, incensed them against me, and set them on to hate, beat, and bruise me. Thus, on a sudden the people were in a rage, and fell upon me in the steeple-house before his face; they knocked me down, kicked me, trampled upon me; and so great was the uproar that some people tumbled over their seats for fear. At last he came and took me from the people, let me out of the steeple-house, and put me in the hands of the constables and other officers, bidding them whip me out of this town. They led me about a quarter of a mile, some taking hold by my collar and some by my arms and shoulders, and shook and dragged me along. Many friendly people being come to the market, and some to the steeple-house to hear me, divers of these they knocked down also and broke their heads, so that the blood ran down from several

of them; and Judge Fell's son running after to see what they would do with me, they threw him into a ditch of water, some of them crying, 'Knock the teeth out of his head.' Now, when they hauled me to the common moss-side, a multitude of people following, the constables and other officers gave me some blows over my back with their willow-rods, and so thrust me among the rude multitude, who, having furnished themselves, some with staves, some with hedge-stakes, and others with holm or holly-bushes, fell upon me and beat me on my head, arms and shoulders, till they had deprived me of sense, so that I fell down on the wet common. When I recovered again and saw myself lying in a watery common, and the people about me, I lay still a little while; and the power of the Lord sprang through me, and the eternal refreshings refreshed me, so that I stood up again in the strengthening power of the Eternal God; and stretching out my arms among them, I said, with a loud voice, 'Strike again; here are my arms, my head, and my cheeks.' There was in the company a mason, a professor, but a rude fellow; he with his walking rule-staff gave me a blow with all his might just over the back of my hand as it was stretched out; with which blow my hand was so bruised, and my arm so benumbed that I could not draw it into me again; so that some of the people cried out, 'He hath spoiled his hand for ever having the use of it any more.' But I looked at it in the love of God (for I was in the love of God to them that had persecuted me), and after a while the Lord's power sprang through me again, and through my hand and arm, so that in a moment I recovered strength in my hand and arm in the sight of them all. They then began to fall out among themselves, and some of them came to me and said if I would give them money they would secure me from the rest. But I was moved of the Lord to declare to them the word of life, and showed them their false Christianity, and the faults of their priests' ministry; telling them that they were more like heathens and Jews than true Christians. Then was I moved of the Lord to come up again through the midst of the people, and go into Ulverston market. As I went, there met me a soldier with a sword by his side: 'Sir,' said he to me, 'I see you are a man and I am ashamed and grieved that you should be thus abused;' and he offered to assist me in what he could. But I told him the Lord's power was over all; so I walked through the people in the market, and none had power to touch me then. But some of the market people, abusing some Friends in the market, I turned me about and saw this soldier among them with his naked rapier, whereupon I ran in amongst them, and catching hold of his hand that his rapier was in I bade him put up his sword again if he would along with me; for I was willing to draw him out from the company lest some mischief should be done. A few days after seven men fell upon this soldier and beat him cruelly because he

SWARTHMOOR HALL

had taken part with Friends and me; for it was the manner of the persecutors of that county for twenty or forty people to run upon one man. And they fell so upon Friends in many places, that they could hardly pass the highways—stoning, beating, and breaking their heads. When I came to Swarthmoor, I found the Friends there, dressing the heads and hands of Friends and friendly people which had been broken or hurt that day, by the professors and hearers of Lampitt the priest. My body and arms were black, yellow, and blue with the blows and bruises I received amongst them that day. Now began the priest to prophesy again, that within half a year we should be all put down and gone."

As the result of his plain speaking at Ulverston, Fox was summoned to the Lancaster Assizes to answer the charge of blasphemy. Forty of the local clergy, with the Vicar of Lancaster at their head, appeared against him. But, notwithstanding the array of theological argument, the charge against Fox could not be substantiated, and one of the magistrates—Colonel West—told him that if he had anything to say to the people he might freely speak it. Fox says that "he was moved by the Lord" to speak, and for the first time in its history the old Crown Court heard the declaration of a religious creed.

Swarthmoor Hall became the headquarters of the Society of the Friends. The travelling preachers—of whom Fox had thirty in 1658, and double that number two years later—sent in their reports to Margaret Fell; and there, at his own expense, Fox built and endowed a meeting-house. In spite of all persecution the Society of Friends continued to increase, and on more than one occasion George Fox saw the Protector, Oliver Cromwell, and urged that the persecution against them might cease. His last interview with Cromwell was three days before that remarkable man died. A month later Judge Fell also died, and was buried beneath his pew in Ulverston Church by torchlight.

Whilst Fox was at Swarthmoor, in 1660, constables were sent to arrest him upon a warrant signed by Henry Porter, Mayor of Lancaster, a man who, like so many others at that time, after having been a strenuous supporter of the Parliament during the Civil War, had veered round and become an equally strenuous supporter of Charles II. The constables carried Fox to Ulverston, where he was kept under a guard of sixteen men, some of whom sat in the chimney lest he should escape that way. When he was brought before the Mayor of Lancaster, Fox was charged with being an enemy of the King, and of endeavouring to raise a new war and embrue the nation in blood. Upon this charge he was committed to prison. Margaret Fell immediately issued an indignant protest against the proceedings of Justice Porter, and this protest being of no avail she instantly proceeded to London to lay this injustice before the King himself. Fox's account shows that the life of the time-server was not an easy one—

"When Justice Porter heard of her going he vapoured that he would go and meet her in the gate. But when he came before the King, having been a zealous man for the Parliament against the King, several of the courtiers spoke to him concerning the plunder of their houses; so that he quickly had enough of the court and returned to Lancaster . . . there I sent him a letter which still further disquieted him, for I reminded him how fierce he had been against the King and his party, how that when he held the castle for the Parliament against the King, he was so rough and fierce against them that favoured the King that he said, 'he would leave them neither dog nor cat if they did not bring him provisions into the castle.' I asked him also whose great buck's horns those were in his house, and where he had both that and the wainscoting from, that he ceiled his house withal; had he them in from Hornby Castle?"

Justice Porter does not seem to have been able to reply to these charges, and was doubtless greatly relieved to find that Margaret Fell had obtained an order from Charles II. that Fox should be removed to London for trial. The writ for his removal was sent to Lancaster; but for the next six months there were heated discussions and arguments among the local authorities as to the escort which nation in blood. No one appeared against Fox; the matter therefore was referred to the King, who ordered his release. Three years later Fox was once more brought up at Lancaster for having refused to take the oath at a meeting of justices at Holker Hall. At these assizes he likewise refused to take the oath and was committed to prison. At the following assizes he was brought up again; and

QUAKER MEETING-HOUSE AT FRANDLY, NEAR WARRINGTON, AND THE OAK TREE UNDER WHICH GEORGE FOX PREACHED IN 1660

should take Fox to London. The duty was obviously the sheriff's, but Fox finally relieved that gentleman of the difficulty by undertaking to carrying his own warrant to London.

Some weeks later the judges at Westminster were greatly surprised to see a grave, plainly dressed man, wearing his hat, walk into their court, and quietly draw from his pocket a writ which charged him with wishing to embrue the again there was the same argument about the removal of his hat and his refusal to take the oath. He was remanded to the next assizes, but before they were due Margaret Fell had also been arrested for refusal to take the oath, and committed to prison in Lancaster Castle.

In September 1664, George Fox and Margaret Fell were brought up together, whereupon Fox begged the judge "to send some one to see my prison, which was so bad that they would put no creature they had in it. . . . Some of the justices went up to see it, but when they came they dar'st hardly go into it for the floor was so bad and dangerous and the place was open to wind and rain." The proceedings were a repetition of the former assizes ; Fox refused to take the oath and was remanded to the next assizes. Colonel Kirby, the sheriff, gave the jailor orders " to keep him close and suffer no flesh alive to come at him, for he is not fit to be discoursed with by men. Then I was put into a tower where the smoke of the other prisoners came up so thick that it stood as dew upon the walls ; sometimes it was so thick that I could scarcely see the candle that it burned, and I being locked under three locks, the under-jailor, when the smoke was great, would hardly be persuaded to come up to unlock one of the outermost doors for fear of the smoke, so that I was almost smothered. Besides, it rained in upon my bed . . . in this manner did I lie all that long cold winter till the next assizes ; in which time I was so starved with cold and rain, and my body so greatly swelled and my limbs much benumbed." Margaret Fell also complained of the state of her prison.

At the March assizes in 1665, a sentence of *præmunire* was passed on George Fox and Margaret Fell, which meant the forfeiture of their estates and imprisonment during the King's pleasure. Fox was sent to Scarborough Castle, where he was imprisoned for two years ; Margaret Fell was kept at Lancaster for four years. The year after her release she and Fox were married. Margaret Fell was considerably older than Fox, and had been a widow for eleven years ; but the union of these two who had worked and suffered together for the cause was singularly appropriate, and for the twenty-one years

it lasted was one of unalloyed happiness to the husband and wife, and a great strength and support to the Society of Friends. Three years after their marriage the *præmunire* against them both was annulled, and their estates were restored to them.

Gradually the persecution of the Quakers ceased, the lawyers being compelled, despite the repressive legislation against Nonconformist sects, to admit that their meetings were legal. At one time there were four thousand five hundred Quakers in prison in England and Wales, two hundred and seventy of these being in Lancaster Castle. Fourteen years later Fox thus records the change in public opinion. He visited Lancaster, and " I found the town full of people, for it was both fair time and the train-bands were met upon a general muster. Many Friends were also in town from several parts of the county, because the quarterly meeting was to be there next day. I stayed two nights and a day at Lancaster, and visited Friends both at their men's and women's meetings, which were very full, large, and peaceful, for the Lord's power was over all and none meddled with us." The rest of George Fox's life was passed between Swarthmoor and London, where he died in Gracechurch Street in 1690, being then sixty-seven. Margaret Fox lived on at Swarthmoor, dying there in 1702 in the eighty-eighth year of her age.

For many years after their deaths the memory of this man and woman who had suffered all for conscience' sake was truly cherished in Lancaster, which had been one of the first towns where a building had been erected for a Quakers' meeting-house. The lintel of the present building shows that it was originally erected in 1677. In 1680 the mayor ordered the door to be locked and set a guard before it, but the Lancaster Quakers—as was their custom when their meeting-houses were shut up or demolished—met in the lane outside. The new meeting-house was built in the spring of 1708. Old William Stout, whose autobiography gives such vivid pictures of life in Lancaster, says: " In the spring of 1708 our meeting-house

THE CHAPEL FOX BUILT AT SWARTHMOOR

not being capable to entertain the general meeting for the four northern counties, it was resolved to pull it down and build it nigh double to what it was, which was committed to Robert Lawson and my care, and in the time of building our meeting was kept in my dwelling house. We got it built and finished in about six months as far as its galleries and ceiling, to the great satisfaction of our friends in the county and others, the whole charge whereof was one hundred and eighty pounds which was thought moderate." William Stout also tells us that there were mostly "forty or fifty Quakers at a time" imprisoned in Lancaster Castle, and amongst them was John Lawson, who administered to many of the imprisoned Quakers. It was to his house in St.

Leonard's Gate that Fox went on his first visit to Lancaster. For speaking in the constable house at Lancaster, Lawson, after being imprisoned until the assizes, was fined twenty pounds, and, on his refusal to pay, was sent to prison, where he remained for nearly a year. It was he who gave the Quakers their cemetery on Lancaster Moor in the year 1660, " for the burial-place of the people of God, Children of Light, such as lived and abode in the truth of God, and for no other purpose whatever."

Quakers in other parts of Lancashire were not all so fortunate with regard to meeting-houses as their brethren at Lancaster. Many of the communities were poor, and, consequently, were unable to afford a building; in other places their numbers were so small that a room in a private house sufficed for their needs. In those communities where poverty made a meeting-house an impossibility, their services were conducted in the open air after the manner instituted by George Fox. But in some places where sectarianism was not strong they were allowed the use of chapels belonging to other Dissenting bodies, as is shown by the notice below, of a Quaker meeting at Ashton in 1822.

Some Members of the Society of FRIENDS, (or People called Quakers,) intend to hold a Public Meeting for Worship, at *the Methodist Meeting House in Ashton tomorrow Evening at Seven O'Clock*

when the company of those who incline to attend will be acceptable.

9 Month 8 1822

NOTICE OF A QUAKER MEETING IN 1822

THE GREAT DUKE of LANCASTER

JOHN-O'GAUNT

OF the many sons of King Edward III., none have left so deep an impression upon history, or occupied so important a place as John of Gaunt, Duke of Lancaster. Even at this distance of time, although the researches of the historians have proved that his character was by no means beyond reproach, the glamour of the martial age in which he lived still clings about his name, which has a lasting monument in the tower, and the magnificent gateway of Lancaster Castle, both built by him.

John of Gaunt was the fourth son of Edward III., and was born at Ghent in Flanders. It was then the custom to call princes by the name of the place in which they chanced to be born, and the future Duke of Lancaster was called John of Ghent, which became corrupted into John of Gaunt. He was born during an interval between two campaigns in the ceaseless wars that raged between England and France in the reign of Edward III., when his mother Philippa had been left at Ghent during the temporary absence of her husband in England; and from this circumstance in later years arose a story as to the legitimacy of his birth.

When he was two years old he was created Earl of Richmond by his father; and when he was fifteen entered upon a career which reads like a romance told by some old chronicler. At an age when princes of to-day are still at school, he and his brother Lionel, Duke of Clarence, accompanied their kinsman Henry, Duke of Lancaster, in an expedition to aid the King of Navarre against the King of France. Henry of Lancaster was John of Gaunt's third cousin, being descended like him from King Henry III., and was regarded throughout Western Europe as a perfect knight. He was brave, courteous, charitable and just, and at once magnificent and personally temperate in his habits. In addition, he was so renowned a captain that he was called the "father of soldiers," and the noblest youths of France and Spain were sent to learn the art of war under his banner. His knowledge of public affairs was no less remarkable than his military talents. He was a wise councillor and held the entire confidence and deep affection of Edward III., himself a brilliant politician and soldier. It is probable, therefore, that John of Gaunt and his brother were placed under the charge of their kinsman that they might be trained in all those complicated matters which in those days of chivalry filled a knight's career. This expedition in aid of the King of Navarre, however, gave the young princes no actual experience of warfare, for ere the English forces could join those of their ally he had patched up a hasty peace.

Those were strenuous times for the armour-clad knights and their followers; and, having returned to England, John of Gaunt very shortly afterwards accompanied his father to Calais, and had his first taste of fighting in a raid made from there into French territory. This was in November 1355, and on the 20th of January in the following year, after a hasty march to the north, the young Prince saw Edward Baliol surrender the crown of Scotland to his father after a brief campaign which was his first experience of actual warfare.

John of Gaunt seems to have been brought up under the care of Henry, Duke of Lancaster, and whether it was from affection, or, as most of his historians relate, from ambition, he married the Duke's second daughter, Blanche, when he was little more than nineteen. Two years after this marriage Henry of Lancaster died, and John of Gaunt, in right of his wife, succeeded to one half of his great estates. Within a year he acquired the whole of the Lancastrian possessions, owing to the death of Maud, his wife's sister and elder daughter of the late duke. He was then created Duke of Lancaster, and resided for some time at Lancaster Castle.

Perhaps the most romantic part of John of Gaunt's career was his campaign in Spain. Pedro the Cruel, King of Castile, had been driven from his kingdom by Henry of Trastamare, and taking refuge at Bordeaux, where Edward the Black Prince was then residing, succeeded in persuading that great soldier to help him to regain the Castilian throne.

The Black Prince asked his father, Edward III., for help, and help being forthcoming, John of Gaunt was despatched with an army, which he led over the Pyrenees into Spain after joining his brother the Black Prince. The English forces marched through Navarre into the kingdom of Castile, and there, after many delays, marches and counter-marches, a great battle took place.

The English vanguard was led by John of Gaunt; that of Castile by the renowned Bertrand du Guesclin, who was famous as a knight and a warrior throughout Christendom. John of Gaunt's onslaught was so successful that the Castilian vanguard was swept away and the great du Guesclin was taken prisoner. In the meantime the Black Prince, who was engaging the main body of the enemy, was in difficulties, and John of Gaunt hastening to his assistance the battle was won. This battle of Najera replaced Pedro the Cruel upon his throne, but it brought no advantage to the English, as the Castilian monarch, with singular effrontery, declined to fulfil any of the promises he had made when seeking the aid of the Black Prince. The Black Prince and his brother vainly waited for Pedro to fulfil his engagements: the soldiers were unpaid and could not be disbanded; provisions were short; therefore the English forces occupied the town of Valladolid, intending to wait until the money owing to them was paid by Pedro. The latter, however, made no effort, and suddenly sickness broke out amongst the English forces. So rapidly did it spread that scarcely a fifth of the army is said to have survived. The Black Prince himself was stricken down; retreat through Spain therefore became essential, and the two brothers, with the remnants of their forces, succeeded in reaching Bordeaux after terrible sufferings and deprivation, the faithless Pedro making no attempt to assist them. Then followed more fighting in France for John of Gaunt, and it was during his absence in that country that his wife, Blanche of Lancaster, died of the plague.

It was in one of the campaigns in France that John of Gaunt played a part which was dear to the writers of mediaeval romances. The city of Limoges, which then belonged to the English, had been delivered up to the French through the treachery of its bishop. The Black Prince was then his father's lieutenant in the French provinces which were owned by England, and the news of the surrender of Limoges roused him to fury. A large force was instantly despatched, the city was completely invested, and after a siege of only six days the English entered, having undermined the walls and made great breaches in them. No quarter was given and 3,000 of the inhabitants were put to the sword, but the men-at-arms of the garrison resisted valiantly. It was the custom in the days of chivalry, as a mark of honour to a worsted foe, to allow the leaders of a beleaguered force to settle the issue by single combat. In admiration of their brave resistance the men-at-arms at Limoges were allowed to go scatheless

on condition that their three leaders met three of the English knights in single combat. The knights chosen on the English side were the Duke of Lancaster, his brother the Earl of Cambridge, and the Earl of Pembroke. Each of the French knights was defeated, and thus became the prisoner of his conqueror until he was released on the payment of a heavy ransom. The bishop who had betrayed the town to the French was taken prisoner, and so infuriated was the Black Prince by his treachery, that he would have had him instantly put to death, but John of Gaunt begged his life.

The Black Prince's health had never recovered from the sickness he contracted during his ill-fated Spanish expedition, and in 1371 he was ordered by his doctors to return to England. He left the Duke of Lancaster as his lieutenant in France, and it was during this representation of his brother that he made his second marriage which brought him again into close connection with Spain.

Pedro the Cruel had died, and upon his death his former adversary, Henry of Trastamare, had recovered the throne of Castile. Pedro's two daughters, Constance and Isabella, had taken refuge at Bayonne, and acting on the advice, it is said, of the French barons, John of Gaunt married the elder, Constance, whilst his brother, the Earl of Cambridge, married the younger sister. The two brothers with their wives returned to England, where the marriages seem to have been celebrated a second time, for it was only after their return to England, that John of Gaunt first styled himself, in right of his wife, King of Castile.

In the year following this marriage a determined effort was made on the part of the French to rid their country of the English. They overran the provinces of Aquitaine and Poitou; the Duke of

Lancaster was at once appointed Captain general and hastily despatched to France at the head of a well equipped army. But although a valiant and competent soldier, John of Gaunt had no capacity as a general. Instead of striking a decisive blow, as he could easily have done, he simply marched his men from Calais to Bordeaux, and as his road lay through a hostile country it was hardly surprising that he fell into a trap. He was allowed to proceed without opposition, but, throughout the whole march his rear was harassed by a body of the enemy whose numbers increased, whilst the number of his own troops gradually diminished. This march lasted from August until the end of the year 1374. He reached the desolate mountain regions of the Auvergne in the beginning of the winter, and here his losses of men and horses were so enormous that he had to abandon his baggage. With the remnants of his half-starved army Lancaster was not in a position to attempt the conquest of Aquitaine. But a curious custom obtained in mediaeval warfare. There being practically no roads, campaigning was out of the question in the winter, and contending generals therefore made engagements when the encounter should take place. Thus, Lancaster made an arrangement with the Duke of Anjou that the armies should meet in battle in the following April. When April came, however, Lancaster seems to have forgotten the engagement, for he returned to England. The French regarded this action as a deliberate breach of faith ; and, again over-running Aquitaine, they conquered the whole province.

Lancaster's return to England had been brought about by the condition of political affairs. His father, Edward III., was rapidly sinking into a premature old age ; his elder brother, the Black Prince, was stricken by the mortal illness contracted in Spain. Neither, therefore, could attend to public affairs, and the Duke took their place. But Lancaster's government was unpopular, owing to increased taxation, his ignominious failure in the conduct of the war with France, and a general belief that the new Ministers appointed by him were embezzling the country's revenues.

The next heir to the throne, after the death of the Black Prince, was his son, Richard of Bordeaux, and seeing that only this child stood between Lancaster and the throne of England, his conduct of affairs gave rise to the suspicion that he was aiming at the Crown itself. The Black Prince himself seems to have shared this suspicion of his brother, for summoning all his failing strength he supported the Parliament in their demand for a reform of abuses. This Parliament was called the " Good Parliament," because of the many reforms that it instituted.

Lancaster's ministers and supporters in the Government were either impeached or dismissed from office. But whilst the Parliament were pursuing their work the Black Prince died, to the grief of the whole nation. The " Good Parliament" petitioned the aged king to recognize Richard of Bordeaux as heir-apparent to the Crown. The young Prince was thereupon presented to them and formally acknowledged by the king as his heir. This action was taken in order to prevent any usurpation by the Duke of Lancaster. The foremost promoter of the reforms and of the acknowledgment of the young prince was William of Wykeham, Bishop of Winchester, and when the " Good Parliament" was dissolved, a month after the death of the Black Prince, and Lancaster once more obtained the supreme powers, the whole weight of his resentment fell upon this prelate. Trumped-up charges of maladministration were brought against him; he was deprived of his temporalities and forbidden to come within twenty miles of the Court.

It was popularly reported, however, that Lancaster's deadly hatred of the Bishop arose, not from his political position but because of the publication by the Bishop of a secret confided to him by Queen Philippa on her deathbed. It was said that the Queen had given birth to a female child at Ghent, which she accidentally overlaid, and that dreading Edward III's. anger, she had substituted for the dead child the son of a Flemish woman. On her deathbed the Queen had confessed this secret to the Bishop of Winchester with the injunction that, should there be a prospect of John of Gaunt succeeding to the throne, he should make the truth known. The Bishop is supposed to have told the story when suspicions were rife that Lancaster was plotting to remove his nephew, Richard of Bordeaux. The story was doubtless a fabrication, but the fact that it found general acceptance clearly indicates the deep unpopularity of the Duke, and the general suspicions as to his intentions.

John of Gaunt was one of the strongest supporters of John Wycliffe, the first English Reformer, but they did not regard the cause which united them from the same point of view. All Lancaster's efforts were directed to restrain the temporal power of the priests; Wycliffe's dream was to reform the priesthood; "Lancaster, whose object was to humiliate it, found a strange ally in Wycliffe, whose aim was to purify the Church—regarding almost with sympathy the Court of Rome as the only counterbalance to the power of the bishops at home. Corrupt in his life, narrow and unscrupulous in his policy, he obtained

some of his ablest support from a secular priest of irreproachable character. Lancaster, feudal to the core, resented the official arrogance of the prelates and the large share which they drew to themselves of the temporal power. Wycliffe dreamed of restoring by apostolical poverty its long lost apostolical purity to the clergy. From points so opposite, and with aims so contradictory, were they united to reduce the wealth and humble the pride of the English hierarchy." When Wycliffe was summoned to answer charges of heresy before the bishops, Lancaster, realizing that it was a subtle challenge by his enemies, the great Churchmen, to himself, accompanied the Reformer to his trial. A dispute speedily arose as to whether Wycliffe had a right to sit or not, which came to a crisis through Lancaster threatening the Bishop of London with personal violence. A riot occurred, and such was the Duke's unpopularity that he only succeeded in making his escape with some difficulty. One of his retainers was badly injured, and the mob, marching to his palace at the Savoy, reversed his coat-of-arms as a mark of indignity. Lancaster's indignation against the city of London for this treatment knew no bounds, and by his persuasion the King dismissed the Mayor and Corporation, and replaced them by others. Shortly afterwards Lancaster's position was entirely altered by the death of his father, Edward III., and the succession of Richard II. to the throne.

During the early years of Richard II's. reign Lancaster was alternately in and out of favour with his nephew. He was given command of a fleet sent against France, but again achieved no success. He was sent as an ambassador to France, and placed at the head of an army sent against the Scots, but once more his lack of enterprise rendered him unpopular, and he was accused of slackness in pursuit and of inflicting more injury on the northern English counties, into which the Scots had penetrated, than upon the enemy. A bitter quarrel broke out between Lancaster and the King in 1384; and Richard, it is said, had decided upon the sudden arrest of his uncle. Warned of his danger, Lancaster fled to Pontefract Castle, which he prepared for a siege. But the King's mother, the Princess of Wales, brought about a reconciliation. It was a hollow reconciliation, however, for Richard's suspicions of his uncle were fully aroused and kept alive by those around him.

Henry of Trastamare having died, in 1379, John of Gaunt renewed his pretensions to the throne of Castile. An opportunity occurred of attempting to gain the Castilian throne with the help of the King of Portugal, and Richard, anxious to be rid of his uncle, lent him all possible assistance with men and money to make good his claim, and on his taking leave placed a crown of gold upon his head, whilst the Queen placed one upon the head of the Duchess. John of Gaunt sailed from Plymouth with an expedition of 20,000 men. On his first entrance into Spain his arms were successful, but when, later, he and the King of Portugal invaded Castile, they met with defeat after defeat. The climate caused sickness to break out amongst the troops, Lancaster himself fell ill and was obliged to leave Spain and retire to Bayonne, thus losing all his conquests of the previous year.

He had married his daughter Philippa, by his first wife, to the King of Portugal, and the Duke of Berri now made overtures to him for the hand of Catherine, his daughter by his second wife, Constance of Castile. The King of Castile, foreseeing that the Duke of Berri would, in all probability, be a future claimant to his throne in the event of the death of his wife's mother Constance, immediately opened negotiations for the marriage of his own son with Catherine. The suggestion pleased the Duke, and a treaty was concluded by which Constance resigned her claim to the throne of Castile in favour of her daughter, who shortly afterwards married the young prince; Lancaster laid aside the title that he had assumed of King of Castile, and received a payment of 200,000 crowns towards the cost of his expedition, as well as an annuity settled upon him and his duchess for their lives.

On his return to England he found King Richard struggling against his other uncle, Thomas of Woodstock, Duke of Gloucester, whose turbulence was the cause of a general disorder throughout the country. Richard appears to have welcomed his uncle of Lancaster's return, and created him Duke of Aquitaine. For the remainder of his life he was on excellent terms with his nephew, with the exception of a short period after he had scandalized the King and the whole royal family by marrying his mistress, Catherine Swynford.

One of the blots on Lancaster's career is the judicial murder of his brother, the Duke of Gloucester. A proposal was made in Parliament for the reform of the King's household, and the Duke of Gloucester, after a personal altercation with the King, retired from Court. By the advice of John of Gaunt, he was shortly afterwards arrested and hurried to Calais, where he was beheaded without any form of trial.

A year before Lancaster's death there occurred that quarrel between his son, the Duke of Hereford, and the Duke of Norfolk, which led to the deposition of Richard II., and ultimately to the Wars of the Roses. It was suggested that the quarrel between the two noblemen should be settled by fighting, but when they appeared in the lists, fully armed, the King threw down his sceptre and stopped the battle, banishing the two men from the country. In the following year John of Gaunt died in London on the 3rd of February 1399 ; and, although Richard had granted permission to the Duke of Hereford to appoint a proxy to receive his inheritance, directly his uncle died he seized upon the whole of his vast estates. It was with the excuse that he came to claim his father's property that the Duke of Hereford returned to England at the head of an armed force. To give colour to this he landed on the coast of Yorkshire and occupied his own castle of Pickering without resistance. So great was the discontent with the rule of Richard that an army speedily flocked to him, the majority of them deserting the King, who,

having crossed from Ireland into Wales, had no alternative but to make submission to his cousin. The unfortunate Richard was taken to London, where he publicly renounced the Crown, and Henry was chosen by Parliament to fill the vacant throne, his claim being based on his being in the right line of descent from Henry III., and on the misgovernment of Richard.

Thus, although John of Gaunt's ambitions for himself were never fulfilled, they were more than realized in the careers of his children. His son became King of England and his two daughters Queens of Portugal and Castile. But the usurpation of the English Crown by Henry, Duke of Hereford and Lancaster, ultimately plunged England into all the horrors of a civil war, which practically annihilated the nobility of the country.

THE ROMANCE OF THE PEEL FAMILY

ALTHOUGH for three centuries the industrial families of England have given members to the House of Commons, and statesmen to the originally a family of Danish extraction, which, after settling at Craven in Yorkshire, migrated to the neighbourhood of Blackburn. At that time the name was

Cabinet, they have only in one instance given England a Prime Minister: and this family was the Lancashire family of Peel.

The Peels are supposed to have been spelt Peele, but the final "e" was dropped by the Robert Peel who was the founder of the great fortunes of the family. Being a thrifty and practical man he economized labour even in writing his signature. He dropped the letter " for no better reason," says his grandson, " than the utilitarian one which he assigned, that it was of no use as it did not add to the sound."

This first Robert Peel was born in 1723, and had an estate which brought him in a hundred pounds a year, and, as was then very common amongst the yeomen of the district, he added to his income by spinning and weaving.

In 1744 he had married Elizabeth Haworth of Lower Darwen, a marriage that not only had a most important effect upon his own life, but upon the whole district of Blackburn. Calico-printing was then in its infancy. Peel's brother-in-law had learnt the trade in London, and coming to Blackburn he persuaded him to give up farming and to start calico-printing, combined with the manufacture of linen. Peel therefore migrated from Peel Fold, at Oswaldtwistle, his paternal home ; and, raising a mortgage upon the property, entered into partnership with his brother-in-law and a man called Yates, the landlord of the Black Bull Inn in Blackburn, as calico-printers. The firm traded as Haworth, Peel and Yates, their works being at Brookside.

The introduction of calico-printing into Lancashire is generally attributed to Haworth and to Peel, but the honour would seem to belong to the Claytons, of Bamber Bridge ; and one of the biographers of the Peel family declares that Peel's firm actually began as weavers, and that cloth-printing was only added to their other business by an accident. Some cloth, he says, had been spoilt in the weaving, and Peel sent it to the Claytons at Bamber Bridge to be printed as handkerchiefs. These were sold at such a profit that the three partners resolved to start operations on their own account as cloth-printers.

But whether the honour of introducing so important an industry into Lancashire lies with Haworth and Peel or with the Claytons, the fact remains that it was Peel who discovered that sugar of lead—used to acetate the alum which was the only mordant used by the first English calico-printers—produced the best calender ; and he likewise was one of the first manufacturers to substitute engraved metal plates for the printing of calico in place of the old blocks of sycamore wood.

There is a charming story told by his grandson of one of his discoveries : " Mr. Peel was in his kitchen making some experiments in printing on handkerchiefs and other small pieces when his only daughter, then a girl, afterwards Mrs. Willock, mother of the postmaster of Manchester, brought him from their garden of herbs a sprig of parsley. It is some proof of taste in so young a girl that she could discern beauty in a common pot-herb, since I believe that the common thought even now about parsley—once like the laurel leaf in honour—is that it was created for a garnish or a fry. She pointed out and praised the beauty—exquisite beauty—of the leaf, and looking by habit of imitation, naturally, to the useful side she said she thought it would make a very pretty pattern. He took it out of her hand, looked at it attentively, praised it for its beauty and her for her taste, and said he would make a trial of it. She, pleased not to be pooh-poohed, as discoverers among geniuses often are, lent her aid with all the alacrity of fourteen. A pewter dinner plate, for such was then the common dinner plate in families of that degree, was taken down from the shelf, and on it was sketched, say rather scratched, a figure of the leaf, and from this impressions were taken. It was called in the family ' Nancy's pattern,' after his daughter. It became a favourite ; in the trade it was known as the

-y

parsley-leaf pattern, and apt alliteration lending its artful aid, gave its inventor the nickname of 'Parsley Peel'."

After nearly thirty years of ever increasing prosperity, during which Peel had used in his cotton manufacturing whatever machinery had been invented, a heavy blow fell upon him. In 1779 came that bitter revolt of the Lancashire weavers and spinners against the use of machinery which they declared enriched the mill-owners whilst it reduced them

The loss was serious, but this founder of the Peel family was a man of indomitable courage and tenacity of purpose. He resolved to start afresh, but " fearing to expose his business again to a similar interruption, and his property again to injury" he removed to Burton-upon-Trent, where he built three mills. His business thereafter prospered exceedingly. But, although driven away by the attitude of the hand-loom workers, he always remained faithful to his native county;

BIRTHPLACE OF THE FIRST SIR ROBERT PEEL

to starvation. Peel had printing-works at Church and mills at Altham which were his sole property, the partnership with Yates and Haworth having been dissolved two years before. In this same year of the workpeople's revolt Peel himself had taken out a patent for a method of " dressing, carding, slubbing, roving and spinning cotton," and for this reason and the eager support he had given to all new machinery, he seems to have been especially singled out by the rioters for vengeance. His mill at Altham, with its costly machinery, was utterly destroyed.

and when, in his old age, he retired from business, he built a house at Ardwick Green, then a suburb of Manchester. Here he died in the year 1795 at the age of seventy-two, leaving a prosperous business at Burton-on-Trent, and an equally prosperous calico-printing business at Church. The future Prime Minister of England, who was a grandson of this Robert Peel, frequently visited him at Ardwick; his remembrance of him was that he was a venerable, fine-looking old man.

The salient points in the first Robert

Peel's character were repeated in his son, the first baronet, and in his grandson the Prime Minister. "He understood thoroughly every branch of the cotton trade," said Sir Laurence Peel, another grandson, "and instructed his sons himself. He loved to impress on their minds the great national importance of this rising manufacture; he was a reflecting man, who looked ahead, a plain-spoken, simple-minded man, not literary, and possessing no refinement in his tastes, free from affectation, and without any desire to imitate the manners or modes of life of a a class above his own. His sons resembled him, and a strong likeness pervaded the whole family."

A story is told of his wife, Mrs. Peel, which goes to show that the future Prime Minister of England inherited not a little of his prescience from his grandmother: "Once, at Burton, the news came whilst Robert Peel was away, that a great financial house had fallen, and that in consequence a run was apprehended upon a bank with which the Peels were connected. The news arrived on a Saturday night, and on the following morning Mrs. Peel came downstairs to breakfast wearing her very best clothes, and insisted upon her daughter doing the same. 'Look as blithe as you can,' she said, 'for depend upon it, if the folk see us looking gloomy to-day they will be all at the bank to-morrow.' So out they sallied to church, and straight on in their ample garments they sailed slowly, serenely, wearing no false colours, saluted and saluting in return, holding their own, making no tacks, neither porting nor starboarding their helms, but proceeding as though they could sweep over any ugly-looking craft which might cross them; and we may fancy some of their humbler neighbours mentally pricing their gowns as they passed with a 'Bless you, they are as safe

as the Church!'—for people will estimate solvency rather illogically by what has been already expended. Who will say that this dame was not fit to be the grandmother of a politic minister?"

Robert Peel had seven sons, but the family rose to distinction and eminence through the third, also called Robert, who was born in 1750, about the time that his father forsook farming at Peel Fold for manufacturing and cotton-printing at Blackburn. From his earliest years the younger Robert was dominated by an ambition to succeed. "Very early in life," says his nephew, Sir Laurence Peel, "and while fortune appeared to shut the door of distinction against him, Sir Robert Peel entertained strong hopes of being the founder of a family; and at the age of fourteen, to the entertainment of his brothers, he avowed his determination to raise himself to rank and consequence in society. He bottomed these hopes on a conviction that any situation in this free country is accessible to a good capacity, aided by prudence and industry."

Like his brothers he was brought up in his father's mills, but all his hours of leisure were employed in study. When he was eighteen he asked his father if he would give him £500 to start elsewhere, as he thought that he and his brother were "too thick on the ground" at Altham and Church. The elder Peel did not accede to the suggestion, and for four more years the ambitious young man plodded on in his father's works. In the meantime his uncle Haworth had dissolved partnership with his brother-in-law, and started business with a man called Yates—who is thought to have been a relative of the Yates of the Black Bull Inn, one of the three partners in the old firm—as calico-printers at Bury on the banks of the Irwell. After a while, more help being needed,

Haworth decided to choose a third partner from amongst his brother-in-law's sons, and finally selected Robert. The firm of Haworth & Yates had only just been started, and on his arrival at Bury the young Robert Peel lodged with his uncle's partner Yates, the sum paid for board and lodging by the junior to the

a day his life was one of hard, incessant labour; he would rise at night from his bed, when there was a likelihood of bad weather, to visit the bleaching grounds; and one night in each week he used to sit up all night, attended by his pattern drawer to receive any new patterns which the London coach, arriving at midnight,

CHAMBER HALL, THE BIRTHPLACE OF THE PRIME MINISTER, SIR ROBERT PEEL

senior partner being only six shillings a week. Yates considered this sum too small and wished it to be increased by a shilling, but against this Peel demurred, and at the outset it seemed that a serious difficulty would arise, but the matter was eventually compromised by the lodger paying an extra sixpence a week!

Sir Laurence Peel gives a vivid picture of his uncle's life at this period. "He was a man of untiring energy. For many

might bring down: for at first they were followers and imitators of the London work, but they soon aspired to lead their masters, and it was ere long apparent to the Londoners themselves that their trade was deserting them and flowing into these new channels.

Eleven years after Peel entered his partner Yates's house he married his eldest daughter Ellen. This was the one romance in a life given up to hard work.

When he had first gone there she had been a little child, and on returning from his day's work at the "Ground," as the print-works on the banks of the Irwell were called, he would take the little girl upon his knee and say to her, "Nelly, thou bonnie little dear, wilt be my wife?" to which the child would readily answer, "Yes," as any child would do. "Then I will wait for thee, Nelly. I'll wed thee and none else." True to his word he waited and worked until she was of marriageable age, and, as one of his biographers says: "Who knows how much of the prosperity of the Bury house may have been due to the young man's affection for the daughter of his partner and his ambition for her sake as well as his own?"

In these days of cheap production and the most finished workmanship, and the small margin of profit which arises from single articles, it is surprising to learn that in the early days of Peel's firm there was for many years a regular demand of 20,000 pieces, of one particular pattern, and that the profit upon each piece was one guinea. The system of printing was most primitive. The patterns, for the most part, consisted of leaves variously arranged, small circles, pippins, clubs, dice and diamonds and spots, flower heads of daisies or buttercups. When more than one colour was to be used the prints received from the hands of the printer only one impression from the block; this was generally the outline. The colours were then laid on by women, of whom a large number were employed. These were called the "pencillers," and Peel built for their special use long ranges of workshops in what are now Peel Street and New Street at Bury. The work was very delicate. One pattern, which was the most costly and beautiful sent out by the firm, was a

chintz pattern upon a white ground; the outline of dark purple was laid on by the block, the remaining colours, two greens, two reds, two blues, a drab and a yellow, were pencilled upon the cloth by the women, every single leaf or object all over the pattern having to be separately touched with a pencil of the colour required. This particular pattern rendered it necessary that the surface of the cloth should be passed over nine times before it was completed.

In these days we should probably consider the patterns very inferior and the colouring very crude, but then the price of a "garment piece," as the fabrics were called which were meant for dresses, containing twenty yards, was from £4 to £5, or 3s. to 3s. 6d. a yard, and even more. Furniture—as chintzes and curtain materials were named—fetched about the same sum.

Peel's energy was unbounded, and two years after he joined the firm he had created a large and profitable trade with the American Colonies and other places abroad. So rapidly had this business increased that it became necessary for the firm to have a shipping house in Liverpool; and when trouble broke out between the mother-country and the American Colonies "it was the chintzes of Peel & Yates, among others, that, previous to the League of Boston, the good citizens of that city prohibited their wives and daughters from wearing; and many American ladies, in their zeal for the public cause, burned their stock of English-printed gowns rather than wear an article of British taxation."

The inventions of Arkwright and Compton by 1779 had entirely revolutionized the manufacture of cotton. From the earliest possible moment Peel and his partner had manufactured calico for their printing-works; and taking advantage of Arkwright's patent—which made it possible to manufacture calico entirely of cotton—and also of Crompton's "mule," in 1784 their works had so extended that they were employing no less than 6,800 people. "The calicoes, which they bleached as well as printed, were manufactured, by weavers whom they hired, out of yarn spun by their own 'hands.' In our own days—days of the division of labour—there is (indeed for a long time there has been) a separation of the business of spinner and manufacturer, of bleacher and calico-printer, but the Bury house performed all four operations, gaining a profit upon each, and thus it came to employ a number of workers, probably much greater than any single firm in the cotton trade of to-day can boast of having in its services."

The various labours of the firm were carried on in what were then considered, immense establishments—Radcliffe Mill, Makin Mill, Hindes and Burrs, White Ash and Summerseat. They had print works at Ramsbottom, bleaching and chemical works between Bury and Radcliffe, and they employed weavers in a large portion of North and East Lancashire and in Yorkshire.

Peel's partner, Mr. Yates, as the firm prospered, removed to Wood Hill, a house with large grounds lying on the opposite bank of the river Irwell to that on which the works were situated. A wooden bridge connected the "Ground" with Mr. Yates's garden, and in an interesting account of the Peel family there is a very pleasant picture in which this bridge plays a part. "But it was not Mr. Yates and his son Edmund alone who realized all the benefit of this mode of communication: it was also over this bridge that Mr. Peel stepped to visit his lady-love in the days of his happy and successful wooing, and when the 'Ground' was silent and the

people had retired from their daily labour, Miss Yates often returned across the bridge with him, and, in the pleasant summer evenings, strolled along towards the higher grounds, whilst he would point out to her with pride and pleasure the rapid rise of quickly extending buildings, all too little for the large and increasing demand that assailed them." Miss Yates is described as "a young girl of sweet disposition, sense beyond her years, pleasing manners, and with a handsome person." In 1783 Peel's long years of waiting were rewarded and they were married. "She was," Sir Laurence Peel says, "an excellent wife, affectionate and sweet tempered, possessed of a good understanding and a sound judgment; she conformed in all things to her husband's tastes and views; and, though naturally inclining to a gayer life, she reconciled herself at once to those quiet domestic habits which were in a manner indigenous among the Peels."

The early years of the marriage were passed in a small house, the yard of which Peel covered with a room "because it would make a large packing-room for printed goods, and they were short of a place for the purpose," thus, with characteristic energy, making his domestic arrangements subservient to his business. Two daughters were born in this small house, but when the third child was born—a son—they had removed to Chamber Hall, a residence more befitting their growing fortunes. Here on the 5th of February 1788, the future Prime Minister was born. So overjoyed was the father at the birth of an heir, that he fell on his knees and vowed "that he would give his child to his country." This vow was fulfilled, and it is amazing to remember that it was made by a calico-printer in what was then an obscure and small commercial town, at a time when gentle birth was almost necessary for entrance into any service of the State, and essential for advancement.

In the year following the birth of this ardently desired son the French Revolution broke out, involving England in deadly perils both at home and abroad. That England passed through this difficult period unharmed by revolution without, and bitter discontent and simmering disloyalty within, was in no small measure due to the simple-minded enthusiasm, the unquestioning and ardent patriotism—backed effectively by their money—of men of this Bury manufacturer's stamp. Robert Peel, in his patriotism and devotion dedicated his son's life to his country, and we shall see how nobly both father and son fulfilled that dedication.

The invention of cylinder-printing on calico gave a further impetus to the ever-increasing prosperity of the firm; and so wealthy did Peel become that he gradually bought the whole of the estate of Drayton Manor, near Tamworth, in Staffordshire, which he pulled down and entirely rebuilt. But he and his family did not desert Chamber Hall, using Drayton only as an occasional residence, although the journey from Bury to Tamworth took " two entire days and a portion of a third to perform " —and this was in 1797!

The rise of Bury was entirely due to Peel's energy and resource. As the firm increased so did the number of workpeople. In one respect Peel was a great benefactor; he took deserted children from the London workhouses, educated them at Bury, and by giving them employment in his works enabled them to earn their living. It is said that, warned by the heavy losses sustained by his father and other manufacturers, he originally bought the land at Tamworth to build cotton mills to be provided with new machinery, as he feared the jealousy of the hand-loom weavers in and around Bury would be provoked against him if he established the machinery there.

Apart from his business concerns Peel took the deepest interest in economic affairs. In 1780 he had written a pamphlet entitled, *The National Debt productive of National Prosperity*, which attracted considerable interest. About the same time the younger Pitt, then Prime Minister, proposed to reduce the duties which at that time existed upon goods brought from Ireland into England. Previously he had placed a duty of a penny a yard on all cotton mixed goods, either bleached or printed, if under three shillings a yard in value, and twopence a yard on all above that value, in addition to the former duty of threepence a yard. This was called the Fustian Tax, and created much discontent and alarm amongst the Lancashire linen manufacturers. Their anger against the tax was aggravated by Pitt's proposal to establish free trade between England and Ireland. They declared, in a petition to Parliament, that the admission of Irish fustians and cottons into England was all that was wanted to completely annihilate the cotton trade in this country, by which so many thousands of industrious and useful subjects got their bread. They complained, too, that the taxes imposed on the fustian and other cotton manufacturers were absolutely ruinous to their trade. The Lancashire manufacturers, it added, " unwilling to submit any longer to the hardships arising from a burdensome tax and from the still more burdensome mode of collecting it, had resolved to discharge their workmen as they brought home their work." This had already been done to a great degree, and so numerous was the body of men thus thrown out of employment that they were begging through the streets in crowds. Moved by these representations the House of Commons went into Committee, and, amongst others, Peel was called to give evidence. It was his answers to the searching questions put to him as to the details of the expenditure incident to the different branches of cotton manufacture, both in England and in Ireland, that first gave him a public prominence outside Lancashire. He pointed out that, owing to the excessive taxes in England, the Irish manufacturers drew a profit thirteen per cent. higher than that drawn by the English manufacturer. He said he employed 6,800 people in his works and paid excise duties to the amount of £20,000 a year. He was asked by the Committee what number of workpeople he would employ if Pitt's Irish proposition were passed into law? His answer was: "Most certainly the same, if not a greater, number —but it would be in Ireland." Peel's evidence was much discussed, and a month later the Fustian Tax was repealed.

Parliament was destined to hear more of this grave and dignified Lancashire cotton manufacturer, for in 1790 he was elected member for Tamworth. He became a warm supporter of Pitt, and although he at first upheld the French Revolution as a temperate reformation, when it became violent and bloodthirsty he denounced it.

England was plunged into war. Pitt had a deficiency of £19,000,000. The people were taxed almost beyond bearing power, and in his dire necessity for supplies, Pitt appealed for contributions to a Loyalty Fund. To this fund Peel gave no less than £10,000; but having done so without consulting his partner, Mr. Yates, he travelled back to Bury in some anxiety as to what Yates would say. "But Mr. Yates had a spirit as loyal as his own. On being told by Peel what he had done, he merely turned round and said: 'You might as well

have made it twenty thousand while you were about it'." In addition to this handsome contribution to the fund Peel armed and commanded six companies of Royal Volunteers at Bury, many of the men being his own workmen.

After ten years of parliamentary life, in which his sound views and his wide commercial knowledge gained him the respect of both parties, he was made a baronet; and two years later he brought in the Act which was the forerunner of all factory legislation, " for the Preservation of the Health and Morals of the Apprentices employed in Cotton and Other Factories."

Throughout the whole of these busy and prosperous years the education of the son whom he had devoted to his country had been Peel's first thought. He carefully trained him from his youngest years for the great part he destined him to play. He was brought up to believe that not only were great things expected of him, but that he could do great things. On Sundays his father, in order to train his memory, set him to repeat the sermon that he had heard in the day. He was taught to give the substance of what he had heard in his own words; and thus, when he was not yet twelve, began the training of the future orator and debater. He was described as a good boy, of gentle manners, quick in feeling, very sensitive; and even when he was at Harrow, Lord Byron, who was his schoolfellow, says: "There were always great hopes of Peel amongst us, both masters and scholars." From Harrow he went to Oxford, where after a very distinguished career he took his degree in 1808.

His father now set about the fulfilment of his vow when the young man was born, and purchased the seat of Cashel, in Tipperary, for him—parliamentary representation in those times being purely a matter of buying and selling in some constituencies. Young Peel entered the house in 1809, and in the following year made his maiden speech, which was declared by old parliamentary hands to be the best first speech since that of Mr. Pitt; and for twenty-one years the proud father had the felicity of seeing the gradual fulfilment of his vow as his brilliant son advanced step by step in his parliamentary career. But he was not spared to see him Prime Minister. He had always said that his son would " never display his talents in their fullness until he held the supreme place."

The name of Robert Peel ranks high amongst those of the Prime Ministers of England. He attained that greatness through his Lancashire blood; and in the story of his brilliant political career may be found the same motives which inspired his father and his grandfather in the conduct of their business at Blackburn and at Bury. The word of " Parsley " Peel, and that of his son throughout their lives, were regarded as being " as good as their bond "; and of their statesman-descendant the great Duke of Wellington said : " I never knew a man in whose truth and justice I had a more lively confidence." Upon the vast stage of public affairs the younger Robert Peel played the same part that his father and grandfather had played within the walls of their mills and factories. They were broad-minded men, deeply religious, but they respected other forms of religion besides their own; Robert Peel, the statesman advocated the removal of the disabilities which prevented Roman Catholics taking any part in public life, and even from serving their country. The Catholic Emancipation Act was the outcome of Peel's early training. His father's first care was the welfare of his workpeople ; " the promotion of the welfare of his countrymen was the absorbing passion " of the Prime Minister's life—a passion that found expression in the repeal of the Corn Laws and the consequent cheapening of the daily bread of the working-man ; and the establishment of the police force to protect all classes against civil disorders. The father and grandfather owed no little of their business success in Lancashire to their financial integrity ; their son and grandson revolutionized the financial system of England and placed it upon a sound basis. A strong sense of justice moved the elder Peels in all their dealings ; the statesman Peel removed from the statute book many of the barbarous and cruel punishments which were a disgrace to our civilization. Thus the seed that was sown in the mills of Blackburn and Bury in the prosecution of cotton manufacture and in cotton-printing bore fruit, for the benefit of all England, at Westminster ; and as the father was the pioneer of our country's commercial greatness, so the son was the pioneer of legislative reform.

Unhappily the great commercial position created by the first Sir Robert Peel, and the political position created by his illustrious son were both lost by the third Sir Robert Peel, a man of great ability, but of a volatile temperament, and whose " inability to accept a fixed political creed prevented him from acquiring the confidence of his associates and of the public." The greater part of the large fortune amassed by his grandfather, the third Sir Robert squandered in reckless extravagance, thus giving an unfortunate illustration to the Lancashire saying " Clogs to clogs in the third generation."

GEORGE ROMNEY

Lancashire Painter

WE usually associate the district of Furness with shipbuilding, mining, and manufactures, but the wild grandeur and romantic loveliness of its scenery once caused it to be called the Calabria of England. It was fitting, therefore, that the birthplace of one of our greatest painters should be in this beautiful part of Lancashire.

George Romney, whose pictures now change hands for many thousands of pounds, was born at Dalton, the ancient capital of Furness, in December 1734, and was thus some ten years younger than Sir Joshua Reynolds, of whom he was destined to become the successful rival. His father was a carpenter, joiner and cabinet maker, and for a man of his position in those days, when money went very much further than it does now, was comparatively wealthy. George was the second son, and, departing from the usual custom then prevalent in Furness, amongst those parents who could afford the expense, by which only the eldest son was educated with a view to taking up a profession, he was sent to school at Dendron, some five miles from Dalton. Here the master, the Rev. Mr. Fell, agreed to teach him the "humanities" for 5s. a quarter, whilst a certain Mr. Gardner took him as a boarder for four pounds ten a year. But the boy's progress was so indifferent, and he showed such little aptitude for learning that his father considered even this extremely modest outlay an unnecessary expense, and when he was eleven years old took him away and placed him in his own workshop.

Romney gave signs of his inclination towards art very early. He had inherited a mechanical skill from his father, and this first found expression in the carving of wooden figures, some of them being portraits of his fellow-workmen. He was passionately fond of music, especially of the violin, and being unable to buy an instrument set to work to make one. When it was completed he was taught to play upon it by a neighbour. A fiddle of his own making became a common present to his boy friends, and one such gift to a former school-fellow called Greene, led to a lasting friendship which was a great help to Romney in later years. Greene became a lawyer of high standing in London, and acted as Romney's adviser in all his business affairs, auditing the painter's confused accounts and directing all his money transactions.

Romney was born a painter, and he taught himself the rudiments of drawing. One of his father's workmen, called Sam Knight, took in an illustrated monthly magazine which he used to hand over to the young artist, who copied the engravings in pencil. A copy of Leonardo da Vinci's *Treatise on Painting* chancing to fall into his hands, Romney copied the illustrations, and with such strength and ability that they attracted the attention of a relative called Lewthwaite, who strongly urged the father to train the boy as an artist. An eccentric dilettante, one John Williams, who lived in the neighbourhood, is also said to have encouraged Romney's aspirations. His natural genius was remarkable. " When Romney first began to paint," says Flaxman, the designer of the beautiful Wedgwood pottery, " he had seen no gallery of pictures, nor the fine productions of ancient sculpture ; but then women and children were his statues, and all objects under the cope of heaven formed his school of painting. The rainbow, the purple distance, or the silver lake, taught him colouring ; the various actions and passions of the human figure, with the forms of clouds and woods and mountains, or valleys, afforded him studies of composition. Indeed his genius bore a strong resemblance to the scenes he was born in : like them it partook of the grand and beautiful ; and like them also, the bright sunshine and enchanting prospect of his fancy were occasionally overspread with mist and gloom."

Few painters have grown up in a district whose scenery is more calculated to foster a natural love for the beautiful. " His father's house," we are told, " stood on a sort of terrace facing the west, and commanding an extensive view of the Irish Sea. From the hill behind, a noble panorama was unfolded. Northward was the estuary of Duddon (afterwards Wordsworth's Duddon) which, with every tide, showed like a fine lake, and was studded with sails. Behind the well-cultivated

high ground on the Cumberland side, and their white farm-houses, rose Black Comb with its mist-clad summit, and to the south-east of this region was the background of mountains which are the pride and glory of Furness."

But Romney's first impulses towards painting were not the expression of the beauties around him, but rather of odd types of humanity. He himself used to say that when quite a boy " one day in church he saw a man with a most singular face, from which he could never take his eyes. He spoke of it when he went home, and his parents desired him to describe the man. He took a pencil, and from memory delineated the face so skilfully, and with such strength of resemblance, that they immediately named the person he meant : and the boy was so pleased with this that he began to draw with more serious application."

Acting upon the persuasion of his relation Lewthwaite or that of Mr. Williams, or of both, the elder Romney decided to start his son upon an artist's career. At that time an itinerant portrait painter named Steele happened to be working at Kendal, and to him Romney was apprenticed, his indentures bearing the date March 20, 1755. Steele has been called a dauber, but this is not correct. He was wild, dissipated, hair-brained, and because of his pretentious airs and love of finery had been nicknamed " Count " Steele, but he had studied under Vanloo, the great French painter in Paris, and was not without ability. For a premium of twenty pounds Romney was to learn " the art and science of painting, and to obey all lawful and reasonable commands," his apprenticeship being for four years.

Romney used to complain that with Steele he had no opportunities for self-improvement because of the incessant drudgery at which he was kept, in grinding colours, and other studio work. But although he may have learnt very little in the way of art from his harum-scarum master, the enforced application and his practical knowledge of grinding colours stood Romney in good stead in later years. A year after Romney's apprenticeship began, Steele persuaded one of his pupils, a young woman of some means, to elope with him to Gretna Green. Romney had been his master's confidant and help in the various arrangements for the elopement, and when it finally took place the excitement had such an effect upon his sensitive and somewhat morbid nature that he fell ill of a fever. Throughout the whole of his illness he was nursed by his landlady's daughter, Mary Abbott, and a tender attachment springing up between the two, they became engaged. The landlady and her daughter were very poor and of a lower social

GEORGE ROMNEY

station than the Romneys, the daughter at one time having been a domestic servant. After his marriage with the heiress at Gretna Green, Steele decided to try his fortune at York, and ordered his apprentice to join him there so soon as he was well enough to travel. Romney, distressed at the separation from his betrothed which this order necessitated, decided upon marriage, and to the great anger of his parents, the ceremony took place in October 1756. The step was most imprudent. Romney had no income

nor the possibility of earning one until his apprenticeship was ended; his family bitterly resented what they considered a *mésalliance*, and all supplies were cut off, despite the young man's assurance that it would prove an incentive to work and a safeguard against youthful follies.

Immediately after the wedding he set out for York, and his wife returned to domestic service. For some time she used to send her husband half guineas hidden under the seal of letters. After remaining for a year in York painting the portraits of such local folk as would sit to him, Steele moved to Lancaster, and here Romney, feeling his powers were being wasted, decided to end the apprenticeship, proposing that a sum of ten pounds he had lent his master should be taken as a consideration for cancelling the indentures. Steele, who was anxious to go to Ireland, agreed to the release, declaring that he did so " in order not to stand in the way of one who, he was sure, would do wonders." During this time of apprenticeship Romney had been forming a style of his own, and when he was freed by Steele started as a portrait painter on his own account, first at Lancaster and then at Kendal. His first recorded work was a sign for the post-office in the latter place—a hand holding a letter. But his painting speedily attracted the attention of some of the local gentry, and amongst the earliest of his

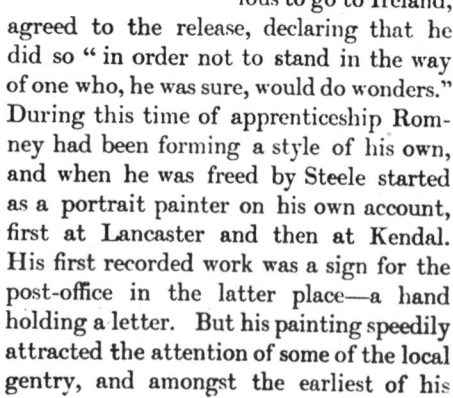

patrons were the Stricklands of Sizergh. He was given free access to the collection of pictures at Sizergh Castle, many of which he copied. It is interesting to note that at this outset of his brilliant career he charged six guineas for a full-length portrait, and two guineas for a three-quarter figure. Yet, although he was happily married, and now had two children —a son who afterwards became the Rev. John Romney and his father's biographer, and a daughter who died at the age of three—Romney was not satisfied with a merely local success. He yearned for the larger field of London. But the means were lacking. In the intervals of portrait painting, therefore, he tried a curious experiment.

Whilst with Steele in York, he had collected a series of prints after pictures by great Dutch painters. From these he painted a selection of copies, and, adding two or three original pictures of his own, he exhibited them in the Town Hall at Kendal, afterwards raffling them at half a guinea a ticket. Two of the originals were scenes from *King Lear*, one "Lear Wakened by Cordelia"—his wife having sat for the figure of Cordelia—and the other, "Lear in the Storm Tearing off his Robes." Another was the scene in *Tristram Shandy*, where Dr. Slop arrives at Shandy Hall, all splashed with mud, at the moment when Mr. Shandy and Uncle Toby are discussing the nature of women. This last picture has a particular interest. When Romney was at York, Laurence Sterne, the author of *Tristram Shandy*, was rector of Sutton, an hour's ride away. He came to Steele's studio to sit for his portrait, and there Romney made his acquaintance. The Dr. Slop in the young painter's picture was said to have been painted from the supposed original of the character, an eccentric medico called Burton who practised at York.

Eighty of the half-guinea tickets were taken, and this sum, added to the savings already made by Romney and his wife, gave them a little capital of one hundred pounds. Romney determined to try his fortune in London, but he hesitated to take his wife and two children upon what seemed a hazardous and doubtful enterprise. Mrs. Romney seems to have acquiesced entirely in his suggestion that she and the children should remain at Kendal until he made an assured position, and with thirty pounds of the hundred in his pocket the young painter set off to conquer the metropolis—and without a single letter of introduction. But he had two friends in London, Greene his old school-fellow, and a man called Braithwaite who was in the Post Office, and through their help he found lodgings.

Here comes in an amazing fact in Romney's history, and one which has never been cleared up satisfactorily. When he arrived in London he made no mention of his wife and children, and accordingly was believed to be unmarried. Romney has been accused of passing himself off as a bachelor, but there is no evidence of his having deliberately stated that he was unmarried. It is probable that, thinking he would have more chance of patronage if it were not known that he had married so rashly, he kept the fact to himself, and having done so had not the moral courage to disclose his wife's existence when he made his success. But whatever the reason, for thirty-seven years he passed as an unmarried man, and deserted his wife for that long period. The curious part of this story is that neither Mrs. Romney nor their son John appear to have resented this treatment; indeed, far from expressing any sense of injury, the son, in his *Life* of his father, justifies his father's conduct with some spirit.

Romney kept his wife well supplied with money, and provided the best education possible for his son, who became a clergyman.

Romney's rise to fame was rapid. He settled in London at a time when it had become the fashion to patronise native artists in place of the foreigners who had hitherto excited the admiration of modish art-lovers. Sir Joshua Reynolds and Gainsborough, especially the former, were reaping a golden harvest, and painting those masterpieces with which their names will be for ever associated. The Royal Academy was not then in existence, but the Society of Arts in some measure filled the same office, and gave great encouragement to young painters, sculptors and architects. A year after his arrival in London, Romney gained the Society's second prize of fifty guineas for a picture called "The Death of General Wolfe." This award was cancelled, some say on the proposal of Sir Joshua Reynolds. Whether this was correct or not, Romney ascribed the disappointment to the great painter, although he had some consolation in this, his first picture exhibited in London, being bought by a wealthy banker who presented it to Governor Verelst, by whom it was hung in the Council Chamber at Calcutta.

The bestowal of the Society's award and its withdrawal caused much comment, and brought Romney's name somewhat prominently before the public. The comment served as an advertisement, and in the following year he had received a sufficient number of commissions for pictures and portraits to enable him to go to Paris for six weeks with his friend Greene, where he studied the wonderful collections of Old Masters in the Orléans Gallery, greatly to the advantage of his art. Despite his sensitive and morbid nature, Romney possessed the true Lancashire grit, and the Lancashire faculty for absorbing and assimilating everything that would help and further his work. Those six weeks in Paris were of incalculable benefit. He had already achieved a measure of success by the sheer force of genius ; now he returned to London with the knowledge of the methods of some of the greatest European painters. And that knowledge found speedy expression in his brush.

Shortly after his return his friend Braithwaite persuaded Sir Joseph Yates, one of the judges of the King's Bench, to sit to him for his portrait. The judge was so pleased with the result that he sent several other lights of the law to the artist's studio.

Romney was ever fortunate in his friends, and whatever may be said of him with regard to his treatment of his wife, he must have possessed qualities which inspired not only affection but admiration. In 1767, he made the acquaintance of Richard Cumberland, a dramatist and a popular writer. Cumberland sat for his portrait (it is now in the National Portrait Gallery), and although Romney's fee was then only eight guineas for a three-quarter length, Cumberland insisted upon giving him ten guineas, at the same time urging him to raise his prices. Not content with this, the dramatist wrote odes to Romney's genius, which, although of a fulsome and inflated nature, brought his name into prominence.

By the time he was thirty-nine Romney was making some twelve hundred a year by his portraits, and therefore felt justified in taking the journey to Italy, then considered indispensable for all artists. In Rome he was greatly impressed by the examples of antique sculpture in the Vatican galleries and elsewhere. Its influence upon his art is strongly marked,

" His fine natural taste readily assimilated its mingled nobility and simplicity, and accepted them as counsels of perfection in art." After two years in Italy, Romney returned to London to find himself somewhat straitened for money. His younger brother, Peter, who had also become a portrait painter and had settled at Cambridge, had got heavily into debt. Romney very generously cleared him of his liabilities and set him up at Southport. But so reduced were his own means by this kindness that he seriously thought of leaving London and establishing himself somewhere in the country. Wiser counsels, however, prevailed, and the painter decided on the bold step of taking a large house with a studio in Cavendish Square, which had become vacant by the death of a Royal Academician. Here, not without some doubts and misgivings, Romney installed himself in 1775. A few weeks later he received a visit from the Duke of Richmond, who was the President of the Society of Arts. The result of the visit was a commission for a three-quarter length portrait of the Duke, and so delighted was the sitter with the picture that he not only ordered several replicas of it, but brought various members of his family to sit to the artist. A whole train of fashionable folk followed the Duke of Richmond to the house in Cavendish Square, and in a comparatively short time Romney was dividing the patronage of the great world with Sir Joshua Reynolds. " All the town," said Lord Thurlow, the Lord Chancellor, " is divided into two factions, the Reynolds and the Romney, and I am of the Romney faction."

Romney's friends and biographers constantly refer to Reynolds's ill-will towards the Lancashire painter. Romney never seems to have given any cause for offence, but Reynolds always spoke of him contemptuously as " the man in Cavendish Square." There never could have been any sympathy between the two men, as Reynolds was of a strong, equable temperament, whilst Romney was weak, ill-balanced and emotional ; but there is little doubt that Sir Joshua resented the brilliant success of a man who encountered him in what he had come to consider his own particular and special province. He certainly on more than one occasion spoke slightingly of Romney's work. Romney, on the other hand, had a sincere admiration for Reynolds's pictures, which he never hesitated to express. Once, when some of his friends had been criticising an imaginative painting by Sir Joshua, he said, " Gentlemen, I have listened to all you have said. Some observations are true, and some are nonsense ; but no other man in Europe could paint such a picture." Again, when told that a portrait of Mrs. Siddons, the great actress, which he had just finished, was generally considered to be superior to Sir Joshua's portrait of the same lady as the Tragic Muse, Romney replied—

" The people know nothing of the matter, for it is not."

Ten years after his settling in Cavendish Square Romney was making nearly four thousand a year. All the great and notable people of the day were amongst his sitters, from Chatham and Burke to Paley and John Wesley, not to mention numerous members of the aristocracy. But he would never exhibit his work at the Royal Academy, which had been founded 1768, with Sir Joshua Reynolds as its president. The ill-will borne against him by Sir Joshua was the cause, and it is a notable fact that no picture of one of the greatest English artists was seen on the walls of the Academy until sixty-nine years after his death, when, in 1871, his beautiful group, " The Lady Russell and Child," was shown. In his persistent refusal to exhibit at the Academy, Romney was encouraged by his friend Hayley, a then popular poet, whose friendship he had made in 1772. Romney relied greatly on Hayley's advice and companionship, and for twenty-two years always spent his summer holidays at the poet's country

" Sonnet to George Romney, Esq.,
On his portrait of me, in crayons, drawn at Eartham in the months of August and September 1792.

Romney; expert infallibly to trace
On chart or canvas, not the form alone
And semblance, but, however faintly shown,

EMMA, LADY HAMILTON, AS A BACCHANTE
(*After Romney*)

house at Eartham in Sussex, where Flaxman, Cowper and Blake were his fellow-guests at various times. Gibbon, of the *Decline and Fall of the Roman Empire*, was also a favoured guest at Eartham, which he called a " little Paradise." During his visit in 1792, Romney did the famous portrait of Cowper the poet, who thus expressed his gratitude—

The mind's impression, too, on every face,
With strokes that time ought never to erase :
Thou hast so pencilled mine, that though I own
The subject worthless, I have never known
The artist shining with superior grace.
But this I mark, that symptoms none of woe
In thy incomparable work appear :
Well ! I am satisfied, it should be so,

Since on maturer thoughts the cause is
  clear ;
For in my looks what sorrow could'st thou
  see,
When I was Hayley's guest and sat to
  thee ? "

Romney's name will be for ever associated with that of Lady Hamilton,
Nelson's "Enchantress." This lovely
woman first sat to him in 1782, whilst she
was living under the protection of Charles
Greville, who was a friend of Romney and
one of his great admirers. To the painter
she became the "divine lady," and from
1782 until 1785, when she went to
Naples, handed over by Charles Greville
to his uncle Sir William Hamilton as if
she were a piece of bric-à-brac, she was
the painter's chief source of inspiration.
He reduced the number of his sitters and
refused commissions, solely that he might
devote more time to a series of studies of
this beautiful creature. Besides making
many portraits and sketches of Emma
Hart, as she then was, Romney painted
her in a variety of characters, the prints
of which are to be met with now in almost
every house. The most popular of these
is "The Spinstress," in which the lovely
Emma is shown sitting at a spinning-
wheel, and as a Bacchante.

After he had settled in Cavendish
Square and sitters flocked to his studio,
whilst their guineas poured into his bank
account, it could have been no consideration of economy that led Romney to continue to separate himself from his wife.
There was certainly no estrangement between them. It may have been that Mrs.
Romney, conscious of her humble origin,
felt herself unsuited to fulfil the duties of
a successful artist's wife in London, but
whatever the cause, the reason given by
scandal—Romney's admiration for Emma
Hart—as the cause of the continued
separation was untrue. Romney's admiration verged upon infatuation, but it was

the artist's admiration for incomparable
beauty, and that the relations between
them were purely platonic is shown by a
letter the lady wrote to Romney after her
marriage to Sir William Hamilton, in
which she addresses him as "My dear sir,
my friend, my more than father."

Romney worked very hard, sometimes
for thirteen hours a day, yet his success
brought him no happiness. He was rich,
he was famous, but he was miserable.
Hayley advised him against this "intem-
perance of labour," but work, whilst it
exhausted his body, was the only solace for
his mind. But even this failed him. One
of his biographers puts the whole situation
very clearly, if with some lack of understanding of Romney's very complex and
morbid nature : "He tried to soothe his
exquisite sensibility by indulging in rap-
tures over the innocence and grace of
other people's children, and in a sentimental worship of the lovely but shame-
less woman who afterwards became famous
and infamous as Nelson's Lady Hamilton,
and whom Romney painted in every conceivable attitude, and in every possible
character from Circe to St. Cecilia. Far
away, in the north, was his own wife, un-
acknowledged and neglected, who might
have brought light and cheerfulness into
the house in Cavendish Square where the
painter moaned and groaned over the
state of his nerves, and could find no
enjoyment in his wealth and fame."

As is the way of hypochondriacal
people, Romney believed that a change of
air would relieve his spirits. He therefore
bought a house at Hampstead to which
he added a studio and a gallery. The
walls were scarcely dry when he entered
into residence, only to find that there was
not sufficient room for all the pictures
and studies he had accumulated. Many
were stood against the damp walls of the
gallery, and were either stolen, or destroyed

—E

by exposure. Flaxman, writing of a visit he paid to Romney at this time, says it "grieved him" to see so noble a collection in a state "so confused, so mangled." This was in 1797, but by the summer of 1798 it was only too clear that the change had been of no benefit. Romney saying a word of his intention to any one, in the summer of 1798 he took the coach for the north, "and after a desertion of nearly thirty-seven years, rejoined, a broken-down old man of sixty-five, the wife whom, at eight-and-twenty, full of hope and strength, he had left behind in

LORD NELSON
(From the painting by Sir William Beechey, R.A.)

had become the victim of a settled melancholia.

A tour in the north with his son did little or no good, and on his return to London the painter complained of dizziness, failing sight, and of a numbness in his hands which prevented him using his brushes. Broken in health, utterly despondent in his mind, his thoughts turned to the wife of his youth, and without the Kendal where once more he sought her." Mary Romney made no reproaches; she received him with the utmost kindness and tenderness, and for the remaining three years of his life nursed him with the greatest care and devotion. For a time his mind remained clear, and in 1800, when his friend Hayley wrote describing an interview he had had with Lady Hamilton and her affectionate inquiries after her old friend, Romney was able to answer, "The pleasure I should receive from the sight of the amiable Lady Hamilton would be as salutary as great, yet I fear, except I shall enjoy more health and better spirits, I shall never be able to see London again. I feel every day greater need of care and attention, and here I experience these in the highest degree." One pleasure Romney looked forward to with eagerness. This was the return of his elder brother James, who had risen to be a colonel in the service of the East India Company, owing to the painter's generous help. But when they met Romney's mind was already clouded.

"Brother," said the Colonel, "do you not know me?"

Romney looked at him, and bursting into tears murmured an incoherent recognition. This was the last effort. He sank into a state of bodily torpor and mental imbecility, and died on November 15, 1802.

He was buried in his native Dalton, but the lay rector refused to allow the monument with which his son desired to perpetuate his father's memory, to be placed in the parish church. It was afterwards put up in Kendal church, and bears this inscription : "To the memory of George Romney Esqre the celebrated painter, who

ROMNEY'S "DIVINE LADY," EMMA, LADY HAMILTON

147

died at Kendal the 15 November, 1802, in the 68th year of his age, and was interred at Dalton, the place of his birth. So long as Genius and Talent shall be respected his fame will live."

The passage of time has proved the truth of this epitaph. An artist's fame, unfortunately, is based upon the money value of his pictures. Romney never received more than one hundred and twenty guineas for a portrait, yet his painting of Caroline, Viscountess Clifden, and her sister, Lady Elizabeth Spencer, was sold ninety-four years after his death for one thousand five hundred guineas.

In appearance Romney was tall and strongly made ; his head was massive. He had a dark complexion, and his eyes were large and penetrating in expression. That he was weak and morbid is shown beyond all doubt ; but at the same time he had many endearing qualities which attracted and held friendship. He avoided general society, being of a very shy and retiring disposition, but his friend Cumberland has left us a picture which shows the man among his friends : " When in company with his intimates, he could give vent to the effusions of his fancy, and harangue in the most animated manner upon the subject of his art with a sublimity of idea and a peculiarity of expressive language that was entirely his own, and in which education or reading had no share. These sallies of natural genius, clothed in natural eloquence, were perfectly original, very highly edifying, and entertaining in the extreme. They were uttered in a hurried accent, an elevated tone, and very commonly accompanied by tears, to which he was by constitution prone." This peculiar sensibility to emotion was also expressed by his brush, for, as it has been written of him, " his slightest sketches have a vivid consistency which is almost peculiar to themselves. His vision was so artistic that his work was complete at every stage. Even the empty canvas about his unfinished heads seems to form an indispensable part in a coherent work of art."

To Romney's " vision " may be attributed his success and fame as a painter, his faults and unhappiness as a man.

WILLIAM ROSCOE

LANCASHIRE men, when they have built up a fortune, rarely devote their hardly won leisure to literature or art. William Roscoe, therefore, stands out as the great exception to the rule. Nor is it frequent that the literary fame which he achieved and which is still associated with his name, is gained by one of such lowly beginnings.

In the middle of the eighteenth century there stood upon the top of Mount Pleasant, which was then a country resort for the people of Liverpool, a small tavern called "The Bowling Green." Here William Roscoe was born in 1753. Both the tavern and the bowling-green beside it—from which it took its name—had been there "from time immemorial." Some sixty years before Roscoe's birth it was the resort of the "quality" of the town, for we read that a neighbouring squire in September 1687 "went with Sir Thomas Grosvenor, Mr. Massey and my son to Liverpool," and "dined with my Lord Molineux at the Bowling Green." But when Roscoe's father kept the inn such highly placed visitors had deserted it, and in order to add to his income he started a market garden.

William Roscoe the elder was an innkeeper pure and simple, a strong, burly man, who delighted in athletics and sport of every kind; it was, therefore, from his mother, "a woman of superior mind and strong affections," that Roscoe inherited his intelligence and his love of books. At the age of twelve his education was completed, and all that he afterwards learnt he taught himself. His mother encouraged him in his love of reading, and, according to his own account, Roscoe took no interest in his schoolfellows or in their games. "I was at this period of my life," he says, "of a wild, rambling and unsocial disposition, passing many of my hours in strolling along the shore of the River Mersey, or in fishing, or in taking long walks alone." When he left school, fortunately for him, he was not allowed to have anything to do with the tavern, but was set to work in his father's market garden. As is very often the case with self-educated men, Roscoe wrote with a touch of pomposity, and had a strong inclination to avoid simple words when he could find long ones to take their place; but this was one of the characteristics of the age in which he lived. His description of the four years he passed in his father's market garden, is a good example of the manner in which he wrote.

"Having quitted school," he says, "and committed my English Grammar to the flames, I now began to assist my father in his agricultural concerns, particularly in his business of cultivating potatoes for sale, of which every year he grew several acres, and which he sold, when produced early in the season, at very advanced prices. His mode of cultivation was entirely by the spade, and when raised early they were considered in that part of Lancashire as a favourite esculent. When they had attained their proper growth, we were accustomed to carry them to the market on our heads, in large baskets, for sale, when I was generally entrusted with the disposal of them, and soon became a very useful assistant to my father. In this and other laborious occupations, particularly in the care of a garden, in which I took great pleasure, I passed several years of my life, devoting my hours of relaxation to reading my books. This mode of life gave health and vigour to my body, and amusement and instruction to my mind; and to this day I well remember the delicious sleep which succeeded my labours, from which I was again called at an early hour. If I am now asked whom I consider to be the happiest of the human race, I should answer those who cultivate the earth with their own hands."

In his wildest imaginings, the clever, intelligent boy as he trudged into the town from Mount Pleasant, with a basket of potatoes on his head, could not have dreamt that one day he would not only represent his native town in Parliament, but would be considered, both during his life and afterwards, amongst the first of her citizens.

To his passion for reading, Roscoe added a talent for carpentering, and made himself a " book-case with folding doors, which served me for many years, and which I filled with several volumes of Shakespeare, a great part of whose historical plays I committed to memory; to these were added the *Spectator*, and other valuable works, which I perused with great pleasure." It is always interesting to trace the causes of great effects. The Royal Institution at Liverpool and the Liverpool Athenæum owed their existence, in no small measure, to Roscoe's love of books and an acquaintance he made as a youth with a china-painter called Mulligan. Besides painting china, Mulligan was a copper-plate engraver, and it was through him that young Roscoe began to take an interest in engravings and pictures. Thus early did he begin to occupy his mind with literature and art, an occupation that resulted in incalculable benefit to his native town.

When he was sixteen Roscoe's parents decided that he ought to follow some profession or trade, that would provide a better livelihood than market-gardening. His love of books instantly led him to decide to be a bookseller. But after a month in a shop at Liverpool he was completely disillusioned, and was articled to an attorney. Although he disliked his profession from the moment he entered it until he left it, Roscoe worked hard, and with such success, that at the age of forty-three he was able to retire with a fortune to enjoy the literature and art he loved so well. Despite his hard work as a lawyer he pursued his studies at every spare moment, making several friends among a little set of clever and cultivated young men, who were doing their utmost to raise Liverpool from the reproach cast upon it—that " it cared for neither art, science nor literature, only for money-getting." Whilst he was still a clerk Roscoe helped this little band in founding a Society for the Encouragement of Art in Liverpool; and it was one of them who first directed his attention to Italian literature, the charms of which " harmonized completely with the rather stately mind which Nature had implanted in the tavern-keeper's son."

When he was twenty Roscoe showed

himself to be a poet as well as a lawyer's clerk. His poem on "Mount Pleasant" gives a clear picture of the difference between the Liverpool of a hundred and forty years ago, and the Liverpool of to-day. From Mount Pleasant the poet looked down upon the town below—

" How numerous now her thronging buildings rise !

Where lenient care allays the weight of grief.
Yon spacious roof, where, hushed in calm repose,
The drooping widow half forgot her woes :
Yon calm retreat, where, secured from every ill,
The helpless orphan's throbbing heart lies still,
And finds, delighted, in the peaceful dome,
A better parent and a happier home."

WILLIAM ROSCOE'S BIRTHPLACE

What varied objects strike the wondering eyes !
Where rise yon masts her crowded navies ride,
And the broad rampire checks the beating tide ;
Along the beach her spacious streets extend,
Her areas open, and her spires ascend."

Then looking down upon the Infirmary (built in 1749), upon the Seamen's Hospital (built in 1752) and the Bluecoat Hospital (built in 1709), he says—

" Hence rose yon pile where sickness finds relief,

This was the view from Mount Pleasant in those days—

" Far to the right, where Mersey duteous pours
To the broad main his tributary stores ;
Tinged with the radiance of the golden beam,
Sparkle the quivering waves ; and 'midst the gleam
In different hues, as sweeps the changeful ray,
Pacific fleets their guiltless pomp display ;
Fair to the sight they spread the floating sail,

Catch the light breeze and skim upon the
    gale;
Till loosening gradual on the stretching
    view,
Obscure they mingle in the distant blue,
Where in soft tints the sky with ocean
    blends,
And on the weakened sight the long, long
    prospect ends."

After poetry came matrimony, a Miss Jane Griffies, the daughter of " a respectable tradesman of Liverpool," being Roscoe's choice ; and it must be admitted that if his love-making was carried on in the same spirit as that in which he wrote to his " dearest Jane," it must have been pompous and heavy-handed in the extreme. He suggested that each should keep a journal, communicating its contents to the other from time to time, and in terms that suggest the perfect prig rather than the perfect lover. " I cannot help pleasing myself with the reflection," he wrote, " what an infinite variety of subjects this intercourse would give rise to. Convinced of the perfect confidence which subsists between us, how freely might our thoughts expand themselves. The desire of pleasing might cause some little attention to modes of expression, whilst the certainty of a natural indulgence would prevent us from being apprehensive about trivial inaccuracies. I own the scheme begins to grow a favourite with me, and I beg my dearest Jane will not overthrow my expectations."

But the cold formality of his letters hid a very real and deep devotion. For some reason that is unknown to us, even whilst he was a lawyer's clerk, he had been obliged to support his father and sister, or as he himself put it, " to screen a helpless parent and a deserving sister from the hardships of an unfeeling world." This duty to his family at one time seemed to make marriage impossible, and apparently there was some suggestion that the engagement should be broken off, for Roscoe in a fit of despair, wrote—

" Some happier youth
(Oh, may he equal me in truth !),
Born under favouring stars, shall gain
That heart thy Roscoe loved in vain."

But at the end of four or five years Roscoe and his " dearest Jane " were united in a marriage that proved to be one of unalloyed happiness. This was in 1781, Roscoe, who was then only twenty-eight, having already made a considerable position for himself as an attorney-at-law, or as we should call it now, a solicitor.

During the next fourteen years his name became known far outside his native town, public attention being first drawn to him by his spirited protests, both in prose and verse, against the slave trade. The fact that these protests came from Liverpool, which profited so largely by this horrible traffic in human flesh, added weight to Roscoe's indignation. When the French Revolution broke out, Roscoe became " the Liverpool Laureate of the new European movement." He wrote a song, " O'er the vine-covered hills and gay valleys of France," which was sung all over England, and was greatly admired by Robert Burns. At the outset the French Revolution excited the profound sympathy of all liberal-minded Englishmen, and the attitude of our own Government was widely condemned. The French people, it was agreed, had risen against an intolerable tyranny, and it ill became the Government or the people of a free country to withhold sympathy or help from those who, after centuries of misery and unspeakable oppression, had thrown off the yoke. Roscoe headed the opposition in Liverpool against the policy of the Government, the motto of this opposition being " Civil and Religious

Liberty all over the World." In his enthusiasm for the cause of liberty, Roscoe did not hesitate to attack the great Edmund Burke himself. However, as the rule of the Paris mob gradually usurped the rule of those who had sought to bring about the regeneration of France, by means of the Revolution, and the guillotine began to do its deadly work, horror took the place of sympathy in the minds of its most ardent English supporters, Roscoe amongst them. And when Louis XVI. and his unhappy Queen, Marie Antoinette, passed beneath the fatal knife, the last spark of sympathy for the Revolution was extinguished in England.

Roscoe was the busiest of men. His business was growing larger each year, but, despite the close attention he gave to it, he found time to interest himself in local politics, to write pamphlets and poems upon an endless variety of subjects, to work at a scheme for the reclamation of Chat Moss, and write his *Life of Lorenzo di Medici*, the great ruler of Florence in the Middle Ages. At that time it was the fashion amongst cultivated people to be interested in Italian history, art and literature; and when Roscoe's book appeared, in 1795, not only did it achieve an instant success, but it made its author famous in all the literary circles of the day. Five years after its publication the Liverpool attorney was in correspondence with some of the foremost men in England. The book went through several editions, and was translated into German and Italian.

From the moment he had been introduced to the charms of Italian history and literature, as a very young man, by a friend in Florence, Roscoe had formed the idea of writing the life of the great Florentine ruler, and it is characteristic of his tenacity of purpose that throughout all those busy years, fully occupied as they were with his business and other interests, he never lost sight of this idea. The study of the subject, and the collection of the material alone occupied several years; in the latter he was greatly helped by the friend in Florence.

A year after the publication of the book, Roscoe, having made a small fortune out of his attorney's business, decided to retire and devote himself entirely to the literature and art which he loved so dearly. Thus, at forty-three, the tavern-keeper's son, who had carried baskets of potatoes on his head to the Liverpool market, had not only won a fortune by hard work, but had gained a commanding position in the world of letters. Truly, a remarkable achievement when it is remembered that he was entirely self-taught.

Shortly after his retirement he bought Allerton Hall, a little estate near Liverpool, and here he settled to enjoy a well-earned leisure amongst his books, his prints and his medals. But after three years the claims of friendship drew him again into business — a business that brought about his ruin. The friend at Florence, who had so materially helped him in collecting the facts for his *Life of Lorenzo di Medici*, was one of the principal partners in a private banking house in Liverpool, the affairs of which, towards the end of the eighteenth century, had become seriously involved. Roscoe's friend died, and it was then discovered that the future support of his family depended entirely upon this bank. The partners approached Roscoe, who at once saved the bank from the pressing danger; they then proposed that he should become a working partner in the business, and believing he could thus help the family of the friend to whom he owed so much, he consented. This is how he came to be called " Mr. Roscoe, the celebrated banker." Notwithstanding the cares of the bank, he still continued his literary labours, and in 1805 brought out his *Life* of the son of Lorenzo di Medici, Pope Leo X.—the pope against whose rule Martin Luther revolted and so created Protestantism. The book had a considerable success, but not so great as its predecessor. Then, for one year, from 1806 to 1807, Roscoe represented his native town in Parliament, being returned as a Liberal by a large majority.

The prosperity of Liverpool was supposed to rest upon the slave trade between Africa and the West Indies, but this in no way affected Roscoe's warm denunciation of the traffic which he considered a disgrace to his constituents, and his speech in the House of Commons was one of those which brought about the Act for the Abolition of Slavery in the British Dominions, since it strengthened the public opinion already formed by the life-work of the great William Wilberforce. The Parliament that passed this Act of humanity was dissolved in 1807, and on Roscoe's return from London a public entry into Liverpool was arranged by his supporters. But his speeches in the House of Commons advocating the abolition of slavery, and the claims of Roman Catholics to the same civic rights as Protestants, had been used by his political opponents to foment the bitterest feeling against him, and for purely political motives they organized a riot at this public entry, in which "strong parties of seamen, chiefly consisting of the crews of vessels lately engaged in the African trade (that is the slave trade), armed with bludgeons and other weapons," played an ugly part. Roscoe's progress through the town from Low Hill was uninterrupted until he reached the south end of Castle Street, when "a scene of riot and confusion then ensued, such as has been rarely witnessed in the town. The horsemen were attacked,

the horses struck with sticks, and the procession obstructed ; but it slowly advanced with difficulty to the north-east corner of Castle and Dale Streets, where Roscoe's bank was then carried on. As Mr. Roscoe was alighting from his carriage, a stone was thrown at him—said to have been aimed from the Town Hall. A voice cried, ' Now is your time ! ' and a violent attack was at once commenced. The horse ridden by Colonel Williams, late commander of one of the volunteer regiments, was stabbed with a knife. Every attempt of Mr. Roscoe to address the crowd was received with groans and uproar, and the assembly finally broke up in disorder." There was more rioting in the evening, during which a young man called Edward Spencer was killed. To a man of Roscoe's refined nature and high ideals such a scene was especially repellent, and he declined to contest the seat, saying : " If the representation of Liverpool can only be obtained by violence and bloodshed I leave the honour of it to those who choose to contend for it." Despite all the appeals of his friends he remained firm in his resolution.

During the next nine years Roscoe lived a happy and busy life, occupied with his banking business, with collecting pictures and engravings, adding to his library, and in promoting a variety of schemes for the encouragement and cultivation of art and literature in Liverpool. Then came the ruin which swept away the fortune he had worked so hard to gain.

In 1816 Roscoe and his partners were obliged to suspend payment. On investigation of its affairs, however, the bank appeared to be solvent—at least, on paper —and a large majority of the creditors readily agreed to Roscoe's own proposal that he should still continue to manage the business and that he should be allowed six years in which to discharge the liabilities. Roscoe immediately gave up his own money, and sold his library and art collections in order to help pay off the debts of the bank. His friends, with great feeling and forethought, bought all the books he had collected for the writing of his two big works, the Lives of Lorenzo di Medici and Pope Leo X., and presented them as a separate collection to the Liverpool Athenæum, which Roscoe

Liverpool for a short while, the certificate being speedily granted.

We have a pen portrait of Roscoe about the time of his return to Liverpool from Chat Moss drawn by that delightful American writer, Washington Irving, during his visit to England. Chancing to be at the Liverpool Athenæum, Irving was attracted to " a person just entering the room. He was advanced in life, tall,

ALLERTON HALL

himself had helped to found some twenty years before. They reserved to him the use of the books, and their removal from the institution during his lifetime.

Four years of the promised six had passed when it was discovered that the debt of the bank could not be paid in that time, and Roscoe, therefore, had no alternative but to go bankrupt. A minority of the creditors opposed the granting of his certificate of discharge—out of sheer spite, it was said; and in order to save himself from arrest, Roscoe went to a little farm he owned on the Chat Moss. But he was only obliged to remain from

and of a form that might once have been commanding, but it was a little bowed by time, perhaps, by care. He had a noble Roman style of countenance, a head that would have pleased a painter; and though some slight furrows on his brow showed that wasting thought had been busy there, yet his eye still beamed with the fire of a poetic soul. There was something in his whole appearance that indicated a being of a different order from the bustling race around him. I inquired his name, and was informed that it was Roscoe. I drew back with an involuntary feeling of veneration. This, then, was an author of celebrity ; this was one of those men whose voices have gone forth to the ends of the earth : with whose minds I have communed, even in the solitudes of America."

A later portrait, written shortly before his death, is given by Mrs. Hemans, who was also a Liverpool woman. Allerton Hall had been given up when Roscoe devoted his property to paying part of

Canova's Psyche in the background, I thought that a painter, who wished to make old age look touching, could not have had a better subject." He died at the "modest brick house," in 1831, of paralysis.

Friends, by subscribing a sum of money, had removed all possibility of Roscoe's later years being harassed by absolute

WILLIAM ROSCOE

the liability of the bank, and Mrs. Hemans found him in "a modest brick house in Lodge Lane, near the end of Bentley Road." "He is a delightful old man," she wrote, "with a fine Roman style of head, which he had adorned with a green velvet cap to receive me in : because, as he playfully said, 'he knew I always admired him in it.' Altogether he put me in mind of one of Rembrandt's pictures, and, as he sat in his quiet study, surrounded by busts, and books and flowers, and with a beautiful cast of

poverty. This was only bare justice, seeing Roscoe's constant benefactions to Liverpool. The debt the great city owes to him is thus summed up by one of his biographers, Mr. L'Espinasse : "The respect which he won from distinguished men at home and abroad, encouraged his fellow-citizens to pay homage to intellect, and directly as well as indirectly, he contributed powerfully to the advancement of culture in Liverpool. As the great mart on the Mersey grew in magnitude, population and wealth, it was chiefly through the influence of Roscoe that it became studded with institutions which fostered something more refining than the love of wealth. The Botanic Garden was almost entirely his handiwork, while the Academy of Arts, the Athenæum, the Royal Institution, the Literary and Philosophical Society, were greatly indebted to him. His private beneficence was great, and he was ever ready to encourage struggling and obscure merit."

Washington Irving, as we have seen, had a profound admiration for Roscoe; and the words he wrote nearly a hundred years ago have a particular significance to-day, when thousands of Liverpool men and women have reaped all the advantages sown for them by Roscoe. "Born in a place apparently uncongenial to the growth of literary talent," says Irving, "in the very market-place of trade; without fortune, family connection, or patronage; self-prompted, self-sustained, and almost self-taught, he conquered every obstacle, achieved his way to eminence, and, having become one of the ornaments of the nation, turned the whole force of his talents to advance and influence and embellish his native town."

THE TOWNLEYS
of Townley Hall

ONE of the most ancient families in Lancashire is that of the Townleys of Townley Hall. If some genealogists are to be believed this family can trace its descent back to the reign of Alfred the Great, to a certain Spartlingus who was said to be the first of the hereditary half-lay, half-clerical Deans of Whalley. But it is not improbable that the genealogists were misled by the marriage in the reign of King John between the elder son of the then Dean of Whalley and the daughter of Roger Fitz-Eustace. The bride brought as part of her dowry the manor of Townley; and from this union the old family traces its direct descent, Townley Hall having been its home for eight hundred years, "a venerable pile with many later additions and alterations, towered, buttressed, and showing on one side thick walls of rude masonry, indicating a great antiquity."

But no particular records have come down to us of any member of the family until the reign of Henry VIII., when Sir John Townley was Sheriff of Lancashire for nine years. This Sir John was neither a hard-hearted nor a bad man, but his miserliness gave him an unhappy reputation. "No one could justly impute to him any infraction of the laws of his country," says one of his biographers. "On occasions he was even capable of performing acts of generosity. Yet he was not loved by his neighbours and the poor feared rather than respected him." In his later years this fear grew into detestation. Even as a boy Sir John had a love of saving, and as he grew up he "seemed beset by a restlessness of disposition which never let him remain contented with what he possessed. If he saw a superior hound or a high-spirited horse, he scarcely slept by night or rested by day till he had made them his own." In the majority of instances he obtained what he desired, and in so doing gained the reputation of being the best man at driving a bargain in the whole country-side. As the years passed Sir John's love of acquisition increased, until it took the form of adding to his domains. He was then past the age of fifty. A large tract of land near his property had been used as common land by the peasants since time immemorial. They pastured their cows upon it, their pigs found a subsistence upon it, and scattered up and down were a number of cottages. Sir John declared this land to be his, and set to work to "lay it in," that is to enclose it. Lawyers were employed to prove his title to the land, and, the necessary authority having been procured, he issued a notice to the peasants that the land was his, that they must no longer, upon any pretext, feed their cattle upon it, and that within the space of three months they must all quit their houses.

In Horelaw and Hollinghey Clough the notice was received with amazement. "They had as much right to their bits of land as John Townley had to his acres," the peasants declared. "The ancestors of most of them had been settled there generations ago. What right had John Townley to turn them out?"

Wherever he went the knight of Townley was met with sullen and threatening looks. More intrepid spirits amongst the peasants advocated an armed resistance, but it came to nothing In the meantime not a single family stirred. The day upon which the notice expired came and passed without incident. The peasants believed that Sir John had only made an idle threat, and finding they would not go, had abandoned his project. But three nights later strange sounds wakened the little community, and hurrying out of doors they found a band of labourers brought from a distance, and protected by a number of men-at-arms, demolishing one of the cottages. On the following morning all the cottages were in ruins and their former occupiers driven away. One poor woman, who had lost her husband only a week before, died of fright and grief.

The land was enclosed and became part of Townley Park.

It is not difficult to imagine the hatred and detestation roused against Sir John by this high-handed action. He may have been within his rights, but the infliction of such hardship and misery upon the poor peasants was scarcely justifiable, and so far as Horelaw was concerned the enclosure was clearly an illegal encroach-ment. We are told that after this transaction Sir John never seemed quite at his ease. He would walk about muttering and talking to himself; and he gave up superintending the alterations made necessary by the appropriation of the land. It is also said that he died crying, "Lay out! lay out!" that is, disappropriate. After his death the peasantry firmly believed that his ghost haunted Townley Hall and the park. They declared that unable to rest because of the appropriation of the common land, it wandered over the very parts taken in, crying in most piteous tones, a warning to his successors—

"Be warned! Lay out! Lay out! Be
    warned!
  Around Horelaw and Hollinghey
    Clough;
  To her children give back the widow's
    cot,
  For you and yours there's still
    enough!"

The Townleys have ever been staunch Roman Catholics, and in consequence they were firm adherents of the House of Stuart from the first assault made upon it by the Parliament to the final overthrow at the Battle of Culloden, a hundred years later. Never did a Townley abandon his faith or flinch from any consequences. When it was a penal offence to be a Roman Catholic, the John Townley who was head of the family—some fifty years after the death of the enclosing Sir John—suffered a bitter persecution, as is shown by the inscription upon his portrait at Townley Hall—"This John about the sixth or seventh year of her Majesty that now is, for professing the Apostolic Catholic Roman faith, was imprisoned first in Chester Castle, then sent to Marshalsea, then to York Castle, then to the Blockhouses in Hull, then to the Gatehouse in Westminster, then to

Manchester, then to Broughton in Oxfordshire, then twice to Ely in Cambridgeshire, and so now of seventy-three years, old and blind, is bound to appear and keep within five miles of Townley

severe measures taken against Roman Catholics after the plot to assassinate Queen Elizabeth in 1583.

Notwithstanding this unswerving devotion to their faith the Townleys escaped

JOHN TOWNLEY, WHO SUFFERED PERSECUTION IN THE REIGN OF QUEEN ELIZABETH

his house, who hath since the statute of '83 paid into the Exchequer £20 the month, and doth still ; (so) that there is paid already above £5,000. 1601."

"The statute of '83" refers to the

confiscation of their estates. They were heavily fined, but seem to have been left in possession of their property, in Lancashire at least, a fortunate contrast to others of the same faith in the county who were deprived of everything.

This immunity from the confiscation that befell some of their neighbours may be traced in John Townley's case to the influence of his half-brother, Dean Nowell of St. Paul's. On one occasion the Lords of the Council directed the Earl of Derby and the Bishop of Chester to allow John Townley to leave his prison for a time, " and upon his own bond in a good sum of money," because of his plea that he had in hand " great causes and suits for land, a marriage to be made in Lincolnshire for his daughter." They granted him this favour because they were " informed that the said Townley (his religion excepted) doth carry himself dutifully and quietly."

Two of this much persecuted Squire of Townley's grandsons, Charles and Christopher, each achieved distinction in two very different ways. Christopher devoted himself to science and antiquarianism and was a member of a remarkable little band of men in the North, who throughout all the troubles and horrors of the Civil War quietly pursued their studies and observations. He spent the greater part of his life in collecting the material for a history of Lancashire, the thirty volumes of which were a mine of information to Dr. Whitaker in the compilation of his history of Whalley. Charles in the course of time became Squire of Townley, and when the Civil War broke out was one of the first of the Royalist Lancashire gentlemen to place his sword at the service of his king. He was with James, Earl of Derby, the " Martyr Earl," when that nobleman made his unsuccessful attack upon Parliamentarian Manchester in 1642, and in the following year when the Parliamentarians stormed Preston we read that " Master Townley of Townley " narrowly escaped, whilst his wife was amongst the ladies who were taken prisoner. Eighteen months later Charles Townley was slain at the fierce battle of Marston Moor, when Cromwell so utterly defeated Prince Rupert and his army.

In the next generation the family showed the same devotion to the Stuarts. Charles Townley, grandson of the Townley who fell at Marston Moor, espoused the cause of James II., so warmly and devotedly that on the passing of the Act of Indemnity in 1690 under James's son-in-law and daughter, William III. and Mary, he was expressly excepted by name from any of its benefits. This Townley was charged with having tried to enlist troops for King James, and with having employed carriers to convey from Barnet, near London, to his house in Lancashire, boxes "full of swords, pistols and carbines," and also with purchasing jack-boots and kettle-drums, to be used in a Jacobite insurrection.

When the attempts were made in 1715 and 1745, to restore the Stuarts to the English throne, the name of Townley once more figured largely in the list of their supporters. In the Rebellion of 1715, which ended so dismally at Preston, the then Squire of Townley, Richard, was one of the Lancashire gentlemen who with the Earl of Derwentwater was forced to surrender. He was carried to London with his companions in misfortune, and there tried for his life. Luckily for him his trial came after Derwentwater and scores of other Jacobites had been condemned and executed. The jury was tired of convicting and hanging, and although it was proved beyond all doubt that he had raised a body of men called " Townley's Troop " to fight on the Pretender's behalf, they accepted his plea that he had been " forced into the rebellion," and acquitted him out of sheer good-nature. Their verdict met with a stern

—5

161

rebuke from the presiding Judge, but it remained unaltered, and Richard Townley returned to Lancashire, none the worse for an adventure in which many of his friends lost their lives and their estates. He died in 1735, and his eldest son, dying in 1742, left a boy of eight, who in late years was to become celebrated as the collector of the Townley Marbles.

Thus, when the Rebellion of 1745 took place the head of the Townley family was

notice of at the Court of Louis XV., and given a commission in the French Army, under Marshal Berwick, the natural son of James II. and Arabella Churchill, sister of the great Duke of Marlborough. After a distinguished career in France, Francis Townley retired to Wales, where the news of the Rebellion of 1745 reached him. Repairing instantly to Manchester, he had many consultations with the leading men of the Jacobite party—which was of consider-

TOWNLEY HALL

a child. But when a Stuart sounded the call to arms it would have been strange if no one of the Townley blood had answered it. Francis Townley therefore, the uncle of the boy squire, and one of the younger sons of the Richard Townley who escaped the gallows thirty years before, following the example of his ancestors, hastened to join the Young Pretender at Carlisle. At this time Francis Townley was thirty-six. When he was nineteen, " by course of misfortune in his family," and also probably because he could obtain no commission in the English Army, since he was a Roman Catholic, he went to France. There, " being a man of spirit and gallant bearing," he was taken much

able strength there—amongst whom was John Byrom, the poet. Now, Townley had a habit, not at all uncommon in his day, especially amongst soldiers, of swearing. The scene of the Jacobite conferences was a small public-house near the village of Didsbury, adjoining a well-known ferry named Jackson's Boat, "and Townley's oaths during these anxious consultations so shocked the worthy Byrom that he ventured upon this poetic reproof "—

" O that the Muse might call without offence,
  The gallant soldier back to his good sense !
  His temporal field so cautious not to lose,
  So careless quite of his eternal foes.
  Soldier, so tender of thy prince's fame,
  Why so profuse of a superior name ?

For the king's sake the brunt of battles
    bear,
But—for the King of kings' sake—do not
    swear ! ''

Francis Townley joined the Young
Pretender at Carlisle on the 17th November, 1745, and marching southward with
him, was at Preston on the 26th, remaining
there for two or three days. We have a
curious narrative of the visit from Harland : " At this time," he says, " it is
conjectured Colonel Townley paid hasty
visits to several of his old neighbours, the
heads of the county families in the district, and, amongst others, there is a
tradition that he visited Gawthorpe Hall,
the seat of the Shuttleworths, between
whom and the Townleys of Townley there
had long existed much friendship and
intimacy. What was his real errand
there it is not difficult to conjecture.
But if it were to incite the Shuttleworths
of the day, with their tenants and dependants, to join in the rebellion, his
arguments were unsuccessful, and he
left the house without any succour, or
the promise of future aid. A few years
ago, during an extensive repair and
renovation of Gawthorpe Hall, the
panelling of a window-sill in one of the
chambers was removed, and there was
found beneath the sill a sum of money in
gold, of which only a few were of English
coinage, the others being chiefly Spanish
pieces, and, it is said, none of later date
than 1745. On examining the window-sill panelling, it was found that after the
wood had been forced up, apparently with
a dagger-blade, and the money hidden,
the panel had been driven into its place
again with the pommel of the dagger,
which had left its dints in the wood. The
reasonable, and indeed the most probable
conjecture is, that Colonel Townley, about
to go southward on a perilous expedition,
and perhaps apprehensive of robbery while
travelling alone through a disturbed
district, had concealed this sum, said
to be about one hundred and fifty
pounds, or one hundred and sixty, in a
place where he rightly deemed it would be
secure and undiscovered, with the intention when peaceful times returned, or when
opportunity served during the struggle
about to commence, to possess himself of
it again, but that time never came."

One hundred and eighty recruits raised
in Manchester became the members of a
regiment called the Manchester Regiment,
command of which was given to the intrepid Francis Townley, and at its head
he marched out of the town with the rest
of the Jacobite forces early in December
1745, upon the famous march to Derby.
On the 8th of the month the Manchester
Regiment re-entered the town in full
retreat.[1] The Manchester men objected
to continuing the retreat into Scotland,
and therefore they were given the task of
garrisoning the town of Carlisle under
Townley, whilst Colonel Hamilton with
some companies of the Duke of Perth's
Regiment was to hold Carlisle Castle. A
few days later the Duke of Cumberland,
George II.'s son, invested the town with a
strong Hanoverian force. The besieged
made a gallant defence, but when six 18-pounders were brought to bear against
them, Hamilton advocated surrender.
Townley, on the other hand, stood out
for defence. " Better," he is declared to
have said, " better to die by the sword
than to fall into the hands of these d——d
Hanoverians." But Hamilton was determined upon submission, and Townley
therefore was compelled, against all his
inclinations, to acquiesce. The only terms
the Duke of Cumberland would grant in
return for surrender were that the garrison should not be put to the sword, but
be reserved for the King's pleasure.

[1] See *The '45*.

Townley, with the other officers, was conveyed to London in a wagon. His name stood at the head of the list of those whom the French Government demanded to be given up as officers in the service of that country—but France and England were at war and the demand was ignored. He was the first of the prisoners arraigned at the trial at Southwark on 16th July, 1746, and although during the trial was firm and undaunted, and when sentence of death was passed against him he was not in the least discomposed, nor did his countenance undergo any change of colour." Amongst the officers of the Manchester Regiment condemned with Townley was Jemmy Dawson, whose execution caused the death of his sweetheart.[1] As he had been the first to be condemned, so Francis Townley was

THE CHAPEL, TOWNLEY HALL

his counsel pleaded that, as he had been sixteen years in the French service and held a French commission whilst with the rebels, he was entitled to the cartel, the Court took this plea as an exaggeration of the offence, declaring that "no man who was by birth a liege-subject of His Majesty was justified in taking up arms and acting in the service of a prince at war with His Majesty." Ten minutes sufficed to decide Francis Townley's fate. "The behaviour of Colonel Townley the first to be executed. "At the end of five minutes after the suspension had taken place, Colonel Townley, even before signs of life had ceased to be extinct, was cut down and stripped. Being laid on the block, the hangman with a cleaver severed his head and put it into a coffin; then taking out his bowels and heart, he threw them into the fire." There was a story current, and long believed, that the head of this unfortunate scion of the

[1] See Shenstone's ballad " Jemmy Dawson."

house of Townley was sent to Carlisle and there exposed over the gateway; it was also said that it was "set up" at Temple Bar in London. But neither of these stories was correct. By the intercession of his friends this last degradation was spared the remains. The head of one Manchester man, a Captain Fletcher, a linen draper living near Salford Bridge, who was executed at the same time as Townley, was placed on Temple Bar, and this has been confounded with that of Townley.

Thus ended the gallant and romantic career of Francis Townley.

One other member of the ancient family achieved a lasting distinction for his name, and one that will be preserved so long as the British Museum exists. This was Charles Townley, nephew to the unfortunate Jacobite Francis. Educated at the Roman Catholic College of Douai in France, he afterwards went to Paris, where he cut a considerable figure in French society, especially in literary and artistic society. From France he went to Italy, and making the acquaintance of Sir William Hamilton, the English Ambassador at the Court of Naples, and afterwards the husband of the famous Emma, Lady Hamilton, and the "enchantress" of Lord Nelson, became smitten with a passion for collecting antique marbles. He collected with such taste and knowledge statues, vases, and terra cotta, that "the contents of the Townley gallery are now amongst the most valuable and valued art-treasures of the British Museum." It is due entirely to the taste and enterprise of this Lancashire gentleman that England now possesses some of the finest treasures of ancient sculpture. His collection was acquired by the nation, by his own arrangement, for the sum of twenty thousand pounds, an amount comparatively trifling when their real value taken into consideration.

Charles Townley spent so many of his earlier years in France, that late in life he used to say he found it easier to express himself in French than in English. But whilst he satisfied his passion for collecting marbles he did not neglect his duty to his tenants and estate. Every summer he spent several months at Townley Hall, and it has been written of him: "Though lavish in his expenditure on the beautiful and the useful, he was personally frugal, and is said never even to have kept a carriage. Dignified, amiable, cheerful, accomplished, uniting to a care for his tenantry and the poor of his estate a splendid cultivation of the beautiful, the figure of Charles Townley appeals to the imagination as almost that of an ideal gentleman of the eighteenth century."

CHARLES TOWNLEY

Lancashire is generally considered to be a county which has contributed more largely than any other to the commercial life of England ; through Charles Townley Lancashire has contributed more superbly than any other county to the art life of the nation.

The old home of the Townleys for so many centuries is now the property of the people of Burnley.

JOHN TOWNLEY, WHO LIVED MOST OF HIS LIFE IN FRANCE
AND WAS A CHEVALIER OF THE ORDER OF ST. LOUIS

166

SIR JOHN BARROW

STANDING upon a gorse-covered bluff, called the Hoad, to the north-east of Ulverstone, is a round tower one hundred feet in height, which looks exactly like a lighthouse. This tower was erected by public subscription to the memory of Sir John Barrow, who was born in a little cottage at Dragley Beck. The cottage represents the lowliness of Sir John Barrow's origin, the tower shows the honour in which he was held when he died.

For nearly two centuries the little one-storeyed cottage had belonged to his mother's family, and it went with her to her husband, who was one of the many sons of an " extensive farmer." Some of these brothers occupied large holdings, but Sir John Barrow's father was an unambitious man and was quite content to cultivate the few fields belonging to the cottage, which supplied all they needed in the way of corn and vegetables, and the grazing for two or three cows. Here John Barrow was born on June 19, 1764. He was an only child, and the little property being their own, his parents were in compara-tively comfortable circumstances, and were therefore able to give him the best educa-tion afforded by the neighbourhood, an education which, as we shall see, Barrow used to the greatest advantage. At the age of eight he was sent to the Town Bank Grammar School at Ulverstone.

The master was "an old gouty gentleman named Ferdinand Hodgson, usually called Fardy by the boys," but—the gout not-withstanding—he had sufficient discern-ment to see that John Barrow was no ordinary boy. A " sort of perambulating instructor " used to teach mathematics during three months of the year in a separate room at the school to those boys whose parents cared to pay " extras," and " from him," says Barrow, " I received instruction in those branches of mathe-matics which are most easily attained under a master, such as algebra, fluxions, and conic sections. Euclid needed no master." The boy had a strong bent for mathematical study, which was fostered by Fardy's successor in the mastership, William Walker, a son of the Robert Walker, the incumbent of Seathwaite, who brought up eight children on a miserably poor stipend, and was immor-talised by Wordsworth.

Robert Walker was curate of Seath-waite for sixty-seven years, " having been presented to the living, which was worth £5 a year, in 1736, living a life of beauti-ful simplicity, usefulness, and piety. . . . Within the communion rails of the church he used to sit, teaching the children of the parish, and spinning for the linen and cloth by which he eked out his scanty living. He died June 25, 1802, in his ninety-third year. He is still

pupils who could assist him in making a survey of that property. Barrow and the schoolmaster's nephew were chosen. The former, in later life, described this expe-

THE "WONDERFUL" ROBERT WALKER

fondly remembered in the district as the 'wonderful Robert Walker.'"

Whilst still at school—which he left at the age of fourteen—Barrow had an opportunity of turning his arithmetical knowledge to good account. The agent of the owner of Conishead Priory asked Mr. Walker to recommend two competent

rience as having been of "incalculable benefit" to him. Indeed, there is a curious fact in Barrow's career not rarely met with. Whatever he learned or did, at some time or another in his life proved of service to him when he least expected it. His own thoroughness and marvellous memory, of course, enabled him to take the fullest opportunity of this good fortune. Thus, as will be seen, a chance study of astronomy paved the way to the high position Barrow afterwards achieved.

"Five or six of the upper boys," he says, "agreed to subscribe for the purpose of purchasing a celestial globe, and also a map of the heavens, which was lodged in the mathematical apartment of Town Bank School, to be made use of jointly or separately, as should be decided on. Our cottage at Dragley Beck was distant a mile or more, yet such was my eagerness of acquiring a practical knowledge of the globe and the map, that I never omitted a starlight night without attending to the favourite pursuit of determining certain constellations and their principal stars, for one, two, or three hours, according as they continued above the horizon. It was a pleasure then, and a profit hereafter." At this time also the clever boy made a valuable friend. An old farmer named Gibson, "living among the hills," had a great reputation locally as a "wise man," and it was said of him, with awe by the countryfolk, that he made his own almanacs and could calculate the date of an eclipse. Gibson employed his leisure time in the study of mathematics and astronomy. One day being sorely puzzled by a problem in geometry, young Barrow decided to consult the farmer-mathematician. He was received most kindly, helped in his difficulty, and made a friend whose advice subsequently determined his career.

When Barrow left school his parents wished him to study for the Church, but he had no inclination in that direction. He was too clever to be content with work at home—cow-keeping, vegetable growing, and ploughing—but as "at fourteen he could not remain living in idleness on his father," there seemed no help for it. At this important point in the boy's career, however, there came an unexpected chance.

A Liverpool lady visiting in the neighbourhood heard of Barrow's remarkable attainments and of his excellent character. Her husband was the "proprietor of a considerable iron-foundry in Liverpool," and the man who helped him in keeping the accounts being old and infirm, he was looking out for an active and intelligent youth to learn the work, and then take its entire charge. The ironfounder's wife, therefore, suggested that Barrow should accept the post, and it was further arranged that he should live with the family, and give lessons to a weakly son of ten. In return, Barrow was to serve for three years, receiving a salary that only provided him with clothes and a little pocket-money. At the end of two years, however, he had proved his capability so satisfactorily that the ironfounder wished to make him a partner; but before the necessary arrangements could be made the owner of the firm died. The widow decided to sell the business, and although the purchaser made him an offer to remain, Barrow thought it best to decline. At the house of his late employer he had frequently met a Captain Potts who had some interest in the whale fishery. Potts was out of health, and being recommended by his doctor to take a sea voyage, thought he could not do better than go on one of his own and his partner's ships to Greenland. Knowing young Barrow to be an agreeable and intelligent companion, Potts invited him to take the voyage, as he then had no occupation, an invitation that was gladly accepted.

Barrow lost no opportunity of picking up knowledge during the voyage, learning navigation, how to take and work out observations, and how to "hand, reef and steer," all of which stood him in good stead years later. On his return to Dragley Beck, bringing two jawbones of a whale which were placed as gate-posts to the cottage garden, Barrow was just in time to attend the funeral of his old schoolmaster, Walker.

But now Barrow found himself in precisely the same position as when he had left school. What work was he to do? His old friend Gibson, the mathematical farmer "amongst the hills," urged him to complete the knowledge he had gained of nautical science, on the wise ground that "without a profession you cannot tell to what good use knowledge of any kind may be applied." The old man also spoke to him of the wide field presented to a young man of talent in London, where he himself had two sons, one of whom was in a high position in the Bank of England. Barrow's ambition was naturally stimulated by this advice, but its gratification presented an insuperable difficulty, seeing he had not the means to travel to London and keep himself there whilst looking for work. So he waited on at Ulverstone, pursuing his studies and looking after the garden of the cottage, but all the while pining for work and independence. He had one offer, that of superintending an estate in the West Indies belonging to a Colonel Dodgson, but when Barrow found that it really meant an overseership of slaves, he declined it. Just as he was beginning to despair, his old friend Gibson received a letter from his son in the Bank of England asking if he could recommend "a north-country youth" who was qualified to teach mathematics to the upper boys of a large school at Greenwich. Gibson immediately proposed Barrow, who, accepting the post joyfully, set out for London. He was engaged for three years at the "academy," which was a preparatory school for the sons of noble-

men and other highly-placed folk, kept by a Dr. James.

The three years at Greenwich were very happy ones for Barrow. He was popular alike with the other masters and the boys, and was an excellent teacher. It will be remembered that as a boy at school Barrow had received some practical instruction in the use of mathematical instruments in the survey of Conishead Priory. He now made a further study in his leisure time, and with considerable advantage. "On arriving in London," he says, "I extended my knowledge of them, so as to draw up and publish a small treatise to explain the practical use of a case of mathematical instruments, being my first introduction to the press, for which I obtained twenty pounds, and was not a little delighted to send it to my mother."

At the end of his engagement at the Greenwich school Barrow was asked to give lessons in mathematics, "and to such as were well advanced in years and knowledge I had no objection." Amongst his pupils was the wife of Sir George Beaumont. He had many friends and passed some years in London giving lessons, a serene and busy existence, only broken by the annual visits he paid to his parents at Ulverstone.

On his return from one of these visits came the turning-point of his career. "One day," he writes, "on my return to town I was honoured with a visit from Sir George Staunton, a gentleman with whom I had not yet had the good fortune to meet, and who introduced himself by saying he was acquainted with several of my friends, and mentioned Dr. Gillies in particular" (an author of some repute at that time), "and some others who were accustomed to meet at the Westminster Library. He said the object of his visit was to know if I had leisure time, and was willing to bestow a portion of it to give instruction in mathematics to an only son, between the age of ten and eleven years, who had been studying the classics under a German gentleman residing in the house. That his son was a lively, animated boy, with more than average abilities and great docility. 'And,' he added, 'from the character I have heard of you, I think you both would be disposed to a mutual attachment.' I thanked him for the obliging offer, and the friendly and courteous manner in which it was introduced, and was ready and most willing to afford his son my best assistance. 'I suppose,' he said, 'you are practically acquainted with astronomy, and know the constellations and principal stars by name? I am a great advocate for practical knowledge.' I answered in the affirmative; and the constellations and astronomy brought vividly to my mind my old friend Mr. Gibson, and the globe and the map of Town Bank School, and I was more than ever persuaded that all is for the best."

All was indeed for the best. The knowledge gained by the boy's interest in astronomy opened the door to a big career for the man. Both Sir George and his son liked Barrow, and the boy was his

LORD MACARTNEY

pupil for some years. The tuition ended, Barrow was asked to accompany an English family to Italy as tutor when he received the most unexpected news.

Owing to the lack of official communications between the Chinese and British Governments the factors employed by the East India Company in China were subjected to gross ill-treatment. Pressed by the Company, which was extremely powerful, and for various other reasons, the British Government decided to send Lord Macartney on a special mission to the Emperor of China with a large suite and handsome presents. Lord Macartney and Sir George Staunton had been old friends in India, and Sir George was appointed Secretary to the Embassy, and his son an attaché.

Both father and son were anxious that Barrow should accompany them, and to his intense surprise the latter heard that Sir George had recommended him most warmly to Lord Macartney as one who would be a useful addition to the suite. Barrow passed a fortnight in anxious expectation, then came word that he was nominated to the Embassy as Comptroller of the Household. The news seemed almost too good to be true to the " whilom assistant in the Liverpool iron-foundry, who had been glad even to make a voyage to the Arctic regions in a Greenland whaler."

At their first interview Lord Macartney gave him a list of the mathematical, philosophical, and scientific instruments, and of the works of art which were to be brought as presents for the Emperor of China, and until the Embassy sailed in September 1792 the happy Comptroller had a busy time.

The Embassy was not unsuccessful, but it did not achieve one of its objects— the establishment of a British ambassador in Pekin. Lord Macartney, however, skilfully evaded, both for himself and his suite, the rule of the Chinese Court that everybody must approach the Emperor on all fours ; a small matter, perhaps, but a point which had considerable influence upon the after relations between that great Empire and this country. Barrow had the satisfaction of seeing all the presents committed to his care—the globes, clocks, glass lustres, instruments etc.—unpacked and arranged in one of the Imperial palaces near Pekin without a single loss or breakage.

Barrow was a man of singularly keen observation. Nothing in that strange country escaped him as the Embassy passed from the coast to Pekin and on its return journey. He made copious notes, and was thus not only able to assist Sir George Staunton in the preparation of the official history of the Embassy, but to give the most interesting and valuable accounts of the then unknown land and its people in his *Travels in China,* his *Life of Lord Macartney,* and later in his *Autobiography,* as well as in numerous articles in the *Quarterly Review.* On two occasions he was asked for advice by the Government with regard to their dealings with China ; another instance of his knowledge proving of service to him long afterwards.

The Embassy returned to England at the end of September 1794, and on their arrival in London, Sir George Staunton begged Barrow to make a home in his house, promising that he himself and Lord Macartney would take care to find some employment for him. Barrow joyfully accepted the kind offer, but begged leave to pay a few weeks' visit to his parents.

The delight with which he was received at Dragley Beck, and the astonishment and pride with which the stories of his Chinese travels were listened to in that remote corner of the world, can easily be imagined.

Three years later Barrow was given another important post. The Cape of Good Hope had been taken from the Dutch, and the then Secretary for the Colonies, Henry Dundas, knowing the Dutch settlers there to be a peculiar and difficult people, thought that a civilian of high rank would be more acceptable to the conquered colony as Governor than a military man. He therefore offered the appointment to Lord Macartney, who accepted it. The former promise was remembered, and Barrow was appointed one of the new Governor's private secretaries.

They landed at Cape Town in May 1797. The Dutch Boers were in a state of revolt against the English rule, as well as at war with the Kaffirs. Lord Macartney therefore at once sent Barrow on a mission which was both political and geographical. He was to pacify the Boers and make a map of the Colony, the only existing map not embracing onetenth part of its area. He had only a scanty equipment for the work, but the surveying at Conishead, and his further studies in London in the use of instruments again came to his aid, and he was able to write, " Between the 1st of July

(1797) and the 18th of January (1798) I had traversed every part of the Colony of the Cape of Good Hope, and visited the several countries of the Kaffirs, the Hottentots and the Bosjesmen, performing a journey exceeding three thousand miles on horseback, on foot, and very rarely in a covered wagon, and full one half of the distance as a pedestrian."

In his dealings with the Boers and the natives, Barrow was most successful, and as soon as. the official reports of his mission reached England they were published at the suggestion of Dundas. Lord Macartney made him Auditor-General of the Cape Colony as a reward. After another mission Barrow took up the work of his new office, and believing that his wanderings were finished, married, in 1799, a Dutch lady, he then being thirty-five. But five years later the Peace of Amiens restored the Cape to the Dutch and Barrow found his occupation gone, and was obliged to return to England. Here he found Dundas out of office, and therefore unable to do anything for him. The former Secretary for the Colonies, however, had been deeply impressed by Barrow's reports, and regarded him as one who might be very useful when his party returned to office. He received him, therefore, with great cordiality and asked him to meet the statesman Pitt at dinner. Pitt also was cordial, and in praising Barrow's book of reports said it corroborated the opinion which he himself had given in Parliament, that the Cape of Good Hope ought never to have been parted with. He suggested, Barrow tells us, "that I had left rather short one portion of the subject which he had always considered of vast importance to this country, and that was, its geographical position with regard to India, as a half-way house between our settlements there and England; as a place of refresh-ment for our shipping and troops; its capabilities for supplying all kinds of produce; its ports and harbours, along a great extent of sea-coast, favourable to commercial enterprise." Such a hint, coming from so great a statesman, was equivalent to a command. "I speedily produced a second volume," says Barrow, "detailing the political, geographical and commercial advantages of this southern part of Africa, which had the effect of producing a second edition of the first volume."

Pitt could have received no more valuable support to his patriotic contention that the Cape should never have been abandoned, and immediately he returned to office as Prime Minister with Dundas as First Lord of the Admiralty, Barrow was one of the first persons whose services were rewarded. He was appointed Second Secretary to the Admiralty in 1804. Two years later the Whigs came in, and Barrow lost his place to make room for a protégé of the new First Lord. But the re-taking of the Cape of Good Hope directed the attention of the Government to Barrow, who knew more about the colony than any man in England, and it was upon their suggestion that he presented a memorial of his services. The Whig Government gave him a pension of one thousand pounds, with the proviso that it was to be lessened according to the salary of any office which he might afterwards hold.

Barrow's services to the country were outside all questions of party. This Whig Ministry was of short duration, and when it fell, Barrow was restored to his post of Second Secretary to the Admiralty, a position he occupied until 1845, under some twelve administrations. He tells us that when Dundas, who in 1804 had become Lord Melville, appointed him to the office of Second Secretary to the

Admiralty he asked if he were a Scotchman.

"No, my lord," Barrow replied, "I am only a borderer. I am North Lancashire."

Whereupon Lord Melville replied that he and Pitt had been so often taunted with giving all the good things of office to Scotchmen that he was glad he had chosen an Englishman for once.

When called to this office under the Admiralty, Barrow showed his gratitude to his old friend the astronomer-farmer Gibson, by seeking out his grandson and making him his private secretary. He served, he tells us, "for forty years, under twelve or thirteen several naval administrators, Whig and Tory, including that of the Lord High Admiral, His Royal Highness, the Duke of Clarence; having reason to believe that I have given satisfaction to all and every one of these naval administrations."

The practical knowledge gained upon his trip to Greenland, and his after study of "nautical science," not only were of great service to Barrow in the Admiralty, but they likewise bred in him a deep interest in Polar exploration. In 1817 he published an account of the movement of icebergs into the Atlantic, and proposed to Lord Melville a plan of two voyages for the discovery of the North-West Passage, a proposal which was the origin of some of the "noblest exploits of seamanship" in the nineteenth century.

The Duke of Clarence, afterwards William IV., had a very high regard for Barrow, and on one occasion gave a striking instance of his reliance on the Second Secretary's capabilities. The Duke was holding a big naval review at Spithead in 1827, when a telegraph message from London—sent by the old method of signalling by semaphore from station to station—was handed to the Admiral in command of the vessel, but not having

his key with him he could not make out the message, which was in cipher.

"Where is Barrow?" the Duke of Clarence cried impatiently.

Barrow was at his elbow. The message was handed to him, with a "What is it? Quick! Quick!"

"Sir," answered Barrow, reading the message, "it is brief, but painfully distressing—Mr. Canning is dead."

Canning was the Prime Minister.

Five years after his accession to the throne as William IV., the Duke made Barrow a baronet, as an expression of his regard for his long services to the country. the honour, it is said, was received with some reluctance.

Great changes took place at the Admiralty during the forty years in which Barrow held his office, and amongst them was an important one for the better management of dockyards, a suggestion made and planned by the Second Secretary. Outside his naval work, Barrow's energies were inexhaustible. He wrote one hundred and ninety-five articles for the *Quarterly Review* on almost every subject except politics, those on Arctic and Chinese matters being the most interesting; nine lengthy books, and his autobiography, as well as preparing for the press innumerable manuscripts from travellers in all parts of the globe. His interest in Arctic discovery first led the Admiralty to assist explorers, and it has truly been said of him, "More than any other man not actually employed in its operations, he had contributed to the splendid results obtained in the nineteenth century." The naming of Point Barrow, Cape Barrow, in the Polar seas, and Barrow Straits, show the estimation in which his interest and friendship were held by the early explorers, and in the interior of the lighthouse-like monument at Ulverstone their names are engraved upon the stone with his own.

When he retired at the age of eighty, amongst the many testimonies given to his official merits, including one from Sir Robert Peel, none gave him keener pleasure than the present of a service of plate, subscribed for by officers who had served in the Arctic expeditions, and accompanied by a letter from Parry and Franklin, Ross and Back, thanking him for the " talent, zeal, and energy " which he had " displayed in the promotion of Arctic discovery." A year after his retirement he published his autobiography.

Sir John had a strong constitution and wonderful health. Only once, before he was eighty, did he consult a doctor, and this was when he was half poisoned in China. Death came to him suddenly and painlessly in his eighty-fifth year. He was buried in London.

Although his brilliantly successful career had carried him far from Ulverstone, Sir John, like so many Lancashire men who have achieved fortune in the greater world, never forgot his native place. By his will he directed the annual subscription he had given for many years to the Town Bank School, in which he had been educated, should be continued. His mother's cottage at Dragley Beck, which he had inherited, was assigned in perpetuity to trustees, who were to use its rent for the education of poor children.

SIR JOHN BARROW

OTHER BOOKS TO LOOK OUT FOR BY

PRINTWISE PUBLICATIONS LIMITED

ILLUSTRATIONS RELATING TO THE HISTORY OF MANCHESTER,
SALFORD AND SURROUNDING DISTRICT ISBN 1 872226 00 0   £2.99

RALSTON'S VIEWS OF THE ANCIENT BUILDINGS OF MANCHESTER (1850)
ISBN 0 904848-06 X   £2.99

PICTURES OF OLDE LIVERPOOL. (Drawings and sketches — Herdman)
ISBN 1 872226 02 7   £2.50

LANCASHIRE HALLS (Margaret G. Chapman). Sketches, photographs and a short history
ISBN 1 872226 03 5   £2.99

MANCHESTER IN EARLY POSTCARDS (Eric Krieger). A pictorial reminiscence.
ISBN 1 872226 04 3   £2.50

CHESHIRE 150 YEARS AGO (F. Graham). Unique collection of 100 prints of Cheshire in early 1800.
ISBN 1 872226 07 8   £4.95

LANCASHIRE 150 YEARS AGO. Over 150 prints reflecting early 19th century Lancashire.
ISBN 1 872226 09 4   £4.95

GREETINGS FROM THE WIRRAL (Catherine Rothwell and Cliff Hayes)
ISBN 1 872226 11 6   £4.95

BRIGHT AND BREEZY BLACKPOOL. (Catherine Rothwell) includes short history of the Tower and the
Piers
ISBN 1 872226 13 2   £4.95

SOUTHPORT IN FOCUS. Glimpses of the town's past (Catherine Rothwell)
ISBN 1 872226 15 9   £2.50

PORTS OF THE NORTH WEST (Catherine Rothwell). A pictorial study of the region's maritime heritage
ISBN 1 872226 17 5   £3.95

SUNRISE TO SUNSET (life story of Mary Bertenshaw)
ISBN 1 872226 18 3   £4.95

STORIES AND TALES OF OLD MERSEYSIDE. (Over fifty stories included)
ISBN 1 872226 20 5   £4.95

STORIES AND TALES OF OLD LANCASHIRE (Cliff Hayes)
ISBN 1 872226 21 3   £4.95

STORIES AND TALES OF OLD MANCHESTER (Cliff Hayes)
ISBN 1 872226 22 1   £4.95

GREETINGS FROM OLD SALFORD. A portrait in old postcards (Edward Gray)
ISBN 1 872226 24 8   £4.95